Philosophy of the Environment

This textbook offers a reasoned and accessible introduction to the philosophy of the environment and the current environmental crisis, designed for scholars and students in both philosophy and the natural and environmental sciences.

The volume addresses the history and meanings of the concept of "environment", provides a theory of the relation between living beings and their environments, and tackles a wide spectrum of key philosophical issues related to the environment and the environmental crisis in a straightforward framework and accessible style. The book's unique approach to environmental philosophy addresses the environment of all living beings and extends beyond environmental ethics to include conceptual history and analysis together with insights from evolutionary and developmental biology, ecology, and environmental and conservation sciences. The book consists of five chapters, each built around a specific thesis drawing upon philosophers and concepts including Georges Canguilhem, Rachel Carson, Donna Haraway, Lamarck's and Darwin's evolutionary theories, Humboldt's theory of nature, and the Gaia hypothesis. The final chapter introduces topics such as environmental denialism and post-natural environmentalism as conceptual tools for better understanding the current ecological crisis.

Targeted at students and scholars in both philosophy and the environmental and life sciences, the book distinguishes itself through its approachable style and choice of topics, which are also well suited to junior researchers who seek to better understand the current environmental crisis.

Elena Casetta is an assistant professor in the Department of Philosophy and Education at the University of Turin, Italy.

Philosophy of the Environment
An Introduction

Elena Casetta

Designed cover image: Elena Casetta

First published 2025
by Routledge
4 Park Square, Milton Park, Abingdon, Oxon OX14 4RN

and by Routledge
605 Third Avenue, New York, NY 10158

Routledge is an imprint of the Taylor & Francis Group, an informa business

© 2025 Elena Casetta

The right of Elena Casetta to be identified as author of this work has been asserted in accordance with sections 77 and 78 of the Copyright, Designs and Patents Act 1988.

All rights reserved. No part of this book may be reprinted or reproduced or utilised in any form or by any electronic, mechanical, or other means, now known or hereafter invented, including photocopying and recording, or in any information storage or retrieval system, without permission in writing from the publishers.

Translated from the original Italian language edition:
Filosofia dell'ambiente, Bologna, Società editrice il Mulino, 2023.

Trademark notice: Product or corporate names may be trademarks or registered trademarks, and are used only for identification and explanation without intent to infringe.

British Library Cataloguing-in-Publication Data
A catalogue record for this book is available from the British Library

ISBN: 978-1-032-76690-4 (hbk)
ISBN: 978-1-032-76687-4 (pbk)
ISBN: 978-1-003-47964-2 (ebk)

DOI: 10.4324/9781003479642

Typeset in Sabon
by Apex CoVantage, LLC

Contents

List of boxes *vi*
Preface to the English translation *vii*
Acknowledgements *viii*

Introduction 1

1 Discovering the surroundings 8

2 Understanding the environment 38

3 Building the human environment 72

4 Conserving nature 105

5 Confronting the crisis 144

Conclusion 166

Index *168*

Boxes

1.1	Lamarck's theory of evolution	13
1.2	Ecosystem services	32
2.1	From Darwin to the extended synthesis	43
2.2	Types of niche construction	59
2.3	The Daisyworld model	65
3.1	Gene expression	75
3.2	Intergenerational responsibility	93
4.1	Aristotle's view on change	107
4.2	Cultural primitivism	124
5.1	The environmental humanities	157

Preface to the English translation

When I decided to translate this book into English, I did not yet fully appreciate how rapidly policies, research, and reflections regarding the environment, environmental management, and nature conservation (and related publications) are progressing. This has meant that, although the English translation of the book would be published relatively soon after the original edition, several updates were necessary. In addition to these updates, which concern both content and some references, I deemed it appropriate to make some changes in two main respects. Firstly, the bibliographic apparatus. For the Italian edition of the book, mainly intended for my students, I favoured bibliographic sources in Italian where available. Similarly, I tried to use concrete examples that readers could identify with. For the translation, I sought to include, where possible, equivalent bibliographic sources in English and to replace "local" examples with more general ones. Secondly, some – although not substantial – changes to the content and theoretical proposals advanced in the book have been made as a result of feedback received from both colleagues and the non-academic public during public presentations of the book, as well as from the reviewers consulted by the publisher to evaluate my editorial proposal, who provided me with useful suggestions and insights.

The introduction and Chapter 1 were translated by Sarah De Sanctis, and I translated the remaining chapters myself. The entire book was then revised by Carolyn Benson, to whom I owe much gratitude for transforming the text into proper English with patience and care. The revision of the text was made possible thanks to the financial support of the Department of Philosophy and Education of the University of Turin. I would also like to thank the editors of Routledge and my colleague Tiziana Andina for believing in this project, and Matt Shobbrook for assisting me during its accomplishment.

Acknowledgements

There are many people to whom I would like to express my gratitude, and for many reasons. Maurizio Ferraris, Biagio Forino, and Diego Marconi supported the original project, helping me to improve and realise it. Lara Barbara, Andrea Borghini, Erica Onnis, and Luca Tambolo lent their acumen to the Italian manuscript. Their valuable criticisms, suggestions, and comments were supplemented by the scientific and human support of colleagues and friends who helped me during the writing process, sending me texts, answering questions, and resolving doubts, discussing specific points, and offering me solutions to the obstacles that arose. My heartfelt thanks go to Carola Barbero, Cecilia Bortolotti, Emilio Corriero, Matteo Di Giovanni, Gabriele Gava, Pietro Gori, Philippe Huneman, Christian Lévêque, Alessandro Minelli, Enrico Pasini, Andrea Roncaglione, Stefano Tiozzo, Vera Tripodi, Achille Varzi, Davide Vecchi, François Walter, and Andrea Wulf. Finally, special thanks go to Stefano, for being by my side. Naturally, the responsibility for any bad choices, errors, or oversights is entirely mine.

Introduction

1 What is the environment?

In 1972, the first global conference on the environment, the United Nations Conference on the Human Environment, was held in Stockholm. As a result of the Stockholm conference, the United Nations Environment Programme (UNEP) was created. UNEP was tasked with producing a report on the state of the environment, the Global Environment Outlook (GEO). In 1995, together with the World Meteorological Organisation (WMO), UNEP gave birth to the Intergovernmental Panel on Climate Change (IPCC), whose most recent report, its sixth, was published between August 2021 and April 2022. In 1992, the second global conference on the environment – the United Nations Conference on Environment and Development, commonly referred to as the Rio Conference or "Earth Summit" – was held in Rio de Janeiro. On that occasion, the Climate Change Convention, which would find its operational expression in the 1997 Kyoto Protocol and the 2015 Paris Agreement, was opened for signature. With these agreements, the industrialised countries – and later the developing countries – committed themselves, at least on paper, to reducing greenhouse gas emissions (Kyoto) and to limiting average global warming to below 2°C compared to the pre-industrial period, aiming for a maximum temperature increase of 1.5°C (Paris). In addition to the Climate Change Convention, the Convention on Biological Diversity (CBD), aimed at the conservation of biodiversity and the sustainable use of its components, was also opened for signature in 1992.

In the space of 60 years, the very same environmental issues that were once the concern of often-mocked minorities had become a top political priority. In the 1960s and 1970s, environmentalists were described as "tree huggers": eccentric, romantic, idealistic characters who were out of touch with the real world with its concrete needs and dynamics.[1] Those who denounced the dangers of pollution faced accusations of hysteria, excessive empathy for other living beings, and communist sympathies – charges levelled, for example, against biologist Rachel Carson, author of *Silent Spring* (1962), the manifesto of modern environmentalism. In the context of a growth-oriented economic model, those who criticised the idea of unlimited economic growth

DOI: 10.4324/9781003479642-1

in the face of limited non-renewable natural resources were accused of promoting "[l]ess than pseudoscience and little more than polemical fiction" (Passell, Roberts, and Ross 1972). It was in precisely these terms that the book *The Limits to Growth* (Meadows *et al.* 1972), a report on the state of the environment (with predictions for the future) written by a group of MIT scientists at the request of the Club of Rome (a non-governmental association founded in 1968 and led by the Italian industrialist Aurelio Peccei), was disparaged in an article in the *New York Times* on 2 April 1972.

Today, things have changed to some extent: although some social groups – in particular younger generations – tend to be more sensitive to environmental issues than others, there is generally greater awareness that the health and quality of our lives, as well as those of species other than our own, depend precisely on the management of environmental issues, around which social, economic, and political conflicts revolve.

Yet in reading the various aforementioned reports, together with the documents produced by intergovernmental scientific organisations (many of which are available online), what stands out is that the meaning of the term "environment" is generally taken for granted – that is, not made explicit. Reference is made to environmental issues, environmental needs and rights, environmental problems, environmental resources, and the like. Sometimes, as in the preface of the first report on the state of the environment (GEO-1), we read of a global environment made up of "social, institutional and economic systems", of marine and coastal environments, and of the urban and industrial environment. At other times, as in the Stockholm Conference Declaration, the environment is identified with the human environment, and it is asserted that "[b]oth aspects of man's environment, the natural and the man-made, are essential to his well-being and to the enjoyment of basic human rights – even the right to life itself" (United Nations 1972).

What exactly is the environment? Do we have reason to treat the Earth as "man's environment" and not, say, as belonging to other species? Does it make sense to focus actions and policies on the human environment, treating it as separate from that of other living beings? What does it mean to say that the human environment is, on the one hand, a natural environment and, on the other hand, artificial? Is the natural/artificial distinction well founded? Could a human-made city park, for example, be a natural or an artificial environment? Or a beaver dam? Can we apply the natural/artificial distinction to the environments of other species? Again, what are environmental resources, and *whose* resources are they? When we say that we need to preserve, conserve, restore, or save the environment, what exactly are we referring to? To the park by our building, to the Amazon rainforest, to the biosphere, to the planet, to natural resources, to the jaguar's environment, or to the jaguar itself? And what kind of action are we talking about? Are preservation and conservation one and the same thing? Why is it that when an ancient forest burns down, we feel we have lost something irreplaceable, as we felt when Notre-Dame de Paris burnt down in 2019?

2 A philosophy of the environment

The concept of the environment[2]

> is in the process of becoming a universal and obligatory means of registering the experience and existence of living things, and one could almost speak of its constitution as a basic category of contemporary thought. But until now, the historical stages in the formation of the concept, its diverse uses, as well as the successive reconfigurations of the relationships in which it takes part, whether in geography, biology, psychology, technology, or social and economic history, all make it rather difficult to make out a coherent whole. For this reason philosophy must, here, initiate a synoptic study of the meaning and value of the concept.
> (Canguilhem 2001, p. 7)

When Georges Canguilhem voiced these ideas in a lecture given in the 1946–1947 academic year at the Collège philosophique in Paris, awareness of the environmental crisis and climate change (or global warming) was still the preserve of the few, and it was not an environment in crisis that Canguilhem had in mind when he stated that the notion was becoming a category of contemporary thought. Yet it is precisely since the 1960s, with the emergence of public consciousness of environmental issues – pollution, overexploitation of natural resources, biodiversity loss, global warming – that the environment has become a category of contemporary thought, to use Canguilhem's words. This book aims to pick up the baton and undertake "a synoptic study of the meaning and value of the concept" in order to better understand the current environmental crisis. The result is a non-neutral treatment, that is, a treatment that takes a specific perspective at the exclusion of others – and this in several senses.

First, as mentioned earlier, this book is written from the perspective of a certain historical moment, the present one: the concept of the environment is particularly relevant today because we have good reason to believe that we are facing an environmental crisis. We therefore need to understand *what* it is that is in crisis and what role our species plays not only in the crisis but also in its management. Investigating the concept of the environment from a present-tense perspective, however, does not exclude (and indeed requires) a historical reconstruction of it that can help to clarify its current meaning and uses.

Second, the notion of the environment is ubiquitous and polysemic: the environment as studied by geography differs in important ways from the environment as studied by physics, biology, economics, computer science, or psychology – to mention but a few of the disciplines that treat the environment as an object of inquiry. Thus, the term does not have the same meaning in the following statements: "Human beings are destroying the environment," "Matilde is uncomfortable when she is out of her environment," or "The market in the digital environment is fragmented." Faced with the multiplicity of possible treatments, I have chosen to focus on the environment of living beings and to concentrate on findings from three scientific disciplines – evolutionary biology, developmental biology, and ecology – paying particular attention to relatively recent areas of research that emphasise the need for greater integration between the three disciplines. The conviction behind this choice is that in order to protect the environment of living beings, including humans, it is necessary to understand it, and this requires examining the relationship between developing organisms and their environments (ecology and developmental biology) over intergenerational time (evolutionary biology).

Third, the following discussion is written from a specific cultural perspective: the point of view is that of Western culture. This is for two reasons, one trivial (this is the culture to which I happen to belong) and one more substantial (the fact that environmentalism is a phenomenon that is typical of Western societies, as we will see). Importantly, in taking the point of view of Western culture, I in no way wish to imply that this is the only one or that it is preferable to others. This point allows me to mention one of the main difficulties I encountered while writing this book: deciding *what to leave out*. Some decisions to exclude certain topics were due to the limits of my expertise. For instance, the decision not to devote a thorough discussion to so-called "Native" or "Indigenous ecologies" was primarily due to my limited knowledge of this complex and multifaceted topic. I recognised the risk of both reducing the discussion to a few shallow pages and mistakenly counterposing an allegedly undifferentiated "we" (Western people) to another allegedly internally homogeneous "them" (Indigenous peoples), along with the related stereotypes (see Jax 2023, pp. 174ff.). Other exclusion decisions were made to maintain the general coherence and aim of the project, specifically that of writing a book on the environment and not, say, on biodiversity, nature, ecosystems, and so forth. Although many of these concepts are related to the environment, I have tried to focus on the latter and have used it as a guide for deciding what to include and what to exclude. This is why, although this book does not contain a section devoted specifically to biodiversity (although there are, of course, mentions of it), it does contain a chapter dedicated to nature conservation understood as the conservation of the natural *environment*. Finally, certain other decisions were motivated by disciplinary considerations. With this book, I have tried to promote a view of the philosophy of the environment that does not conflate the philosophy of the environment with environmental ethics. Accordingly, I did not embark on an explicit discussion of either the main positions or the main topics of environmental ethics (for those who are interested in environmental ethics, many books are available; I particularly recommend DesJardins 2013 and Attfield 2018).

Fourth, environmental philosophy, as understood here, takes the form of an inquiry into the concept of the environment. This enquiry is not intended to promote a particular ethical perspective and seeks as far as possible to avoid assuming one: even though the concept of the environment has been criticised as hopelessly anthropocentric (think of the title of the Stockholm Conference, devoted to the "human environment"), there are good reasons – which will be set out throughout the book – to reject this conclusion. Indeed, although our environmental concerns are primarily directed at the environment of our own species, the thesis that underlies this book is that it is impossible to manage the human environment without understanding the various ways in which living beings interact with their surroundings and without considering the extent to which the former are both products and creators of the latter.

A final caveat for the reader. There are many possible ways of engaging in the philosophy of the environment: one could write a manifesto defining the principles and objectives of the discipline, or offer a critical review of the concept of the environment in the history of philosophy, or propose a discussion of key contemporary philosophical positions on the environment. While not excluding these approaches, the philosophy of the environment as understood in this book is primarily a form of conceptual negotiation. As Roberto Casati explains, in conceptual negotiation "we try to build an explanation or a narrative that allows us to recompose a conceptual *tension*" (Casati 2022, p. 6). Conceptual negotiation is a necessary practice whenever a major change requires us to rethink, and possibly modify, our established beliefs, ideas, and habits. The changes in question may be grounded in different sources, among which scientific discoveries undoubtedly play a major role (think of the Copernican Revolution, which removed the Earth from the centre of the universe and offered a planetary model that was at odds with both everyday experience and Ptolemy's elegant mathematical model; or consider the Darwinian Revolution, which deprived a supposed "designer" of nature of its explanatory role). Our everyday language reveals how hard it is for old ideas and habits to die: sentences like "The sun is setting over the horizon" and questions such as "What are mosquitoes for?" show the extent of the need to negotiate between our perceptual (we see the sun going down) and cognitive (we think teleologically) systems, on the one hand, and the scientific image of the world, on the other. The tools of such negotiation are many: they include (historical) conceptual analysis, mental experiments, examples, and arguments.

It is hard to deny that the current climate crisis is bringing about extreme changes that necessitate conceptual negotiation and a search for compromise between these concepts and our established ideas and beliefs about the world, including our place and role in it. The environmental crisis has meant that notions such as "environment" and "nature" must be rethought, as must our relationship with other species. Understanding the philosophy of the environment through the lens of conceptual negotiation is an approach that is both ambitious and modest: it is ambitious insofar as it involves arbitrating between different actors and fields of research, straddling the past (established ideas and beliefs), the present (the environmental crisis), and possible futures. It is modest insofar as it is a preliminary exploration: as understood in this book, environmental philosophy does not offer norms of behaviour or solutions to the crisis. What it does offer, however, is a historical and conceptual basis for elaborating such norms and solutions at both a personal and an institutional level, as an individual or as a community endeavour.

3 Structure of the book

The book consists of five chapters, each built around a specific thesis.

The first reconstructs a history of the concept of "environment". Its guiding thesis is that the modern concept of the environment was born, together with the organism–environment dyad, from the combination of the concept of a *medium*, stemming from Newtonian mechanics, and the concept of external conditions or circumstances, in use in evolutionary biology.

Based on the history traced in the first chapter, the second chapter engages in a systematic treatment of the environment of living beings. Its guiding thesis is that the concept of environment is constitutively relational: the environment always belongs to something or someone, and the relationship at issue is a complex web of linear and cyclic causal relationships, on both a local and a global scale.

The third and fourth chapters deal with the environment of a particular species, *Homo sapiens*, and are devoted to the artificial and natural components of that environment, respectively, according to the characterisation of the human environment proposed by the Stockholm declaration mentioned earlier. Humans, like all other species, are subject to the action of their environment and construct their own environment. Whether the traditional natural/artificial distinction represents an adequate heuristic tool for dealing with such a construction is a matter of debate.

The first four chapters offer a systematic treatment – albeit partial and perspectival – of the environment of living beings and the human environment as a special case, thus providing a possible key for better understanding the current environmental crisis. The fifth and final chapter offers suggestions for thinking about the present situation. The background thesis of the final chapter is that there are good reasons to believe that the current environmental change constitutes a crisis that calls for a rethinking of both environmentalism and the traditional concept of nature.

Notes

1 The non-violent practice of hugging trees to prevent them from being felled dates back to an event known as the "Khejarli Massacre". In 1730, the soldiers of Maharaja Abhai Singh were sent to Khejarli, a village inhabited by the Bishnoi community (a religious sect whose daily life revolves around 29 precepts, many of which focus

on environmental protection), with orders to cut down the village's trees – considered sacred – to build a new palace. To stop this, a woman named Amrita Devi hugged one of the trees, refusing to move, and was consequently beheaded. Her three daughters took her place and were killed in the same manner. The massacre continued, resulting in the death of 363 Bishnoi. Upon hearing of their sacrifice, the maharaja revoked the deforestation order and instituted a ban on cutting the trees of the Bishnois, who are regarded by many as among the first environmentalists in history. Their actions inspired the Chipko movement (chipko = to hug), an organisation led by women from various villages in northern India, which fought against commercial deforestation in the 1970s and 1980s. Tree hugging has thus become a method of non-violent environmental activism that is still practised today in various parts of the world (one place to read about this and other non-violent action methods is the Global Nonviolent Action Database).
2 Canguilhem uses the French term *milieu* (which, like the French *environnement*, can be translated as "environment"). The relationship between *environment* and *milieu* will become clear in Chapter 1.

References

Attfield, R. (2018) *Environmental Ethics: A Very Short Introduction*. Oxford: Oxford University Press.

Canguilhem, G. (2001) 'The living and its milieu'. Translated by J. Savage, *Grey Room*, 3, pp. 6–31.

Carson, R. (1962/2002) *Silent Spring*. Boston, MA: Houghton Mifflin Harcourt.

Casati, R. (2022) *Philosophy as Conceptual Negotiation*. ffhal-03937758f. Available at: https://hal.science/hal-03937758/document

DesJardins, J.R. (2013) *Environmental Ethics: An Introduction to Environmental Philosophy*, 5th edition. Belmont, CA: Wadsworth.

Jax, K. (2023) *Conservation Concepts: Rethinking Human–Nature Relationships*. London: Routledge.

Meadows *et al.* (1972) *The Limits to Growth*. Falls Church, VA: Potomac Associates – Universe Books.

Passell, M., Roberts, M. and Ross, L. (1972) 'The limits to growth', *The New York Times*, 2 April, Section BR, p. 1.

United Nations (1972) *Report of the United Nations Conference on the Human Environment*. Available at: www.un.org/en/conferences/environment/stockholm1972 (Accessed 14 June 2024).

1 Discovering the surroundings

As Rachel Carson writes, "[t]he history of life on Earth has been a history of interaction between living things and their surroundings" – that is, their environment (Carson 1962/2002, p. 5). This chapter aims to explore the historical semantics of the term "environment", including its etymology and the changes in meaning it has undergone over time. Its focus is limited to Western culture, centring on a significant phase in the birth and development of the concept from the late 17th century to the early decades of the 20th century. This period was marked by great intellectual activity and advancement, as the Scientific Revolution challenged the Ptolemaic–Aristotelian paradigm and established a predominantly mechanistic view of the natural world. This in turn fostered the emergence of the modern sciences, including the appearance of biology in 1802.[1] The modern concept of "environment", understood as part of the *organism–environment* pair, was formed during this period.

The reconstruction I will offer is a proposed interpretation of complex events that span various disciplines and will thus inevitably be partial and tentative. The main two guiding principles of this interpretation are as follows: first, the notion that the concept of environment arose as a reaction to the theoretical limitations of the traditional concept of nature, which called for a *relational* concept that emphasised the interplay between organisms and their surroundings; second, the hypothesis that the concept of environment also emerged to explain phenomena that revealed the interdependent network of relationships among the various components of the biosphere, as well as humanity's role in that network. These phenomena, such as the relationship between deforestation and climate change and, more generally, the consequences of technical advancements for the natural world, were starkly revealed as a result of specific historical circumstances: the Industrial Revolution and naturalists' voyages around the world. Indeed, the 18th and 19th centuries were marked by environmental exploration and discovery, with naturalists being taken as guests on government-funded naval exploratory expeditions thanks to a shared interest on the part of the state and the scientific community. However, this period was also marked by the transition to a fossil fuel–based energy regime, as our species witnessed the rise of the Industrial Revolution.

DOI: 10.4324/9781003479642-2

Discovering the surroundings 9

Drawing on the reconstruction presented by philosopher Georges Canguilhem (1904–1955), this chapter explores the historical development of the concept of environment, tracing its origins in Newtonian mechanics (Section 1.1) and following its evolution through Lamarck's evolutionary theory and Humboldt's theory of nature (Section 1.2). I then identify as a crucial moment the explicit formulation of the concept of environment and the organism–environment dyad by positivist philosophers Auguste Comte (1798–1857) and Herbert Spencer (1820–1903) (Section 1.3). Next, in addition to outlining the Darwinian view, I explore a non-evolutionary perspective on the relationship between organisms and their environment. Whereas Darwinian evolutionary biology views this relationship in terms of the organism's adaptation to the environment, the Estonian biologist Jakob von Uexküll (1864–1944) instead views it in terms of the organism's construction of its environment (Section 1.4). Lastly, I discuss ecology, the scientific field that emerged specifically to study the relationship between organisms and their environment (Section 1.5).

1.1 The concept of environment

The recent pandemic, which had a dramatic effect on our species, vividly highlighted the impact of human activities on nature. During government-imposed lockdowns to deal with the health emergency, the water in city canals became clear again, dolphins were seen swimming in harbours, and the air became cleaner due to decreased car and aeroplane traffic. In other words, slowing down our activities seems to have benefitted the environment.

The terms "environment" and "nature" are often used interchangeably, as in the previous paragraph. Indeed, it seems reasonable to say that slowing down our activities has a positive impact on the environment, and it is undeniable that water, the sky, and dolphins are all part of nature. However, let us consider for a moment the unwanted guest responsible for the situation described earlier: a virus of the genus *Betacoronavirus*. It, too, is part of nature, perhaps more so than the water in city canals, whose flow is partially determined by our activities. Yet, we do not view its proliferation as positive; rather, we have implemented strategies to limit its spread, such as seeking medicines to counteract its effects on our health and developing a vaccine.

Hence, there is a substantial difference between nature and environment: whereas the former can be seen as a class of entities – natural objects and processes – the latter has a *relational* character. The environment always belongs *to* someone or something. Although both *H. sapiens* and SARS-CoV-2 are, in the same way, part of nature, their environments are not the same. On the contrary, the problem is that *H. sapiens* provides an ideal environment for the virus: it thrives within human cells, using their metabolism to multiply and live.[2] However, this parasitic activity typically results in the death of the host cell (hence the term *virus*, meaning venom in Latin).

The concept of environment is certainly more recent than that of nature. If we look at the etymology of the term, we find that "environment" is imported from the French *environnement*, which means surrounding. In general, the origin of the term is similar in various European languages: the Italian *ambiente* comes from the Latin *ambiens, -entis*, present participle of *ambire*, meaning to go around, to surround. The prefix *amb* (often shortened to *am* or *an*) means around, on both sides, on all sides, as does the prefix *en* in the French *environnement* and the English *environment*, as well as the prefix *um* in the German *Umwelt*. Originally, therefore, the term functioned as an adjective, as in the *Surgery of Gabriel Falloppio*, where it is advised that the "ambient air" (*aere ambiente*) is one of the primary causes of inflammation (Falloppio 1603). By extension, the term is also used as a noun, to indicate the fluid – air or water – surrounding a body. For example, it appears in the final addendum to Giacomo Pergamini's *Memorial of the Italian Language* (1602/1688), where we read that the term "environment" (*ambiente*), "as termed by experts in Philosophy, refers to the Air, insofar as it surrounds bodies, in which they are found as in a place". Similarly, in the *Universal Critical Encyclopedic Dictionary of the Italian Language* by the abbot Francesco Alberti di Villanova, we read that "environment" (*ambiente*) is "that liquid substance which surrounds something, commonly referring to the air" (Alberti di Villanova 1797–1805).

In his 1704 treatise *Opticks*, Isaac Newton (1642–1726) makes use of the concept of a fluid to explain action at a distance. In his 1952 essay "The Living and Its Milieu", Georges Canguilhem suggests that the history of the concept of environment begins precisely with Newton (Canguilhem 2001). Action at a distance is one of the most controversial issues in the history of mechanics. In a world made only of corpuscles of matter, how is it possible for two celestial bodies to act on each other without touching, as evidenced by gravity? Yet gravitational attraction – as well as magnetic attraction and vision – seem to prove that action between bodies can occur even without physical contact. The explanation proposed in Newton's *Opticks* is that there is a fluid, the aether, that acts as an intermediary between bodies. Imagine you are in the dark and see a light in the distance. On one side you have a light source, on the other side your eye. Between the two bodies, for Newton, there must be a subtle fluid – the aether – that acts as a medium, as an *intermediary between the two centres*, the light source and the eye (cf. Altamirano 2016, pp. 129ff.).

According to Canguilhem, the theory of fluid as medium was adopted by French biology in the second half of the 18th century (this is not surprising considering that in *Opticks* this theory explained a physiological reaction, namely the reaction of eye muscles to light). In French biology, as we shall see, the term used to refer to the fluid as medium is "milieu" (*mi-lieu*, middle place) – an expression that is still used today, even outside the French language, to refer to the environment, often in the social and cultural sense of the word. The term – which I will keep in French – is used in Lamarckian evolutionary theory alongside "external circumstances" or "habitation circumstances". It was from the unification of the two concepts, *milieu* and *circumstances*, that the modern concept of environment was born.

1.2 Circumstances

That external circumstances – what we now call "environmental factors" – have an impact on living things is an ancient idea: at the beginning of his treatise *On Airs, Waters, and Places*, Hippocrates (c. 460–377 BCE) encouraged medical students to check a place's exposure and position relative to winds and sunrise, the nature of the waters (marshy, mountainous, or brackish), as well as the humidity or dryness of the soil. As Hippocrates writes, it is the consideration of these factors, together with diet and, more generally, lifestyle, that enables the physician to know the nature of a place and the particular diseases that dominate the area. According to the medical conception of the time, the external circumstances that influence the health of patients and their physiology include not only natural factors but also the products of human action: cities and wars affect the state of people's health in the same way as water, soil, food, and the stars do.

External circumstances and their causal influence on organisms would also be central to theories of evolution, where they would take different names: in addition to "circumstances" we find, for example, the expressions "surrounding circumstances", "natural circumstances", "external conditions", "places of habitation", and "conditions of life". As these terminological variations help to show, the concept of *circumstances* – like that of *milieu* – is fundamentally relational: circumstances are *around* something and can be more or less favourable to it.

The road that leads from the idea of *multiple* external circumstances influencing the lives of individual organisms to the notion of environment, understood as a whole in its relation to the living, is far from simple, linear, or immediate, as we shall see, and passes through two semantic shifts. One of these, to which I have already alluded, consists in the fusion of the concept of circumstances and that of *milieu*; the other is instead represented by the unification of the multiplicity of circumstances in a unitary concept. The result of these two shifts is the modern concept of environment, understood as part of the *organism–environment* pair.

1.2.1 Surrounding circumstances

When natural philosophers of the 17th and 18th centuries spoke of *evolution*, they usually meant embryogenesis: the development of the embryo. To them, evolution was the process by which organisms acquire their own form, through the growth and differentiation of their parts according to a given developmental trajectory. Some – like the preformationists – held that the formation of new features in the course of development was simply the unfolding of characteristics already contained (*preformed*, in fact) in the sperm, egg, or zygote. Others – like the epigenesists – held that development was an evolutionary process in which qualitatively new features emerged from formless matter.

There was thus consensus that organisms evolve (develop). As for species, however, by the late 17th century the idea had been established that their numbers were fixed by divine creation and had not changed since then. Some naturalists, however – including Erasmus Darwin (1731–1802), Charles's grandfather – rejected fixism, believing that species had indeed transformed over time, a fact that empirical evidence (e.g. fossil findings) seemed to confirm. However, it was Jean-Baptiste de Lamarck (1744–1829) who elaborated the first systematic theory of the transformation, or evolution, of species. Initially a fixist, around 1800 Lamarck began to develop the belief that species transform, by virtue of both a natural tendency toward greater complexity or perfection and the adaptation of organisms to external circumstances (Box 1.1).

The idea that organisms adapt to external circumstances is thus at the heart of the first systematic theory of evolution, set forth in the *Zoological Philosophy* (1809). According to Lamarck, external circumstances, which may be favourable or unfavourable to development and survival, are primarily the abiotic (non-living) characteristics of places: climate, sunlight, type of water or soil, temperature, humidity, air, and so on.

But how can circumstances, which are *external* to organisms, exert causal action on vital functions such as growth, development, and the regeneration of parts, which originate within them? The explanation adopted by the French naturalist is the Newtonian mechanistic view we saw in the previous section: it is through the fluid, the *milieu* (which Lamarck uses almost always in the plural, *milieux*), that external circumstances can exert causal action on organisms. Fluids, in fact, are able to convey the goings-on of external circumstances and penetrate organisms: as we read in the Preface to *Zoological Philosophy* (Lamarck 2011, p. 5), "subtle and ever moving fluids contained in the environment (*milieux*) incessantly penetrate these organised bodies".[3]

At the same time, Lamarck points out, *milieux* are also a specific type of circumstance, indeed the most influential, because they can act directly on organisms. As he explains in Chapter VI of *Zoological Philosophy*, for example, amphibians and cetaceans habitually live in dense *milieux*, where highly developed limbs would hinder movement: that is why their limbs are very short.

According to Lamarck, therefore, circumstances greatly influence the development of organisms and, consequently, the transformation of the species to which they belong over time. The concept of environment began to take shape precisely from the encounter and mutual interpenetration of the concept of *milieu* and that of *circumstances*, whose causal effects on organisms is the subject of Lamarckian theory. In other words, the concepts of *milieu* and external circumstances ultimately aim to express the same idea: that what surrounds organisms shapes them, or, if you will, that organisms – their physiology and behaviour – are as they are due to the causal action of what surrounds them.

BOX 1.1 Lamarck's theory of evolution

The term "transformism" is generally used to refer to the Lamarckian theory of evolution, to distinguish it from the theory of evolution by natural selection. Unlike the latter, for which the evolution of life proceeds in a tree-like fashion from a common origin, for Lamarck each line of descent arises as a result of an episode of spontaneous generation. The earliest forms of each species are simple and gradually become more complex over time (in this sense species transform: worms *become* vertebrates over generations). The most complex species today, in other words, are the oldest. Four explanatory mechanisms underlie this transformation: (i) the causal influence of external circumstances on organisms, (ii) the action of the medium, (iii) an internal force within nature that drives the complexification process; and (iv) inheritance (see La Vergata 2003; Taylan 2020).

(i) According to Lamarck, external circumstances influence the habits of organisms, that is, the repetition of the same acts over a long period of time. These, in turn, affect the structure of the organism, its components, and their organisation. If circumstances change, so do habits and, consequently, organisms themselves. Put differently: a change in circumstances can lead to the emergence of a new need in an organism and cause it to adopt a new behaviour that involves a different use of a pre-existing organ. Prolonged use of this organ will lead to its strengthening, which in turn will imply a reorganisation of the parts that make up the organism. A different change in circumstances may instead induce an organism to discontinue the use of a certain organ, the size of which will tend to decrease until the organ disappears altogether.

(ii) External circumstances can act on organisms through the *milieux*, the fluids in which they are immersed, according to the Newtonian model. More precisely, for Lamarck, nature is pervaded by subtle fluids – such as caloric (a hypothetical fluid that is responsible for the different temperatures of bodies) and electricity. Through the *milieux* that surround organisms and are able to penetrate them, such as air and water, external fluids mechanically excite the fluids inside organisms, giving rise to vital movements.

(iii) To explain why life forms become more complex over time, Lamarck introduces a "vital power" or "power of nature" that drives them to grow, develop, and become more complex. This force is an intrinsic property of living matter which, operating together with (i), the influence of external circumstances, produces the transformation of species over time. It is worth noting that, while the term "vital

> power" suggests a vitalist interpretation of Lamarck's thought, according to some authors (see, for instance, La Vergata 2003), there is nothing vitalist or finalistic about Lamarck's idea, since the tendency to complexification cannot be considered apart from its basis in (ii), fluid mechanics.
> (iv) In order for the changes in organisms caused by external circumstances and the vital power to result in the transformation of species over time, it is necessary for these changes to be inheritable, that is, transmissible to descendants. Today we know that, as a rule, the changes acquired by an organism during its lifetime are not transmissible. Like most of his contemporaries, however, Lamarck believed that characteristics acquired in the course of life through the use and disuse of organs could indeed be inherited. Thus, he posited a very close link between development (of organisms) and evolution (of species).

It is worth recalling a choice of terminology on Lamarck's part to which I have already alluded. In *Zoological Philosophy*, one sometimes finds the expression *circonstances d'habitation* (literally "habitation circumstances"). This clearly contains a reference to inhabitation – a reference that would become explicit in the concept of habitat (third person singular of the Latin *habitare*, to dwell, to inhabit) typical of contemporary ecology:

> We therefore define "habitat" as the resources and conditions present in an area that produce occupancy – including survival and reproduction – by a given organism. Habitat is organism-specific; it relates the presence of a species, population, or individual (animal or plant) to an area's physical and biological characteristics. Habitat . . . is the sum of the specific resources that are needed by organisms. Wherever an organism is provided with resources that allow it to survive, that is habitat.
> (Hall, Krausman and Morrison 1997, p. 175)

As with "environment", there is no single, universally accepted definition of "habitat" (the one just given resulted from a critical analysis of the literature). The main difference between the two terms, which are often used synonymously, is probably that "habitat" comes from scientific ecology, and thus it is normally used within that discipline and has a more limited polysemy.

More generally, in Lamarckian – as well as Humboldtian, and later Darwinian – discourse, we can identify an early use of concepts that would become central to scientific ecology, a field that will be discussed at the end of this chapter. Furthermore, the texts of the French naturalist also contain a foreshadowing of environmentalist thought. This should come as no surprise: Lamarck wrote in the midst of the Industrial Revolution, marked by the introduction of steam engines (produced through fossil fuels), unprecedented population growth, and the massive conversion of prairies and forests into arable land (consider the fact that between the 19th and the mid-20th century, some 17 million square kilometres of prairie land were converted to other uses, mainly cultivation; see McNeill 2000). The following passage is emblematic of Lamarckian environmentalism:

> With a short-sighted selfishness toward his own interests, with a tendency to enjoy whatever he has at his disposal, in a word with disregard for his own and his fellows' future, man seems to be striving for the annihilation of his own livelihood and the destruction of his own species. By destroying everywhere the great plants that protected the soil to satisfy his immediate activity, man rapidly renders sterile the land he inhabits, causes the springs to dry up, drives away the animals that find sustenance there, and causes large parts of the globe, once fertile and populated, to be now bare, barren, uninhabitable and deserted.... Man seems destined to exterminate himself after making the Earth uninhabitable.
>
> (Lamarck 1820, p. 154, note 1)

1.2.2 Environmentalism before the environment

Based on Lamarck's theory, in the first half of the 19th century naturalists took an interest in studying the influence of external conditions on organisms and the correspondence between certain external conditions and certain types of organisms. A central figure among them (not only for the history of the concept of environment but also, as we will see in the course of the book, for reflection on the contemporary environmental crisis and the birth of environmentalism) was undoubtedly the German naturalist, philosopher, and explorer Alexander von Humboldt (1769–1859). Described by his contemporaries as the most famous man of his era after Napoleon, he is now considered the founder of phytogeography,[4] a forerunner of ecology and environmentalism, and was one of the first naturalists to hypothesise a link between human activities and climate.

Humboldt adopted an innovative approach compared to the botanical studies of his time, which centred on individual plants or plant types and focused on description and classification. Instead, his method was quantitative and statistical, and his investigation focused on the *causes* of the distribution, composition, and geographical spread of plant communities (groupings of plants of different species inhabiting a given territory according to given geobotanical regularities). Why do we find similar plant communities in certain kinds of areas, even when they are far apart? What is the reason for such regularity? According to Humboldt, the answer was to be found in the causal action exerted by external circumstances: climate, temperature, and atmospheric pressure. Humboldt's thought brought out the idea of a correlation between organisms and between organisms and their environment – a concept that would be characteristic of modern scientific ecology. Indeed, the

Danish botanist Eugene Warming (1841–1924), considered one of the founders of the discipline, would equate the ecological approach with the study of how plants and vegetal communities adjust their structure and behaviour to external factors such as the available quantity of heat, light, nourishment, and water (see Acot 1988, p. 48).

Humboldt's proto-ecological insights were largely the result of his explorations around the world (cf. Wulf 2015). If exploration voyages provided naturalists with new lenses through which to view the world, the Industrial Revolution taking place in Europe, along with the exploitation of natural resources in the colonies, was beginning to raise suspicions that many of our species' activities had negative consequences for other species, and indeed for humanity itself.

On his most important journey, Humboldt spent five years exploring different areas of the Americas. Together with his friend and travelling companion, French botanist Aimé Bonpland, he travelled more than 9,000 kilometres on foot, horseback, and canoe, traversing the territories of present-day Venezuela, Colombia, Ecuador, Peru, Cuba, and Mexico. He was thus able to compare the vegetation of these places with that of Europe, noting that regions with a similar climate in different parts of the world were populated by similar plants. He depicted this insight – accompanied and supported by measurements of altitude, temperature, humidity, and the chemical composition of the air, which he had meticulously collected at every step – in an illustration that became famous: the *Naturgemälde*. Humboldt himself called it "a microcosm on one page".[5]

The illustration reproduces the Chimborazo volcano in present-day Ecuador (a volcano that Humboldt climbed, becoming the first person in the world to reach an altitude of 5,917 metres). Chimborazo is drawn in a cross section, with the plants (as well as the fungi and lichens that interact with them) distributed according to altitude. Arranged in columns to the left and right of the image are details and information about what is depicted. This arrangement made it possible to consider a particular altitude of the mountain and to draw connections with other information in the table, so as to relate the different plant and animal species present at different altitudes to temperature, humidity, and atmospheric pressure. In turn, this information could be compared with similar information about other major mountains of the world, listed next to the Chimborazo outline. While such correlations may seem trivial today, at the time this was an innovative approach: as historian Andrea Wulf put it, Humboldt was the first to look at "vegetation through the lens of climate and location: a radically new idea that still shapes our understanding of ecosystems today" (Wulf 2015, p. 89).

Explorations of distant parts of the world also allowed Humboldt to develop another kind of insight, making him a forerunner of environmentalism in his own right. It was during his long journey through South America in particular that he was able to observe the environmental consequences of colonial rule. And it was at Lake Valencia, Venezuela, that he hypothesised the existence of a link between human activities and climate.

Lake Valencia, which Humboldt and Bonpland reached in 1800, was located in a valley renowned for being green and lush. As local residents told the two travellers, however, water levels were rapidly dropping, large areas that had been under water until two decades earlier were now intensively farmed fields, and the coastline kept receding. The inhabitants' hypothesis was that an underground outlet was draining the lake, but Humboldt – based on the empirical data collected – proposed a different explanation, namely that the cause instead lay in the felling of the surrounding forests, the consequent exposure of the soil, and the redirection of water to irrigate the fields. Whereas in the past forests had protected the soil from the sun and reduced evaporation, logging had dried up the soil and was draining the lake. *Everything was connected*:

> When forests are destroyed, as they are everywhere in America by the European planters, with an imprudent precipitation, the springs are entirely dried up, or become less abundant. The beds of the rivers, remaining dry during a part of the year, are converted into torrents, whenever great rains fall on the heights. The sward and moss disappearing with the brushwood from the sides of the mountains, the waters falling in rain are no longer impeded in their course: and instead of slowly augmenting the level of the rivers by progressive filtrations, they furrow during heavy showers the sides of the hills, bear down the loosened soil, and form those sudden inundations, that devastate the country.
> (Humboldt 1814–1829, quoted in Wulf 2015, pp. 57–58)

It was thus at Lake Valencia that the idea of *anthropogenic climate change*, that is, change resulting from human activities, was first formulated. More broadly, Humboldt pointed to three ways in which human activities affect climate: deforestation, reckless irrigation, and the "great masses of steam and gas" produced by industrial centres (Humboldt 1843, quoted in Wulf 2015, p. 213). The hypothesis of a correlation between atmospheric gases and the Earth's temperature was later tested experimentally in 1856 by the American scientist Eunice Foote (1819–1888), who related changes in the types and amounts of atmospheric gases – including carbon dioxide – to warming and climate change, concluding that an increase in CO_2 in the atmosphere would increase the Earth's temperature (Foote 1856).

Humboldt's thought thus anticipates very current themes and considerations, such as a systemic view of nature and an appreciation of the environmental impact of human activities. He also acknowledged the relationship between socio-political and environmental conditions, so much so that he actively fought against slavery and the exploitation of human beings and natural resources by colonising countries. However, he did not explicitly address the *environment* in his work. The concept was in the air, as it were, but

18 *Philosophy of the environment*

had not yet been born. Humboldt's reflections were in fact a reflection on nature, which he saw as a living network of relationships, an interconnected and harmonious whole that requires science as much as art and sensibility to be understood. In such a whole made up of interrelated parts, a change in one component can have unpredictable consequences on another, as well as on the entire system. Within such a view of nature, in which the study of the relations between organisms and external circumstances plays a central role, we catch a glimpse of the modern concept of environment. Its official birth, however, would occur in another context, as I will now illustrate.

1.3 The birth of the environment

The birth of the modern concept of environment was made possible by two conditions: first, the synthesis initiated by Lamarck between circumstances and *milieux*, and second, the fusion of the various factors that constitute circumstances into a single, unified concept. These conditions were realised through the work of two philosophers, Auguste Comte and Herbert Spencer, the founder and a leading exponent (respectively) of the movement known as *positivism*, according to which philosophy must be configured as positive knowledge that, following the model of the sciences, restricts itself to experimentally ascertained facts and data.

We have seen that for Lamarck, the *milieux* are both what conveys the causal action of circumstances and a particular type of circumstance – indeed the most important kind, able to affect organisms directly. In 1838, Auguste Comte proposed a general biological theory of the *milieu* (using the term in the singular, unlike Lamarck) in the 40th lecture of his *Course on Positive Philosophy* (1838). This work – along with Charles Lyell's (1797–1875) *Principles of Geology* of 1830 – played a key role in spreading Lamarck's evolutionism after the French naturalist's death (cf. Galera 2017).

In presenting his theory, Comte explicitly states that he uses the term *milieu* to designate "sharply and quickly, not only the fluid in which the organism is immersed but, in general, the overall set of external circumstances, of whatever kind, necessary for the existence of each organism", asserting that life "constantly presupposes the necessary correlation of the two indispensable elements, an appropriate organism and a suitable *milieu*" (Comte 1838, p. 301, note 1).

Comte's polemical target was the conception held by the vitalist Xavier Bichat[6] (1771–1802), for whom life was nothing more than the set of functions that oppose death. Bichat's conviction was in fact that a living organism is a kind of reaction centre, an island of resistance against the forces of decay and decomposition that, time and again, assail it until they prevail with the death of the organism itself (cf. Haigh 1975). This view completely overlooked "one of the two inseparable elements whose harmony necessarily constitutes the general idea of *life*" (Comte 1838, pp. 288–289). In proposing his theory of the *milieu*, Comte thus sought to propose a new conception of life. A living being is not only an organism composed of certain parts organised in a certain way, but also one that is in a given relationship with its surroundings, with "such an arrangement of external influences as will also admit of (the vital state). The harmony between the living being and the corresponding *medium* (as I shall call its environment) evidently characterises the fundamental condition of life" (Comte 1838, p. 289).

Life, then, cannot be understood as abstracted from its surroundings, and a living organism cannot be understood except in relation to the environment. For Comte, this relationship is – we would say today – a feedback relationship: the environment cannot modify the organism without the latter's exerting a corresponding influence on it, inevitably modifying it. However, in general, feedback is rather negligible, according to Comte, and can be reduced to the Newtonian principle of action-reaction. The only exception to this is our species, which, through collective action, is able to radically modify its *milieu*.

There is no need to go further into the details of Comtean theory here. What I would like to emphasise is a semantic shift: a plurality of factors (external circumstances) is subsumed under a single concept, designated by Comte as *milieu*. *Milieu* is a relational concept (a *milieu* is always *of* someone or something), and the relationship in question is a feedback relationship: the organism modifies its *milieu*, and this in turn modifies "its" organism. The result of this relationship is a correspondence between its two terms. Hence the *organism–environment* dyad, which would also be applied outside the biological sphere (for example in the humanities, and specifically in sociology, a discipline of which Comte is considered the founder).

Studies on the relationship between the organism and its *milieu* are central to the work of French physiologist Claude Bernard (1813–1878), the founder of modern experimental physiology. We are indebted to Bernard for both the development of a systemic view of the study of living things and the concept of homeostasis, though not for the term itself, which was coined by American physiologist Walter Cannon (1871–1945). Both elements will be important for the remainder of this book, and thus it is worth discussing them here, albeit briefly.

According to Bernard, to understand a living being it is necessary to know not only its structure, the order of its different parts, but also its organisation, that is, how the different parts and the processes in which they participate are related to each other and to the whole organism. The functioning of the organism depends on this organisation (cf. Bich 2012; Mossio and Bich 2017).

The interactions between the parts and processes that take place within organisms (in what Bernard calls the *milieu intérieur*, the internal environment) cannot, however, be understood in abstraction from the external environment: as he wrote in the 1865 *Introduction to the Study of Experimental Medicine*, "the conditions necessary to life are found neither in the organism nor in the outer environment, but in both at once" (Bernard 1957, p. 75). Put differently, it is only in the interaction between organism and external environment that vital phenomena emerge.

20 *Philosophy of the environment*

While organisms cannot be separated from their environment, they nevertheless exhibit a degree of independence from it. This is because their internal environment, where organic processes take place, is different from the external environment, and one of its distinguishing characteristics is precisely the ability to keep its properties constant in the face of changes in the latter. This ability of organisms is now called "homeostasis" and is defined as a process of self-regulation by which an organism (or, more generally, a biological system) maintains internal stability in the face of changing external conditions. It is through its capacity for homeostatic regulation that an organism can keep its internal conditions fairly constant and thus adapt to a changing and often hostile external environment.

The use of the organism–environment dyad was consolidated outside France through the work of Herbert Spencer (cf. Pearce 2010a, 2014). When Spencer, who embraced the relational view of external circumstances promoted by Lamarck and Humboldt, read the English translation of Comte's *Cours de philosophie positive*, he found a new conception of life that responded to that view. Comte's proposal, focusing on the correspondence between organism and environment, thus became the heart of Spencer's *Principles of Psychology* of 1855. For Spencer, as for Comte, life cannot be understood as abstracted from the environment, and this applies not only to physiological changes and processes but also to intelligence and the mind:

> the life of the organism will be short or long, low or high, according to the extent to which changes in the environment, are met by corresponding changes in the organism. Allowing a margin for perturbations, the life will continue only while the correspondence continues; the completeness of the life will be proportionate to the completeness of the correspondence; and the life will be perfect only when the correspondence is perfect.
>
> (Spencer 1855, p. 376)

In Spencer's *Principles*, the Comtean term *milieu* becomes *environment*, a word that Comte's translator took from the historian and philosopher Thomas Carlyle (1795–1881), who had coined it in the late 1820s to translate the Goethean *Umgebung*. (However, the organism–environment dyad, corresponding to *Organismus–Umgebung*, seems to be absent in German texts prior to Comte and Spencer's reception.)

At this point, *environment* spread throughout the English-speaking world, both in the natural sciences and in the humanities. Due to Spencer's popularity and influence – with some considering him the most famous philosopher of his time[7] – his works were translated into a variety of languages and read around the world, even outside the scientific community. His popularity contributed significantly to the spread of the term and the organism–environment pair beyond English-speaking countries as well.

Comte and Spencer's role in the construction of the modern concept of environment was to conceptually unify external circumstances with Lamarck's *milieux*, on the one hand, and to unify these circumstances with each other into a single, cohesive concept, on the other. In this way, the two philosophers enabled the emergence and spread of the organism–environment dyad, a new object of study not only for the natural sciences but also for the humanities. Of course, the emergence and establishment of a new concept does not imply the disappearance of previous ones – in this case, circumstances or *milieux*. As a rule, old concepts tend to coexist with new ones at least for a time, being used interchangeably (before eventually, but not necessarily, becoming semantically established). This is the case with "circumstances" and "environment", which were generally used as synonyms by Spencer and his contemporaries (see Pearce 2010a). I will do the same in the next section, where I illustrate the theory of evolution by natural selection.

1.4 Adaptation and construction

At the same time that Comte and Spencer were establishing the organism–environment dyad in philosophy, the theory of evolution by natural selection was being developed in biology. This theory enriched the concept of environment, which was still typically referred to as "external circumstances", by introducing a new function: natural selection. In the theory of evolution by natural selection, it is the environment that determines whether a particular "proposition" of the organism, such as a random variation in its physiology or behaviour, is beneficial to that organism. In the former case, it will be *selected*, that is, preserved and transmitted; in the latter, it will be lost. The correspondence mentioned by Comte and Spencer is thus interpreted in terms of the adaptation of organisms to the environment by means of natural selection. In the early 20th century, Jakob von Uexküll proposed a different interpretation of the relationship between organism and environment. He explained this correspondence not through natural selection but rather by resorting to a form of construction that, as we shall see, can be defined as "transcendental construction".

1.4.1 Natural selection

It was mainly to follow in the footsteps of his hero Humboldt – whose work he took with him on the Beagle, a British navy brig adapted for reconnaissance activities – that young Charles Darwin (1809–1882) embarked on the voyage following which he would develop his theory of evolution by natural selection. The voyage lasted five years and enabled him to explore the islands (including the famous Galapagos) and the continent of South America. A few years later, another naturalist, Alfred Russell Wallace (1823–1913) – also inspired by Humboldt's adventures and by those of Austrian ethnographer Ida Laura Preiffer (1797–1858) and Darwin himself (see Van Wyhe 2019) – explored first Brazil and then the Malay Archipelago. Independently and at the same time as Darwin, he reached the same conclusions regarding the origin of the diversity of living forms.

The theory of evolution by natural selection proposed by Darwin and Wallace contains a conception of external circumstances that differs in important ways from Lamarckian theory. The most important such difference is that their causal influence on organisms is exercised primarily (though not only) *a posteriori*. Another difference worth mentioning is that while Lamarck focuses on abiotic environmental factors, for Darwin and Wallace a prominent role is played by biotic factors, that is, other organisms. To understand the relevance of these two differences, it is necessary to consider the theory in further detail.

We have seen how, for Lamarck, changes in organisms – which I shall call "variations" – result from the use or disuse of certain organs in response to environmental changes (Box 1.1). In this view, the organism responds to the demands of the environment, we might say. Accordingly, variations adapt the organism to the external circumstances in which it lives. For Darwin and Wallace, by contrast, variations arise randomly and therefore are not necessarily guaranteed to enable the organism to live well in its circumstances. To use more technical language, according to the theory of evolution by natural selection, there is no certainty that a given variation will increase the fitness – the ability to survive and reproduce – of the organism that carries it compared to one that has no such variation.

Organisms that carry variations that make them fit for their environment will be able to pass them on to their offspring; such characteristics will thus become prevalent within a species over an evolutionary timescale. In a herd of gazelles running away from a lion, the slowest one will be caught, while the one with the *longest leg* variation, being faster than the other members of the herd, has a better chance of surviving and reproducing, thus transmitting its trait to subsequent generations. This is the central point of the theory of evolution by natural selection: the causal role of external circumstances in modifying organisms, present in Lamarck, is complemented by a different one, which becomes primary. External circumstances function as a kind of sieve or testing ground for variations, which arise quite independently of them: this is how the mechanism that Darwin and Wallace called "natural selection" works.

Unlike Lamarck, who focuses on abiotic external circumstances, the theory of evolution by natural selection also acknowledges the role of other organisms. The lion is part of the gazelle's external circumstances, just like grass, soil type, and air temperature. Similarly, the gazelle is part of the lion's external circumstances: a resource just like water or other prey. An organism, then, finds itself living in a certain environment, but it is also part of the environment of other organisms, as a resource or predator, as a competitor for the same resource, or as a collaborator to obtain it. Darwin's work thus brings forth the idea of an infinitely complex network of relationships between organisms and the environment. It is a dynamic but balanced network, where the number of individuals of each species remains roughly constant because

> in the long-run the forces are so nicely balanced, that the face of nature remains for long periods of time uniform, though assuredly the merest

> trifle would give the victory to one organic being over another. Nevertheless, so profound is our ignorance, and so high our presumption, that we marvel when we hear of the extinction of an organic being; and as we do not see the cause, we invoke cataclysms to desolate the world.
>
> (Darwin 1859, p. 73)

The preceding quotation suggests that Darwin did not express concern about the impact of human activities on the environment, in contrast to Lamarck and Humboldt. Indeed, Victorian-era optimism and belief in progress are evident in Darwin's vision, which portrays nature as being in a state of equilibrium despite the "struggle for existence" described in Chapter III of *Origin*. For example, predator populations do not increase excessively to the point of wiping out all prey and starving to death, and forests can recover after being cut down. If a species becomes extinct, another will take its place. The issue of the balance of nature and the struggle for existence, which are central to ecology, will be discussed in more detail in Section 1.5.

1.4.2 *The surrounding world*

Whereas Darwinian evolutionism explains the correlation between organisms and their environment as the result of natural selection, Jakob von Uexküll, an anti-Darwinian, proposes a radically different explanation: organisms fit their environment (*Umwelt*) because the latter is their own subjective construction. It is worth devoting some space to Uexküll's theory – as dated as it is in some respects – because it anticipates, at least in part, the much more recent theory of niche construction to which we will turn, starting in the next chapter, to illustrate the feedback relationship between organisms and their environment.

Uexküll's polemical target is what he calls the "physiologist": the promoter of a mechanistic conception of the relationship between the organism (he generally speaks of animals) and its surroundings. To the physiologist, he writes,

> every living thing is an object that is located in his human world. He investigates the organs of living things and the way they work together just as a technician would examine an unfamiliar machine. The biologist, on the other hand, takes into account that each and every living thing is a subject that lives in its own world, of which it is the center.
>
> (Uexküll 2010, p. 45)

To understand the theory of *Umwelt* – environment, or literally, *surrounding world*[8] – we need to look at Uexküll's overall goal: the grounding of biology in a Kantian basis (cf. Eldridge 1928; Guidetti 2021). As he wrote in the introduction to his most important work, *Theoretical Biology*, published in 1920, "[a]ll reality is subjective appearance. This must constitute the great, fundamental admission even of biology" (Uexküll 1926, p. xv). Uexküll's position becomes clearer in the context of the following quote, taken from the *Critique of Pure Reason* (1781) by Immanuel Kant (1724–1804):

> everything intuited in space or in time, hence all objects of an experience possible for us, are nothing but appearances, i.e., mere representations, which, as they are represented, as extended beings or series of alterations, have outside our thoughts no existence grounded in itself. This doctrine I call transcendental idealism.
> (Kant 1998, p. 511)

Phenomena – Uexküll's "subjective appearance" – are the objects of experience, objects *as* they are known by a subject, based on the information gathered from their senses and cognitive structures.

Uexküll's *Umwelt* theory, presented in his 1907 manifesto *Die Umrisse einer kommenden Weltanschauung* (*Outline of a Future Worldview*) and his later work *A Foray into the Worlds of Animals and Humans* of 1934, explored the idea that the environment is a subjective representation in the Kantian sense, that is, a *transcendental construction* shaped by the subject's perceptual and operational faculties.

Let us delve into this position in a little more detail. Uexküll views animals as subjects whose primary activities are perception and action. According to him, everything an animal perceives constitutes its perception world (*Merkwelt*), and everything an animal does constitutes its effect world (*Wirkwelt*). The perception and effect worlds together make up the *Umwelt*. As organisms of the same species share similar perceptual, cognitive, and operative faculties, each species, including humans, has its own *Umwelt*.[9]

However, intraspecific differences are more significant for the human species, and each human subject has its own unique *Umwelt*. Moreover, Uexküll, in *A Foray into the Worlds of Animals and Humans*, argues that humans have augmented their eyes through instruments to the point that even the most remote stars, denizens of the ocean depths, electrons, and light waves are included in their environment.

A given *Umwelt* "corresponds" to a given organism because it results from the establishment of *functional cycles* between the organism and the objects of its perceptions and actions. To simplify, the idea is as follows. Imagine that a wave hits Matteo's optic nerve, resulting in his perception of the colour blue. Matteo will then project his perception onto the object (e.g. a ball). The sensation of blue becomes the property of being blue. The same is true for actions: in response to sensory stimulation from the ball, the subject (Matteo) will project graspability onto it. This applies to every property of the ball. By establishing a series of object/subject/object functional cycles with the ball, Matteo's *Umwelt* will include it as an object (with its blue colour, graspability, and so on). Of course, the more functional cycles an organism can establish, the richer its *Umwelt*.

To illustrate his thesis, Uexküll uses the example of a tick. From a human perspective, the life of a tick may seem rather unremarkable: it lingers on a branch or blade of grass waiting for a host, typically a mammal, to pass by; when it does, the tick drops onto it, sucks its blood, and eventually drops to the ground, lays its eggs, and dies. Uexküll argues that the tick's environment comprises three perception and three effect marks (features), which the tick attributes to the mammal based on the stimuli it receives. Specifically, the butyric acid emitted by the passing mammal is transposed as an olfactory mark that triggers the tick's action of leaving the branch (effect mark); the collision with the mammal (effect mark) causes the tick to sense its skin (tactile mark) and to begin "exploring" the mammal (effect mark) until it finds a hairless area (thermal mark) and punctures it.

In this process,

> something miraculous happens. Of all the effects emanating from the mammal's body, only three become stimuli, and then only in a certain sequence. From the enormous world surrounding the tick, three stimuli glow like signal lights in the darkness and serve as directional signs that lead the tick surely to its target. . . . *The whole rich world surrounding the tick is constricted and transformed into an impoverished structure that, most importantly of all, consists of only of three features and three effect marks – the tick's environment [Umwelt]*. However, the poverty of this environment is needed for the certainty of action, and certainty is more important than richness.
>
> (Uexküll 2010, p. 51, emphasis added)

The environment of a certain type of organism, according to Uexküll, consists of the elements of the surrounding physical world that are salient to that type, which "glow like signal lights" because they are what the organisms can perceive and what determine their possibilities for action and the effects they produce. Today we know that the indicators, or *environmental cues*, that enable a living being to reach "its target" play a fundamental role in the life and development of every organism, as well as in the functioning of ecosystems.

Although much of the biology on which Uexküll based his theory of the environment is now clearly outdated, some of his ideas – such as the notion that living things pick up cues from their environment – are still extremely relevant today. For example, as we will see in Chapters 3 and 5, anthropogenic climate change is causing the reliability of environmental cues to wane for many species. Uexküllian theory also helped to generate new areas of inquiry, such as ethology (the comparative study of animal behaviour) and biosemiotics (the study of signs and meanings in living systems).[10]

The idea that physical features *become* features of the environment of organisms *relative* to their capability of perception and action was independently developed by the ecological psychologist James J. Gibson (1904–1979).

In his *Ecological Approach to Visual Perception* of 1979, Gibson introduces the term "affordance" to mean

> something that refers to both the environment and the animal in a way that no existing term does. It implies the complementarity of the animal and the environment. . . . The affordances of the environment are what it offers the animal, what it provides or furnishes, either for good or ill.
> (Gibson 1979/1986, p. 127)

For example, Gibson continues, if, relative to the size and weight of the animal, a surface is nearly horizontal, flat, and sufficiently extended, then the surface affords support. The same surface, however, does not afford support for water bugs; for them, a different kind of surface will do the job. While properties such as being horizontal, flat, extended, and so on, are physical properties of a surface that can be measured using the standard measurements of physics, affordances have to be measured relative to the animal.[11]

A common feature that emerges from the different positions examined thus far is the idea of a *correspondence* or *harmony* (to use Comte's words) between an organism or species and its environment. The theories advanced by Lamarck, Darwin, and Wallace, on the one hand, and by Uexküll, on the other, seek to answer how such correspondence is achieved. Humboldt's work focuses on how it is structured at the level of populations and biological communities and on what its dynamics are. These questions are addressed by a specific science: ecology. As we will see in the next section, ecology is defined as the overarching science of the organism's relations with its environment.

1.5 The foundation of ecology

The history of ecology – from the Greek *oikos* (home, dwelling) – is shaped "more (like) a bush with multiple stems and a diffuse rootstock than a tree with a single, well-defined trunk and roots" (McIntosh 1985, p. 7). This science has both ancient and recent origins, with early roots tracing back to Aristotle and his student Theophrastus in *Enquiry into Plants*. The diffuse rhizome of ecology also encompasses many of the great naturalists of the 18th and 19th centuries, including Lamarck, Darwin, and Humboldt, as well as Georges-Louis Leclerc de Buffon (1707–1788) and Carl Linnaeus (1707–1778).

The history of ecology has been reconstructed in various ways. While some emphasise the Darwinian origins of the discipline (Cooper 2003), others stress the role of botanical studies and Humboldtian thought (Acot 1988). As we shall see, the term "ecology" was coined in 1866, but institutional recognition of the field did not occur until the early 20th century with the founding of the British Ecological Society (1913) and the Ecological Society of America (1915).

1.5.1 The science of the struggle for existence

To better understand the domain of ecology, we need to take a step back and return to the theory of evolution by natural selection.

Darwin and Wallace embraced the theory put forth by English economist Thomas Robert Malthus (1766–1834). In his 1798 *Essay on the Principle of Population*, Malthus argued that a population of individuals – considered in isolation and with infinite resources in terms of space and food – has the potential to grow geometrically (1, 2, 4, 8, 16, 32, 64, . . .), while livelihood production grows arithmetically (1, 2, 3, 4, 5, 6, 7, . . .). As population growth outpaces resource production, there will be a crisis point at which resources for subsistence will no longer be sufficient to support geometric population growth.

So, like the human species, all species tend to grow geometrically; but then how is it, Darwin wonders in the third chapter of *Origin*, that, all things considered, species are largely demographically stable and one does not expand disproportionately at the expense of others? The theory of evolution by natural selection adopts the mechanism hypothesised by Malthus: since more individuals are born for each species than can survive, a crisis point will be reached where a *struggle for existence* will keep population growth in check.

When Darwin speaks of a "struggle for existence", he uses the expression "in a large and metaphorical sense, including dependence of one being on another" (Darwin 1859, p. 62). In fact, we should think of the struggle for existence not (or at least not only) as a direct physical confrontation over some scarce resource, but rather as that set of strategies (conscious or not) that organisms enact to survive and reproduce.

Having a beak shape that differs from that of other birds in the population will allow its bearer to access a different type of resource, increasing its chances of survival; a seed that is more palatable than others will be more easily eaten and transported far away; an individual born with a bigger build or greater behavioural flexibility will have a better chance of surviving a harsh winter. All of these strategies are understood only within a complex network of relationships: a plant fights drought with a particular leaf shape but also competes with other plants to disperse its seeds; in this competition, it may benefit from the cooperation of birds (for example if it has more palatable fruits) or the wind (if it has lighter, more volatile seeds).

Ernst Haeckel (1834–1919), a German naturalist and follower of Humboldt and Darwin, believed that a new discipline was necessary to study the Darwinian struggle for existence, which he called "ecology". In his 1866 work, *General Morphology of Organisms*, Haeckel presented ecology as a branch of biology, specifically physiology, and provided the first definition of it: "By ecology, we mean the whole science of the relations of the organism to the environment including, in the broad sense, all the 'conditions of existence'" (quoted in Stauffer 1957, p. 140) – that is, what we have previously called "circumstances".[12]

The preceding definition, as can be seen, includes the term "environment". However, it is interesting to note that Haeckel does not use the German equivalent of "environment" (*Umwelt* or *Umgebung*). If we were to translate the definition literally, it would become: "By ecology, we mean the whole science of the relations of the organism to the external world that surrounds it (*umgebenden Aussenwelt*) including, in the broad sense, all the 'conditions of existence.'" As previously noted, the emergence of a concept – especially the concept of environment – is not always a linear or punctual process, especially when the terms that convey it and bear witness to it belong to different disciplines, languages, and cultural traditions.

External conditions, Haeckel continues, play a fundamental role in the physiology of organisms, which must adapt to them. He distinguishes between two types of external conditions: inorganic and organic. Inorganic conditions include physical and chemical properties of the environment, climate (light, heat, humidity, and atmospheric electricity), nutrients, water, and soil. Organic conditions refer to the set of relationships an organism has with other organisms with which it interacts, which can either benefit or harm it. Haeckel writes:

> Each organism has among the other organisms its friends and its enemies. . . . The organisms which serve as organic foodstuff for others or which live upon them as parasites also belong in this category of organic conditions of existence. The study of such relationships has been neglected by physiology, which has not addressed the relations of the organism to the environment, the place each organism takes in the household of nature, in the economy of all nature. . . . The theory of evolution explains the housekeeping relations of organisms mechanistically . . . and so forms the monistic groundwork of ecology.
> (Haeckel 1866, quoted in Stauffer 1957, pp. 140–141)

Studying the relationship between organism and environment thus means, for Haeckel as for Darwin, investigating both the network of relationships between organisms and their biotic and abiotic environment and the "place" each living form occupies within that network – that is, its place within the economy of nature.

1.5.2 *The economy of nature and the idea of balance*

It was the Swedish naturalist Carl Linnaeus, founder of modern taxonomy, who defined the concept of the economy of nature to which Darwin and Haeckel would refer about a century later (see Bondì and La Vergata 2015; Egerton 1973).

As we read in *Oeconomia Naturae* of 1749, for Linnaeus the economy of nature was the "all-wise disposition of the creator in relation to natural things, by which they are fitted to produce general ends, and reciprocal uses" (Linnaeus 1749, p. 31, quoted in Pearce 2010b). In this providential organisation, the balance between births and deaths maintains a roughly constant numerical proportion of different species. In addition to this, there is a complementary relationship between the functions and purposes of living forms. For instance, moulds stimulate the decomposition of dead plants to nourish the soil, which in turn provides new nutrients to plants. A fallen tree is not wasted, because it is colonised by other organisms such as worms, fungi, and insects.

Divine wisdom has ordained that all creatures should continually produce new individuals (propagation) to preserve the species and has stipulated that death and decay are always compensated by the reuse of organic matter by other organisms. Propagation, preservation, and destruction are the mechanisms that maintain the economy of nature – a state of equilibrium equivalent to bodily health for a single organism. In speaking of "economy" – beyond household (*oikos*) management – Linnaeus was in fact thinking of animal economy, which studies how body parts contribute to the functioning and health of the whole. He likely also had in mind an analogy between the organs in an animal and the species in a station, that is, in what we now call "habitat" (see Egerton 1973). Just as organs cooperate to maintain the health of an animal, interrelationships between plants and animals are aimed at the good of nature as a whole.

Darwin adopted the Linnean principle of the economy of nature, with the difference that the ordering principle is not external – that is, God – but internal to nature itself. Through the struggle for existence, organisms adapt to different environments and acquire different functions in relation to those environments, each coming to occupy its own place in the balance of nature by means of natural selection. Perhaps Linnaeus had also thought of the superorganismic metaphor, but Darwin was the one who explicitly put it in writing: "The advantage of diversification in the inhabitants of the same region is, in fact, the same as that of the physiological division of labour in the organs of the same individual body" (Darwin 1859, p. 115).

The Linnean and later Darwinian economy of nature is a variation of the idea, as old as it is vague, of the "balance of nature". The belief that nature is in equilibrium has characterised Western thought since its origins, but the idea has rarely been explicitly defined, likely because it has always been a kind of underlying assumption rather than an actual hypothesis or fully formulated theory (cf. Egerton 1973). For the same reason, it is hard to find a rigorous formulation of it. Without claiming to be exhaustive or precise, I will therefore assume that the idea of the balance of nature consists in the belief in an orderly and self-regulating nature, one that is demographically quite stable, characterised by recurring trends and regular processes, and capable of regaining stability following perturbations. In short, it is the belief that nature is able to balance things out.

From a contemporary perspective, two questions arise at this point: What is the place of human beings within the economy of nature? And is the belief in the balance of nature well founded? If we accept the Linnean idea, humans, like all other organisms, fall within the divine organisation of nature and are therefore subordinate to it. However, they occupy an honourable role, so to speak: all natural entities were created for their benefit and use. Thus, humans must fulfil their assigned task, which is to use other species for their own benefit. To do so, they must eliminate undesirable species and increase the populations of those that are useful. Created in God's likeness, human beings will fulfil their duty not by merely observing but by acting so that natural resources enrich the human economy.

Despite being potentially detrimental to the environment (this was the beginning of the first Industrial Revolution), human activities are considered part of the overall balance within the Linnean perspective. This is because they are seen as an expression of ingenuity in administering the natural resources granted by God. Historian Daniel Worster (1994) views Linnaeus as one of the earliest representatives of an "imperial" view of nature, where natural entities and processes are seen as mere resources to be exploited for human benefit. In a less critical and more general sense, the Linnean perspective is one of the earliest expressions of the idea that nature is a collection of *resources* that humans should *manage* (I will return to this in Chapter 4).

By contrast, Humboldt subscribes to a holistic view of nature, which regards it as a harmonious and organic whole, a living network of interdependent elements of which humans are an integral part. This viewpoint acknowledges that human activities can disrupt the overall balance and have an adverse impact on other natural entities and processes, as well as on human health and the planet as a whole. Humboldt's perspective, which combines holism with an understanding of the link between human history and the environment, would be pivotal to the emergence of environmentalism in Europe and the United States as we will see in Chapter 4.

For now, let us see whether the belief in a natural balance is well founded. I have already mentioned that the idea of equilibrium is more of an implicit assumption than a scientific hypothesis or theory. It is also often implied in ecology, environmental management, and conservation practices (for which ecology is the science of choice). In the words of ecologist Daniel Botkin:

> This idea of nature forms the foundation of twentieth-century scientific theory about populations and ecosystems. It is the basis of most national laws and international agreements that control the use of wild lands and wild creatures, just as it was an essential part of the 1960s and 1970s mythology about conservation, environment and nature.
> (Botkin 1990, p. 9)

Were it not for Botkin's use of the term "mythology", one could be excused for assuming that this idea is sound and supported by empirical data and substantial consensus from the scientific community. Yet, this is not the case at all – quite the contrary. The reason is mainly that, as this is not a clearly formulated hypothesis or theory, it is not clear what observations and data could support it. One of the few attempts to express the idea in the form of a scientific theory was the plant succession theory advocated by Frederic Clements (1874–1945), one of the founders of scientific ecology.

According to Clements (1916), communities of plant species tend to go through a series of successive developmental stages, much like how organisms are born, develop, reach adulthood, and then stabilise in an optimal state of equilibrium and self-regulation, called *climax*. In the absence of external disturbances, plant communities would maintain this state indefinitely. Human activity, considered an external disturbing factor, can jeopardise both the attainment of climax and its continuation. Once the disturbing factor is removed, the trajectory toward equilibrium is resumed, and a climax state regained.

Clements's theory became a veritable paradigm for scientific ecology (which in its early days focused on plant communities and only later on ecosystems) and an integral part of non-expert thinking about nature. This is what we are referring to, perhaps unknowingly, when we say that natural systems are normally in a state of balance that human actions tend to disrupt and that these would remain stable in our absence. As mentioned earlier, however, much of contemporary ecology brands the balance of nature as an ideology due to the absence of direct and convincing empirical evidence (see Blandin 2009).

It could be argued, however, that there is some consensus at least regarding the more modest formulation of the idea of equilibrium in terms of the demographic stability proper to nature's economy. Yet, in the work of another founder of ecology, Charles Elton, we read:

> The balance of nature does not exist, and perhaps never has existed. The numbers of wild animals are constantly varying to a greater or lesser extent, and the variations are usually irregular in period and always irregular in amplitude. Each variation in the numbers of one species causes direct and indirect repercussions on the numbers of the others, and since many of the latter are themselves independently varying in numbers, the resultant confusion is remarkable.
> (Elton 1930, quoted in Simberloff 2014, p. 17)

The idea of the equilibrium of nature therefore experienced a crisis within scientific ecology even before the mid-20th century and has now been replaced, at least in part, by more dynamic views – such as nature as a *flow* – based on the observation that balance in nature is rare and that change, rather than stability, seems to be the rule (see Kricher 2009). This shift – in both terminology and vision – has not been particularly successful outside the scientific sphere, however. In fact, the idea of natural balance continues to persist in non-scientific thinking and is generally an implicit assumption of natural environment conservation policies and practices.

An emblematic example of how this idea still guides conservation practices today is that of ecological engineering, defined as "the process of designing systems that preserve, restore, and create ecosystem services . . . which are the goods and services humanity extracts from the ecosystem" (Matlock and Morgan 2011, p. 1). Ecological engineering aims to ensure that ecosystems continue to provide their services, from food to water, from disease control to the spiritual benefits of a walk in the woods (Box 1.2). This can be done, for example, by *restoring* ecosystems that have been damaged by human activities or by *designing* and building ecosystems aimed at becoming reliable providers of a desired service.

As philosopher of biology Philippe Huneman (2011) notes, this presupposes the idea of a stable nature. Ecosystem restoration, for example, assumes that human intervention has altered what would otherwise have been an optimal equilibrium (recall Clements's climax) and that the lost natural balance can be recovered. In ecosystem design, on the other hand, ecological engineering aims to produce stable ecosystems (or at least ecosystems that require management interventions to maintain stability, such as the proportion of species present) to ensure the availability of services.

Goals such as the restoration and establishment of stable ecosystems do not align with current knowledge about how ecosystems function and may be unattainable if formulated in this way. A more promising approach, from the perspective of ecosystems in perpetual flow, is the concept of *persistence*, whereby an ecosystem can persist over time *despite changes and perturbations*. According to some authors, this ability to persist can be measured in terms of *resilience*,[13] that is, "a measure of the persistence of systems and of their ability to absorb change and disturbance and still maintain the same relationships between populations or state variables" (Holling 1973, p. 14).

BOX 1.2   Ecosystem services

In the now classic article "The Value of the World's Ecosystem Services and Natural Capital" (Costanza *et al.* 1997), ecosystem services are defined as the goods (such as food) and services (such as waste assimilation) that human populations derive, directly or indirectly, from ecosystem functions.

The concept was introduced in the late 1970s to illustrate the economic value of the material and spiritual benefits of ecosystems and thus to promote their conservation (Braat and de Groot 2012). The economic and human welfare arguments are, in fact, generally effective, even for those who do not care about environmental issues *per se*. For example, if it could be shown that ecosystems provide us with goods and services for which we would otherwise have to pay, say, $33 trillion a year, it is reasonable to expect that we would put more effort into keeping ecosystems healthy so that they continue to provide their services (the monetary estimate – with its limitations, as the article warns – is found in Costanza *et al.* 1997).

Such forms of "monetising nature" and, more generally, the concept of ecosystem services have faced a number of criticisms and related possible responses (see Maris 2014 and Schröter *et al.* 2014).

From an ethical standpoint, for example, the concept has been criticised for being anthropocentric and for attributing instrumental value to nature (i.e. only in reference to the satisfaction of human needs). Such criticisms could be answered, for example, by saying that the attribution of instrumental value does not exclude the attribution of intrinsic value and that anthropocentric values can simply provide additional reasons to preserve ecosystems. Moreover, while it is true that the current concept of ecosystem services is anthropocentric (a service *to* humans), ecosystem functions can, at least in principle, be related to the satisfaction of needs that affect not only humans but also other species (a similar claim can be made for the concept of natural resources, as we will see in Section 4.3.1). A stronger criticism concerns the fact that the transition from function to service is not well founded. Not every ecosystem function is a service (some may be disservices), and to think otherwise is simply the result of a teleological view of nature. Moreover, ecosystem services are the result of a reification that is not possible because ecosystem functions and components are in constant interaction.

Another type of objection concerns the use of economic metaphors (capital, goods, services) to promote the exploitation of nature on the part of humans. Such terms position us as consumers of nature, from which we are increasingly alienated and separated. This type of criticism could be answered – perhaps somewhat less convincingly – by saying that the concept can instead offer a way of reconceptualising the relationship between humans and nature, emphasising the former's dependence on the latter.

Notes

1 As is perhaps obvious, this is a conventional date, corresponding to the first appearance of the term in its modern meaning in printed texts (on the birth of biology see Minelli 2019; Zammito 2018).
2 It is unclear whether viruses are living beings, since they do not have a metabolism of their own. However, there is some agreement among scholars that, like all entities that can multiply, carry mutations that affect their fitness, and transmit those mutations, viruses evolve through natural selection.

3 The Cambridge edition of Lamarck's work, to which I refer here, renders *milieux*, *environnants*, and *circonstances* as "environment".
4 The term "phytogeography" – or plant geography – was coined by Humboldt himself in the *Essay on the Geography of Plants* (written with Bonpland in 1807; see Humboldt and Bonpland 2010) and is the science of the causes of the distribution, geographic spread, and composition of plant communities.
5 Quoted in Wulf (2015, p. 88). The *Naturgemälde* is contained in the *Essay on the Geography of Plants*.
6 It should be noted that Comte's physiology was characterised by its proximity to Bichat's ideas and that Bichat's method influenced Comte's approach to the study of social phenomena and the development of his positivist philosophy. However, Bichat was wrong, according to Comte, to see living beings as independent of the external world, although it was understandable that such a view "could have seduced the genius of Bichat" (Comte 1838, p. 293). For more on Bichat's vitalism and theory of life, see Huneman 2023, part I.
7 As biologist D'Arcy Thompson put it, "[n]o philosopher of modern times, not Kant himself, has exercised in his lifetime so wide a dominion" (1913, p. 3). Spencer's enormous influence began to decline rapidly in the early 20th century, however, mainly because of the use made of his theories in the political and social spheres. For Spencer, in fact, Darwinian natural selection – which I will discuss shortly – also applied to societies and social classes, and his theory was invoked to justify colonial exploitation, political conservatism, and ruthless economic competition (the phrase "survival of the fittest", which is often used misleadingly, is Spencer's). In recent times, especially in the fields of moral philosophy and sociology, attempts have been made to rehabilitate Spencer's thought. See, for example, Weinstein (2019).
8 The term *Umwelt* appeared in the German scientific context in Friedrich Ratzel's work *Anthropogeographie* in 1899 (see Feuerhahn 2009).
9 One may ask whether – and to what extent – perception must be conscious in order to speak of an *Umwelt*. While Uexküll primarily focused on animals, the concept can be extended to plants. Although plants lack a nervous system and do not perceive the world in the conscious, intentional manner that animals do, they still interact with their environment in complex and adaptive ways. In this sense, plants can be said to have an environment defined by their unique ways of perceiving and responding to their surroundings (Forestiero 2009).
10 Unfortunately, *Umwelt* theory was also invoked to support utterly reprehensible ideologies, particularly the doctrine of *Blut und Boden* (blood and soil), relating to the supposed link between a "racially pure" population and its native soil, which was used by the Nazis to justify their policies (see Stella and Kleisner 2010). The extent of Uexküll's ideological alignment with Nazism remains a subject of debate among historians. Whether the *Umwelt* theory can be separated from the context in which it was developed is the subject of *Uexkülls Umgebungen* by Gottfried Schnödl and Florian Sprenger (2021) (who answer in the negative).
11 Gibson's affordances inspired the idea of the *affordance landscape* by Denis M. Walsh (2014, p. 223), which is defined as "the complete set of conditions experienced by an organism as impediments to, or as conducive to, its goal of survival and reproduction".
12 It is worth noting that while ecology is strictly linked to evolution, in terms of both its origin and its objects, its integration within the Modern Synthesis has been the (perhaps yet to be accomplished) result of a tortuous path (see Huneman 2019; and Box 2.1).
13 On the relation between the concept of resilience and the balance of nature paradigm, see Delettre and Korniliou (2022) and Barbara (2024).

References

Acot, P. (1988) *Histoire de l'écologie.* Paris: Presses Universitaires de France.
Alberti di Villanova, F. (1797–1805) *Dizionario universale critico enciclopedico della lingua italiana.* In Lucca, dalla stamperia di Domenico Marescandoli, t. I.
Altamirano, M. (2016) *Time, Technology and Environment.* Edinburgh: Edinburgh University Press.
Barbara, L. (2024) 'Resilience and the shift of paradigm in ecology: A new name for an old concept or a different explanatory tool?', *History and Philosophy of the Life Sciences*, 46 art. n. 2. https://doi.org/10.1007/s40656-023-00600-8.
Bernard, C. (1957) *An Introduction to the Study of Experimental Medicine.* Translated by H. Copley. New York: GreeneDover Publications.
Bich, L. (2012) 'Il concetto di "milieu intérieur": ruolo e implicazioni teoriche in un approccio sistemico allo studio del vivente', in Cianci, E. (ed.) *Quaderni del CERCO. Epistemologie in Dialogo? Contesti e costruzioni di conoscenze.* Rimini: Guaraldi, pp. 179–210.
Blandin, P. (2009) *De la protection de la nature au pilotage de la biodiversité.* Versailles Cedex: Éditions Quae.
Bondì, R. and La Vergata, A. (2015) *Natura.* Bologna: Il Mulino.
Botkin, D.B. (1990) *Discordant Harmonies: A New Ecology for the Twenty-First Century.* Oxford: Oxford University Press.
Braat, L.C. and de Groot, R. (2012) 'The ecosystem services agenda: Bridging the worlds of natural science and economics, conservation and development, and public and private policy', *Ecosystem Services*, 1(1), pp. 4–15.
Canguilhem, G. (2001) 'The living and its milieu'. Translated by J. Savage, *Grey Room*, 3, pp. 6–31.
Carson, R. (1962/2002) *Silent Spring.* Boston, MA: Houghton Mifflin Harcourt.
Clements, F. (1916) *Plant Succession: An Analysis of the Development of Vegetation.* Washington: Carnegie Institution of Washington.
Comte, A. (1838) *Cours de philosophie positive, Tome troisième, contenant la philosophie chimique et la philosophie biologique.* Paris: Bachelier.
Cooper, G.J. (2003) *The Science of the Struggle for Existence: On the Foundations of Ecology.* Cambridge: Cambridge University Press.
Costanza, R. *et al.* (1997) 'The value of the world's ecosystem services and natural capital', *Nature*, 387, pp. 253–260.
Darwin, C. (1859) *On the Origin of Species by Means of Natural Selection, or the Preservation of Favoured Races in the Struggle for Life.* London: John Murray.
Delettre, O. and Korniliou, A. (2022) 'From balance of nature to stability and resilience: Disuse and persistence', *Philosophia Scientiae*, 26(1), pp. 53–72.
Egerton, F.N. (1973) 'Changing concepts of the balance of nature', *The Quarterly Review of Biology*, 48(2), pp. 322–350.
Eldridge, S. (1928) 'Review of theoretical biology, by J. von Uexküll', *The Journal of Philosophy*, 25(2), pp. 53–56.
Elton, C. (1930) *Animal Ecology and Evolution.* Oxford: Oxford University Press.
Falloppio, G. (1603) *La chirurgia di Gabriel Falloppio modonese, fisico, chirurgo, & anathomico celeberrimo. Tradotta dalla sua latina nella lingua volgare . . .*, presso Giacomo Anton. Somascho.
Feuerhahn, W. (2009) 'Du milieu à l'Umwelt: enjeux d'un changement terminologique', *Revue philosophique de la France et de l'étranger*, 199(4), pp. 419–438.
Foote, E. (1856) 'Circumstances affecting the heat of the sun's rays', *The American Journal of Science and Arts*, 22, pp. 382–383.
Forestiero, S. (2009) 'Ambiente, adattamento e costruzione della nicchia', in Casellato, S., Burighel, P. and Minelli, A. (eds.) *Life and Time: The Evolution of Life and its History.* Padova: Cleup, pp. 253–283.

Galera, A. (2017) 'The impact of Lamarck's theory of evolution before Darwin's theory', *Journal of the History of Biology*, 50(1), pp. 53–70.

Gibson, J.J. (1986/1979) *The Ecological Approach to Visual Perception*. Hillsdale, NJ: Lawrence Erlbaum Associates.

Guidetti, L. (2021) 'Meccanicismo e realtà fenomenica nel mondo degli esseri viventi. Ernst Mach e Jakob von Uexküll', *.S&F_scienzaefilosofia.it*, 25, pp. 278–298.

Haeckel, E. (1866) *Generelle Morphologie der Organismen . . . 2 Vols*. Berlin: Reimer.

Haigh, E. (1975) 'The roots of the vitalism of Xavier Bichat', *Bulletin of the History of Medicine*, 49(1), pp. 72–86.

Hall, L.S., Krausman, P.R. and Morrison, M.L. (1997) 'The habitat concept and a plea for standard terminology', *Wildlife Society Bulletin*, 25(1), pp. 173–182.

Holling, C.S. (1973) 'Resilience and stability of ecological systems', *Annual Review of Ecology and Systematics*, 4, pp. 1–23.

Humboldt, A. von (1814–1829) *Voyage aux régions équinoxiales du Nouveau Continent fait en 1799, 1800, 1801, 1802, 1803 et 1804*. Paris: N. Maze.

Humboldt, A. von (1843) *Asie centrale, recherches sur les chaînes de montagnes et la climatologie compare*. Paris: Gide.

Humboldt, A. von and Bonpland, A. (2010) *Essay on the Geography of Plants*. Translated by S. Romanowski. Chicago: Chicago of University Press.

Huneman, P. (2011) 'About the conceptual foundations of ecological engineering: Stability, individuality and values', *Procedia Environmental Sciences*, 9, pp. 72–82.

Huneman, P. (2019) 'How the modern synthesis came to ecology', *Journal of the History of Biology*, 52(4), pp. 635–686.

Huneman, P. (2023) *Death: Perspectives from the Philosophy of Biology*. London: Palgrave-Macmillan.

Kant, I. (1998) *Critique of Pure Reason*. Translated and edited by P. Guyer and A. Wood. Cambridge: Cambridge University Press.

Kricher, J. (2009) *The Balance of Nature: Ecology's Enduring Myth*. Princeton: Princeton University Press.

Lamarck, J.-B. (1820) *Système analytique des connaissances positives de l'homme*. Paris: Chez l'Auteur et Belin.

Lamarck, J.-B. (2011) *Zoological Philosophy: An Exposition with Regard to the Natural History of Animals*. Translated by H.S.R. Elliott. Cambridge: Cambridge University Press.

La Vergata, A. (2003) 'L'Ottocento: biologia. Da Lamarck a Darwin', in *Enciclopedia Treccani on-line*. Available at: www.treccani.it/enciclopedia/l-ottocento-biologia-da-lamarck-a-darwin_%28Storia-della-Scienza%29/ (Accessed 14 June 2024).

Linnaeus, C. (1749) 'The oeconomy of nature [defended by I. Biberg]', in *Miscellaneous Tracts Relating to Natural History, Husbandry, and Physick*. Translated by B.R. Stillingfleet and J. Dodsley. London, pp. 31–108.

Lyell, C. (1830) *Principles of Geology*. London: J. Murray.

Malthus, T.R. (1798) *An Essay on the Principle of Population*. London: J. Johnson.

Maris, V. (2014) *Nature è vendre. Les limites des services écosystémiques*. Versailles Cedex: Éditions Quae.

Matlock, M.D. and Morgan, R.A. (2011) *Ecological Engineering Design: Restoring and Conserving Ecosystem Services*. Hoboken, NJ: John Wiley & Sons.

McIntosh, R. (1985) *The Background of Ecology: Concept and Theory*. Cambridge: Cambridge University Press.

McNeill, J.R. (2000) *Something New Under the Sun: An Environmental History of the Twentieth-Century World*. New York: Norton & Co.

Minelli, A. (2019) *Biologia. La scienza di tutti i viventi*. Udine: Forum.

Mossio, M. and Bich, L. (2017) 'What makes biological organisation teleological?', *Synthese*, 194, pp. 1089–1114.

Newton, I. (1704) *Opticks: Or, a Treatise of the Reflexions, Refractions, Inflexions and Colours of Light*. London. Printed for Sam. Smith and Benj. Walford, Printers to the Royal Society, at the *Prince's Arms* in St. Paul's Church-yard.

Pearce, T. (2010a) 'From "circumstances" to "environment": Herbert spencer and the origins of the idea of organism–environment interaction', *Studies in History and Philosophy of Biological and Biomedical Sciences*, 41, pp. 241–252.

Pearce, T. (2010b) '"A great complication of circumstances": Darwin and the economy of nature', *Journal of the History of Biology*, 43(3), pp. 493–528.

Pearce, T. (2014) 'The origins and development of the idea of organism–environment interaction', in Barker, G., Desjardins, E. and Pearce, T. (eds.) *Entangled Life: Organism and Environment in the Biological and Social Sciences*. Dordrecht: Springer, pp. 13–32.

Pergamini, G. (1602/1688) *Il memoriale della lingua italiana del sig. Giacomo Pergamino da Fossombrone*. In Venetia, appresso Gio. Battista Ciotti senese.

Schnödl, G. and Sprenger, F. (2021) *Uexküll's Surroundings*. Translated by M.T. Taylor and W. Yung. Lüneburg: Meson Press.

Schröter, M. et al. (2014) 'Ecosystem services as a contested concept: A synthesis of critique and counter-arguments', *Conservation Letters*, 7(6), pp. 514–523.

Simberloff, D. (2014) 'The "balance of nature": Evolution of a panchreston', *PLoS Biology*, 12(10), p. e1001963.

Spencer, H. (1855) *The Principles of Psychology*. London: Longman, Brown, Green, & Longmans.

Stauffer, R. (1957) 'Haeckel, Darwin, and ecology', *The Quarterly Review of Biology*, 32(2), pp. 138–144.

Stella, M. and Kleisner, K. (2010) 'Uexküllian *Umwelt* as science and as ideology: The light and the dark side of a concept', *Theory in Biosciences*, 129(1), pp. 39–51.

Taylan, F. (2020) 'The rise of the "environment": Lamarckian environmentalism between life sciences and social philosophy', *Biological Theory*, 17(1), pp. 4–19.

Thompson, D'A.W. (1913) *On Aristotle as a Biologist, with a Prooemion on Herbert Spencer*. Oxford: Clarendon Press.

Uexküll, J. von (1907) 'Die Umrisse einer kommenden Weltanschauung', *Die neue Rundschau*, 18, pp. 641–661.

Uexküll, J. von (1926) *Theoretical Biology*. Translated by D.L. Mackinnon, D.Sc. London: K. Paul, Trench, Trubner & Co. Ltd.

Uexküll, J. von (2010) *A Foray into the Worlds of Animals and Humans: With a Theory of Meaning*. Minneapolis, MN: University of Minnesota Press.

Van Wyhe, J. (2019) *Wanderlust. The Amazing Ida Pfeiffer, the First Female Tourist*. Singapore: NUS Press.

Walsh, D.M. (2014) 'The affordance landscape: The spatial metaphors of evolution', in Barker, G., Desjardins, E. and Pearce, T. (eds.) *Entangled Life: Organism and Environment in the Biological and Social Sciences*. Dordrecht: Springer, pp. 213–236.

Weinstein, D. (2019) 'Herbert Spencer' in Zalta, E.N. and Nodelman, E. (eds.), *The Stanford Encyclopedia of Philosophy*, Summer 2024 edition. Available at: https://plato.stanford.edu/archives/sum2024/entries/spencer/ (Accessed 14 June 2024).

Worster, D. (1994) *Nature's Economy: A History of Ecological Ideas*. Cambridge: Cambridge University Press.

Wulf, A. (2015) *The Invention of Nature: Alexander von Humboldt's New World*. New York: Alfred A. Knopf.

Zammito, J.H. (2018) *The Gestation of German Biology: Philosophy and Physiology from Stahl to Schelling*. Chicago and London: The University of Chicago Press.

2 Understanding the environment

What do we mean when we talk about the environment? The most immediate way to answer this question is to consult a dictionary for an up-to-date definition. In the Cambridge Dictionary online, for example, the entry for "environment" reads: "The air, water, and land in or on which people, animals, and plants live." It is clear, however, that definitions, while fundamental, often leave us unsatisfied: where is the correspondence between organism and environment discussed in the previous chapter? And are we sure that the living world consists only of humans, animals, and plants? Doesn't a bacterium also have an environment? Definitions rarely trace the needs for which a particular concept was introduced, or the semantic changes through which it was formed and transformed. Consequently, although they are a possible starting point for understanding a concept, it is necessary to go one step further.

In the first chapter, we delved a little into historical semantics and saw that the history of the concept of the environment – even in the brief and prospective reconstruction provided – is rich and complex. Bearing in mind what emerged in that reconstruction, this chapter will offer a possible philosophical analysis of the concept in its contemporary uses, in the spirit of the conceptual negotiation outlined in the introduction to the volume. The starting point will be a list of statements that exemplify various current uses of the term "environment". These will serve as a leitmotif for three chapters: the present one, which is devoted to the environment of living beings in general, and the two following chapters – Chapters 3 and 4 – which focus instead on the human environment, understood as a particular case of the environment of living beings.

After an introductory section (Section 2.1), which highlights the semantic richness of the contemporary concept of the environment and circumscribes the study, Section 2.2 defines the spatial and temporal boundaries of the environment of living beings. Section 2.3 then presents an explanation of the correspondence between living beings and their environment in adaptive terms, followed by a discussion of the notion of causation, including the distinction between linear and cyclic causation. While the former characterises explanations of the correspondence between living beings and their

DOI: 10.4324/9781003479642-3

Understanding the environment 39

environment in terms of adaptation, the latter includes constructivist explanations (Section 2.4), such as niche construction theory (Section 2.5), the theory of the biosphere, and the Gaia hypothesis (Section 2.6).

2.1 Surrounder and surrounded

Looking at the list of sentences in Figure 2.1, we can begin to draw conclusions regarding current uses of the term "environment". The first is that the term is used both in everyday language and in scientific disciplines. In fact, although the sentences on the list are all part of our everyday language, they also refer to phenomena the study of which is pertinent to different disciplines, and often to more than one discipline. For example, sentence 1 has to do with a phenomenon studied in chemistry, whereas sentences 2 to 6 involve biology and ecology, to which are added, in sentence 3, the sciences of conservation and environmental management and, in sentences 5 and 6, ethology and biosemiotics. Sentence 6, like sentence 8, also involves systems science, cybernetics, climatology, geology, and geography. Sentences 7 to 9 then have implications that require the intervention – in addition to the disciplines already listed – of the human sciences: anthropology, but also economics and law, human geography, environmental history, and ethics.

A second feature that stands out is that some of the sentences are not emotionally neutral. While sentences like 1, 2, 4, 5, and 6 are merely descriptive

1. Red wine should be served at room temperature.
2. Organisms are adapted to their environment.
3. Many species are threatened with extinction due to the disappearance of their environment.
4. The environment determines the development of organisms.
5. The mole moves easily in its environment despite being virtually blind.
6. Living things construct their environment.
7. The environment of the Amazon tribes is in danger of disappearing due to deforestation.
8. "An increase of 2°C compared to the temperature in pre-industrial times is associated with ... a much higher risk that dangerous and possibly catastrophic changes in the global environment will occur."
9. "A healthy natural environment can also provide us solutions ... [for] some of the impacts of climate change."

Figure 2.1 Different uses of the term "environment" in an extremely broad sense (light grey background), a broad sense (grey background), and a narrow sense (dark grey background). The quotation in sentence 8 comes from the European Commission website, while that in sentence 9 comes from the European Environment Agency website.

and do not arouse any particular emotion, when we read that many species are on the verge of extinction or that the environment of Amazonian tribes is threatened by deforestation, our emotional reaction will likely be different: we are likely to feel a sense of sorrow for something that, if lost, will be lost forever. Perhaps images of lush nature come to mind, arousing our reverence or scientific curiosity. Reading that rising temperatures may have catastrophic consequences for the global environment, or that the natural environment can help us in addressing the impact of climate change, is likely to provoke, on the one hand, a feeling of uncertainty and fear for the future, of helplessness, and, on the other hand, hope and a call to action: something can and must be done! Sentences mentioning the disastrous consequences of global warming may, however, also provoke a very different reaction. Many people – including some quite famous ones – think, for example, that anthropogenic climate change and the biodiversity crisis are hoaxes perpetrated by politicians with the complicity of the scientific community. Statements such as 3, 8, and 9 will arouse in so-called environmental deniers – whom we will discuss in the last chapter – the desire to expose the scam, to unmask the conspiracy.

In short, the notion of the environment is in some ways elusive: not only because of its various meanings and uses but also because it conveys scientific, ethical, emotional, religious,[1] economic, political, and social aspects at the same time. Despite their diversity, however, the uses exemplified by our list of sentences all have a more or less explicit common trait: the environment always *belongs to* something or someone. As mentioned in the previous chapter, in fact, "environment" literally conveys the idea of something that "goes around", that "surrounds", and in order for there to be something to surround there must be something or someone to surround. The concept of the environment is a formal concept: it applies whenever there is an x – something that surrounds – and a y – something that is surrounded (and which can in turn surround something else, z), regardless of the nature of x, y, and z.

On the basis of the nature of the surrounded, we can distinguish between an *extremely broad*, a *broad*, and a *narrow* sense of "environment" (represented, in Figure 2.1, by the different grey tones of the background). In an extremely broad sense, the environment is that which surrounds something, regardless of the nature (living or non-living) of the surrounded. In this book, however, we are mainly concerned with the environment in the broad[2] (the environment of living things) and narrow (the environment of a particular type of living thing, humans) senses. It is normally in its narrow sense that the environment is the object of environmental philosophy and environmental studies. If, for example, we consult one of the most widely used textbooks in American university courses on environmental studies,[3] we read in the first few pages that "the environment is *our* basic life-support system. It provides the air we breathe, the water we drink, the food we eat, the land we live on" (Park 2001, p. 5, Box 1.1 emphasis added). Yet, at least from a biological point of view, human beings are but one species among many, and, as we will see, *the narrow sense cannot be considered separately from the broad sense*, except for the sake of convenience of investigation.

2.2 The prebiotic soup

The environment of living things has not always existed: if there is no environment without the surrounded, then the environment of living beings also arose at a certain point in the history of the Earth. It should also be noted that it might never have arisen, because life might never have emerged, or perhaps it would have been completely different if the first living things had had a radically different biology.

We can identify the environment of living beings with the biosphere,[4] the layer of the Earth's surface that supports life. It has temporal boundaries, which may be difficult to individuate precisely but which coincide with the origin of life on Earth, at least 3.5–3.7 billion years ago. Before that, there was only the geosphere, which includes the atmosphere (the envelope of air surrounding the Earth), the lithosphere (the Earth's crust and part of the upper mantle), and the hydrosphere (all of the water on Earth, in different states of aggregation).

Originally, Earth was a rocky globe with shallow seas, surrounded by an atmosphere likely composed of methane, ammonia, water, and hydrogen – nothing organic. Yet, if these substances are put together in an ampoule and energy is supplied (for instance in the form of electrical discharges), after about 20 days it will be discovered that something interesting has happened. The ampoule will contain a large number of molecules that are more complex than those originally introduced: organic acids, amines (organic molecules derived from ammonia), and amino acids (the building blocks of proteins). These new molecules will contain carbon, the element present in all forms of life: unlike the molecules originally placed in the ampoule, they will be *organic molecules*.

It is thought that something similar happened on Earth. First, organic molecules formed, according to a process of the kind just described. These organic molecules accumulated in the *prebiotic soup*,[5] concentrating locally, perhaps in the foam that dried around the coasts of the seas or in oceanic hydrothermal springs, fractures in the depths of the oceans from which geothermally heated water pours out. Under the influence of solar energy, these molecules combined to form larger molecules, macromolecules. At some point, by chance, one of the macromolecules acquired a peculiar ability: it could generate copies of itself. This molecule was the ancestor of DNA (Dawkins 1976, chapter 2).

It was therefore certain external circumstances (certain chemicals in certain proportions, solar energy, and then the different concentration of organic molecules in the primaeval soup) that made possible the appearance of life on Earth and, with it, its environment, the biosphere. The "surrounder" (water, the sun, inorganic molecules . . .) exerted a causal influence on the surrounded (inorganic molecules), leading to the formation of more complex, organic molecules, until the appearance of DNA and the handful of single-celled organisms from which the entire biodiversity of the planet originated.

In the definition of "biosphere" we also find an indication of the spatial boundaries of the environment of living beings. The biosphere in fact extends from a few kilometres in the atmosphere to the deep hydrothermal springs of the ocean (Thompson, Thompson and Gates 2024). Within its boundaries, the strategies for dealing with the struggle for existence mentioned in the previous chapter manifest themselves in all their variety. To give an idea of their radical diversity, it is enough to think that, while on the Earth's surface life depends on solar energy, which plants and certain bacteria (cyanobacteria) are able to store in the form of chemical energy, at the boundaries of the biosphere, in those hydrothermal springs mentioned in the definition, life is independent of solar energy. There, for example, can be found bacteria that use sulphur compounds – highly toxic to other organisms – to produce organic material through a process called "chemosynthesis". If we wish to find life on other known planets, it is these "extremophile" organisms, living in environmental conditions that are extreme for us, that we should probably look for. On Venus, for example, with no water and an atmosphere composed mostly of carbon dioxide, life as we know it is impossible. However, it cannot be ruled out that some layers of the planet's atmosphere may harbour life in the form of microorganisms capable of living in an acid medium and at extremely cold or warm (for us) temperatures (Merino *et al.* 2019). A certain environment "corresponds" to certain organisms: those conditions that are extreme for most plants and animals may be altogether comfortable for other living things.

2.3 The ecological environment

One of the most amazing features of the biosphere is the diversity of forms in which life occurs: there are millions of different species, and the organisms that form them have morphological and behavioural characteristics that make them adapted to the environments they inhabit. In the previous chapter, we reviewed explanations for such adaptation, some of which, for different reasons, have been disproven. The Lamarckian explanation has been refuted because variations acquired in the course of life cannot be passed on to offspring, and the Uexküllian explanation has been rejected because it is non-evolutionary. However, although these theories are not entirely correct, they contain useful and important insights for understanding how the correspondence between organisms and environments is realised, as we shall see. For example, certain variations acquired in the course of life, such as social and cultural variations, *can* be passed on to offspring. The Lamarckian theory is therefore incorrect in general but is possibly valid when applied to the right field, that of cultural evolution. A similar point can be made about Uexküll's theory: admittedly, adaptation occurs through evolution by natural selection, a process that the Estonian biologist did not allow for. The *Umwelt* theory, however, provides important insights into the correspondence between organisms and the environment in the course of their life and development.

Today, the best explanation available for understanding the process by which organisms adapt to their environment is the theory of evolution by natural selection. Of course, this has partially changed since its original formulation: in the current version of the theory, for example – the Modern Synthesis (see Box 2.1) – the mechanisms of inheritance and the origin of variations, which were unknown to Darwin and Wallace, are known.

BOX 2.1   From Darwin to the extended synthesis

Darwin and Wallace were as much in the dark about the source of variations (what is it that produces them?) as they were about the material basis of inheritance (by means of what are they transmitted?). It was the evolutionary biologist August Weismann (1834–1914) who refuted the Lamarckian theory of the inheritance of acquired traits and realised that the material basis of inheritance lies in chromosomes. The botanist and Augustinian friar Gregor Mendel (1822–1884), on the other hand, discovered the mechanisms of the transmission of hereditary traits and postulated that discrete factors (genes, as the Danish botanist Wilhelm Johannsen would call them in 1909) were at the basis of these traits. (Weismannian) Darwinism and Mendelian theory converged in the Modern Synthesis, the version of the theory of evolution by natural selection elaborated between the 1920s and the 1940s (Jablonka and Lamb 2005, chapter 1).

At least in its early stages, the Modern Synthesis consisted mainly of population genetics, based on the laboratory study and mathematical modelling of changes in gene frequencies within populations. As put by one of its main protagonists, the Soviet-born geneticist Theodosius Dobzhansky (1900–1975), "[e]volution is a change in the genetic composition of populations. The study of mechanisms of evolution falls within the province of population genetics" (Dobzhansky 1937/1951, p. 16). In this context, organism–environment interaction as such seems to take a back seat in evolutionary biology, replaced by the genes–environment pair (Lewontin 1983/1985). The former continues, however, to be central within developmental biology and is the subject of ecology (note, however, that the story, as always, is more complicated than can be presented in a few lines; see for instance Pievani 2005; Eldredge 1995; Huneman 2019).

Within the Modern Synthesis, therefore, the paths of evolutionary biology, developmental biology, and ecology tend to diverge. An important exception is the work of the developmental biologist Conrad Hal Waddington (1905–1975), who was strongly influenced by the process philosophy of Alfred North Whitehead (1861–1947). Waddington, focusing on the dynamic organisation of organisms and the interaction between the parts and between the parts and the whole, worked towards a better integration of genetics and development. He showed that organisms' development is interconnected with the environment and that they are able to adapt to their environment throughout their development by changing their phenotype and behaviour. He thus introduced the term "epigenetics" to refer to "the branch of biology which studies the causal interactions between genes and their products which bring the phenotype into being" (Waddington 1975, p. 218) (cf. Box 3.1).

Inspired by Waddington's work and integrative intentions, there have been calls since the 1980s for greater coordination between the study of evolution, the study of development, and the study of the environment. These have led to the creation of new disciplinary fields such as Evo-Devo (Evolutionary Developmental Biology) (Minelli 2007; Hall 1999), Eco-Devo (Ecological Developmental Biology) (Gilbert and Epel 2008), and their synthesis, Eco-Evo-Devo (Ecological Evolutionary Developmental Biology) (Gilbert, Bosch and Ledón-Rettig 2015). These demands have also led to the proposal of a new research programme, the Extended Evolutionary Synthesis, which emphasises the need to move beyond the Modern Synthesis towards a new, *more extended* theoretical synthesis that can better account for findings from developmental biology and ecology and better integrate them within evolutionary biology (Pigliucci and Müller 2010). In the integrated view advocated by these disciplines and research agendas, certain phenomena – such as phenotypic plasticity and niche construction, which will be central to the next chapters of this book – are considered particularly relevant because they illustrate the inseparability of the evolutionary process from the developmental process, and the inseparability of both from the environment (Gilbert 2001; Laland *et al.* 2008). Furthermore, while the Modern Synthesis recognises the genetic system as the only inheritance system, the Extended Evolutionary Synthesis generally accepts the existence of multiple inheritance systems. For Jablonka and Lamb (2005), for example, in addition to genetic inheritance, there is also epigenetic inheritance (see Box 3.1), behavioural inheritance, and symbolic inheritance. For niche construction theorists, on the other hand, ecological and cultural inheritance are central (Odling-Smee and Laland 2011).

The process of adaptation can be divided – following the philosopher of biology Robert N. Brandon (1990) – into three steps: selection, reproduction, and development.

Let us start with selection. Suppose that in a given population sharing the same environment, in generation g_1 there are some individuals that are taller than others and that, in virtue of this, they are more reproductively successful than the short ones (perhaps because they survive longer, or because they are more fertile). We would say that such organisms are *better adapted* to their environment than short ones and are therefore *selected for* by the environment. It is important to emphasise that adaptation is a relative concept, as Darwin illustrated: *it is only in a certain environment* that a trait confers greater reproductive success on its bearer. For example, it is only in a certain context that greater height is an adaptive trait for plants: in a dense forest, taller plants can receive more sunlight and thus have more energy for seed production. Adaptedness is not a property that an organism has in itself but a relational property that an organism has by virtue of its relation to an environment, a "property-in-an-environment", in Brandon's words (1990, p. 46). The first step of the process is therefore the selection of variations (greater height, in our example) that make their bearers better adapted than others to the environment in which they find themselves.

The second step is reproduction. Today we know, unlike Lamarck, Darwin, and Wallace, that it is not height that is directly transmitted through reproduction from parents to offspring (see Box 2.1). What is transmitted is a particular genotype (for the sake of simplicity, we will use "genotype" and "genome" as synonyms to refer to the genetic makeup of an organism). If height is a trait that increases the fitness of its bearer in generation g_1 and is inheritable, generation g_2 will display an increase in the frequency of the genotype *tall* compared to the previous generation. However, this does not *ipso facto* mean that the new generation will have a greater number of tall organisms than the previous one. The information contained in the genotype must be translated into an actual organism, a phenotype. The genotype *tall* may or may not manifest itself to varying degrees, depending on the environment in which the organism develops. A third step is therefore required to close the circle: the organism must *develop*. As the organism evolves, genotypic variants *can* be expressed as phenotypic differences on which selection can act.

Before going any further, a brief but important excursus on the concept of information is needed. What exactly does it mean to say that a DNA sequence contains information? In this book, we will follow Eva Jablonka and Marion Lamb's proposal (2005, chapter 2) that for something (a *source*) to contain information, there must be some kind of *receiver* capable of responding to and interpreting it. The nature of the receiver is not relevant: it can be an organism or an artefact (thus the receiver's reaction and interpretation need not be conscious or intentional). What is important is that this reaction and interpretation causes a change in the functional state of the receiver and that this change is not random but related to the form and organisation of the source. For example, a train timetable contains information in the sense that the functional state of the person reading it (e.g. staying at home or leaving immediately) changes as a result of reading it and in a way that is consequential to what is written on the timetable (the form and organisation of the source). Similarly, the length of daylight contains information for the flowering of a plant, and a genotype for the development of an organism.

The whole adaptation process takes place in what Brandon calls "the ecological environment". This consists of "those factors in the external environment that *affect* the organisms (or the populations or the species)" (Brandon 1990, p. 47, emphasis added). Not all features of the external environment (the set of physical, chemical, and biological factors surrounding an organism or set of organisms) are in fact causally relevant to organisms. For example, the relative position of Mars and Venus during the germination of seeds is likely irrelevant to their development, fertility, and reproduction, although Mars and Venus are part of the seeds' external environment (Brandon 2012). By contrast, the chemical composition and humidity of the soil will play an important role. Thus, unlike the external environment, the ecological environment is always defined with regard to organisms and, more specifically, with regard to a particular population or species. Returning to our list of sentences, it is the ecological environment to which sentences 2, 3, and 4 refer specifically: a particular species is adapted to a particular ecological environment (and not another) and is at risk of extinction if that environment changes drastically. The development of organisms of a particular species is influenced by certain factors and not others.

More precisely, Brandon defines the ecological environment as "those features of the external environment that affect the organisms' contribution to population growth" (Brandon 1990, p. 49). Why restrict the causal influence of the ecological environment to population growth? On the one hand, it must be remembered that Brandon's approach is an evolutionary one: his is a theory of the environment as it is understood in the theory of evolution by natural selection, and central to evolutionary theory is the concept of fitness, that is, the ability of organisms to survive and reproduce. On the other hand, it can be pointed out that according to the position we took in the previous chapter on the Darwinian origins of ecology (Section 1.5), the ecological environment is the theatre of the struggle for existence, and it is in this theatre that reproduction plays a fundamental role. For example, if a species continues to reproduce even when resources are scarce, it will have to either compete with other species that use the same resources or develop new capacities that allow it to access different resources. If the predators of a certain species disappear from the ecosystem, that species will grow disproportionately, requiring more resources to sustain itself and potentially causing the extinction of other species. Population growth is central to so-called population dynamics (territorial occupation, migrations and invasions, competition for resources, cooperation) and thus to the Darwinian struggle for existence.

The growth rate of a population depends on the "contributions" of its members: for a population to grow, its members must survive and reproduce, and this in turn depends on the ecological environment. Let us consider an example. The rabbit was introduced to Australia from Europe in the mid-19th century, when 12 pairs were released on a farm in Victoria to provide game for hunters. From the initial few individuals, the population grew exponentially (rabbits can produce more than four litters a year, each with about five offspring: today there are an estimated 200 million rabbits in Australia), but not everywhere (for example, rabbits survive longer – but produce fewer offspring – in the arid regions of Australia than in the Mediterranean). This exponential growth was followed by a stabilisation of population growth: as the population increases, the available resources decrease such that the number of offspring that can be fed decreases and those that survive are less robust (Ricklefs 1990, chapter 4).

2.3.1 Example: Invasive species

The example of rabbits raises an important environmental issue: the biodiversity crisis. How exactly biodiversity should be defined is the subject of much debate. For the sake of simplicity, we will use the most common definition, found in the text of the 1992 Convention on Biological Diversity (CBD), the most important global treaty for the conservation of biodiversity. According to the CBD, biodiversity is "the variability among living organisms from all sources including, *inter alia*, terrestrial, marine and other aquatic ecosystems and the ecological complexes of which they are part; this includes diversity within species, between species and of ecosystems" (CBD 1992, Art. 2). There is substantial agreement among the scientific community that a massive loss of biodiversity is currently taking place at the global level. According to the Intergovernmental Science-Policy Platform on Biodiversity and Ecosystem Services (IPBES), invasive species are among the five key drivers of this loss, along with land/sea use change (e.g. the conversion of grasslands to croplands), the direct exploitation of natural resources, climate change, and pollution. Invasive species are species that occur outside their native geographic range, are able to reproduce without human intervention, and thus occupy an increasing proportion of the new area. Over time, as in the case of rabbits, the population growth of the new species tends to stabilise, but often at the expense of the native biodiversity of the area. To give just one example: the latest IPBES report (Díaz *et al.* 2019, p. 27) states that a single invasive pathogenic species, the amphibian fungus *Batrachochytrium dendrobatidis*, has already caused several extinctions and threatens nearly 400 amphibian species worldwide.

Invasive species are often introduced – voluntarily or involuntarily – as a more or less direct consequence of human activities. For example, while rabbits were deliberately and directly introduced into Australia from Europe, *Batrachochytrium dendrobatidis* likely originated in the Korean Peninsula in the 1950s and was inadvertently spread around the world by human activities, particularly the unrestricted global trade in amphibians (O'Hanlon et al. 2018). The spread of invasive species can sometimes be the indirect result of human activities, and this is particularly true of climate change. For instance, the reduction in ice cover as a result of global warming allows more light and oxygen to penetrate the water below, favouring the spread of aquatic plants (as has happened with the invasion of the thread-leaved water-crowfoot – *Ranunculus trichophyllus* – in several lakes in the Himalayas) and the colonisation of lakes by piscivorous fish, which can lead to the decline of native populations of small-bodied fish (Rahel and Olden 2008).

Two things are worth noting before proceeding. The first is that invasiveness, like adaptedness, is a "property in an environment": a species is not intrinsically invasive but only becomes so under certain environmental conditions – for example when its traditional predators or competitors are absent. Second, in addition to a purely descriptive use of the term "invasive species" – such as the use I have tried to adopt here – the term is also used axiologically in conservation discourses. Terms such as "invasive", "alien", and "exotic" are typically contrasted with "native" and "endemic", with the former having negative connotations. More generally, as the ecologist Kurt Jax notes, discussions about invasive species "are sometimes highly emotional, not the least as they are connected to various metaphors that allude to (undesired) human immigration or even xenophobia and 'nativism'" (Jax 2023, p. 159, Box 4.1).

2.4 The selective environment

We have said that the ecological environment consists of those features of the external environment that influence the contributions of organisms to population growth. Some of these features will *differentially* affect the reproductive contribution of different genotypes, that is, cause a particular genotype to spread more in one population than another. These factors make up the selective environment, which can be illustrated by the following example.

2.4.1 Example: The peppered moth

The classic case of selection in action of the peppered moth (*Biston betularia*), used in biology textbooks to explain the theory of evolution by natural selection, will help to illustrate the selective environment. In the area around Manchester, England, in the middle of the 19th century, at the height of the Industrial Revolution, the peppered moth populations were almost entirely light-coloured (the *typica* variant), although occasional dark specimens (the *carbonaria* variant) could likely be spotted. By the middle of the 20th century, however, the situation was the reverse: populations of *Biston betularia* in polluted areas consisted mainly of dark moths, with rare light-coloured individuals, while in unpolluted areas the light-coloured moths predominated. What happened? To hypothesise an answer, we need to look at changes in the selective environment of the moths, in this case due to human activity.

B. betularia usually rests on the trunks of birch trees. These are covered with lichens, which provide perfect camouflage for the pale phenotypic variant, allowing it to escape the sight of birds, which consequently prey mainly on the dark variant. The selective environment of the moths therefore includes (at least) birds and birch trees: it is these that caused the increase in the reproductive propensity of the light variant (as it had a better chance of surviving). However, as air pollution increased due to the widespread use of coal as fuel (hence the name of the dark form, *carbonaria*), the lichens disappeared and the trees became covered in soot. The light variant no longer blended in with the tree trunks and became more visible to predatory birds. As a result, the frequency of the light-coloured form (together with its genotype) declined, generation after generation, in favour of the dark one and its genotype. The selective environment had changed, and so had the frequency of the two variants in the population. However, the correspondence between organisms and their environment was maintained: whereas the light-coloured moth populations were better adapted to the old environment, the dark populations were better adapted to the new one. This correspondence is not always achieved: if there had not been a dark form and environmental conditions had remained unsuitable for the light form, the peppered moth might have become extinct. With the introduction of the first environmental laws to combat air pollution in England in 1950, lichen populations (which had been used to monitor air quality since the second half of the 19th century onwards) began to cover tree trunks once again, and since then the frequency of the *typica* has increased and that of the *carbonaria* has decreased.

The case of the peppered moth not only illustrates the concept of the selective environment but also shows how humans and their activities (in this case pollution) are part of the selective environment of *B. betularia*, on a par with birds and their activities (predation). In the same way, the population dynamics of the invasive species illustrated in the previous example depend on human intervention: although species migrate and move, the occupation of new areas that are very different and distant from their areas of origin is mainly linked to globalisation. This should make it clear that, as emphasised at the beginning of this chapter, the human environment cannot be considered in isolation from the environment of other living things. At the same time, the environment of living things includes humans, and its functioning cannot be understood otherwise.

2.5 The developmental environment

The selective environment determines the differential replication of genotypes. In Brandon's reconstruction of the adaptation process, however, this is only one part of the story, as we have seen. Whereas what is transmitted from one generation to the next is the genotype, it is the phenotype – the realised organism, as it were – that is the object of selection. Put more metaphorically, the genotype needs to be *translated* into the phenotype, but this translation process leaves much room for interpretation. The development of the organism is in fact determined by a set of environmental factors which Brandon, for ease of analysis, separates from the selective environment and calls *the developmental environment.*[6]

Two main views on the development of organisms can be distinguished. On a fairly standard view, which biologist and geneticist Richard Lewontin (1929–2021) calls "superficial Darwinism", "the development of an individual organism is an unfolding or unrolling of an internal program" (Lewontin 1983/1985, p. 89). According to superficial Darwinism, Lewontin explains, if the complete DNA sequence of an organism were known and a sufficiently powerful computer were available, it would in principle be possible to "compute" the organism. In other words, the information for the production of the phenotype would be contained almost entirely in the genotype, which determines the timing and the details of the formation and differentiation of cells and organs. The environment would intervene mainly, if not exclusively, a posteriori, by testing the realised phenotype through natural selection. In its most radical versions, superficial Darwinism is clearly a reductionist position: if the genotypes are known, the phenotypes can be predicted, and genotypes can be studied in the laboratory (a simplified environment with few variables) in replicable experiments, usually carried out on a few hand-picked model organisms.

However, it is clear that model organisms are precisely that: *models* (i.e. they cannot reflect and exhaust the diversity of living things). Moreover, in the real world outside the laboratory, changes are often unpredictable, variables virtually uncontrollable, and interactions potentially infinite. At the beginning of the 21st century, the need for a different, less gene-centric approach – one inspired by the spirit of the research of the first experimental embryologists, who sought to understand how the environment, and not just factors intrinsic to the organism, determines the development of organisms – resulted in the formation of the new discipline of Ecological Developmental Biology (or Eco-Devo, see Box 2.1) (Gilbert 2001). This new approach sought not to deny the causal role of genes in determining phenotype but rather to rethink the extent of that role, to place it in a broader network of causal interactions, and to take it out of the geneticist's laboratory and return it to the ecological environment.

As we read in the introduction to the first edition of the now classic Eco-Devo handbook: "The relationships between developing organisms and their environments is crucial for our world's future. We need to understand the former if we are to protect the latter" (Gilbert and Epel 2008, p. xiv). At a time in history when addressing environmental issues is becoming increasingly urgent and unavoidable, the perspective of ecological developmental biology seems to be preferable to that of superficial Darwinism. Indeed, it places the ecological environment in the foreground and understands it as a "normal agent in producing phenotypes", as the title of the first chapter of the aforementioned handbook puts it. For Eco-Devo, the environment does not merely determine whether a certain phenotype is more adapted than another through natural selection. Rather, it intervenes throughout the entire developmental process by means of signals that, once interpreted by the organism, become information that determines the process itself. Organisms possess *phenotypic plasticity*, defined by biologist Mary Jane West-Eberhard (2003, p. 34) as "the ability of an organism to react to an environmental input with a change in form, state, movement, or rate of activity".[7]

2.5.1 Example: Sex determination

From a biological point of view, a mammal's sex is determined by the composition of its sex chromosomes, that is, by factors intrinsic to the organism. In many species of fish, turtle, and alligator, however, sex determination depends on extrinsic abiotic factors, such as the incubation temperature of the eggs, or extrinsic biotic factors, such as the presence of predators or potential mates. A familiar example is the red-eared slider turtle (*Trachemys scripta*), a popular pet in North America and other parts of the world. If, at a certain stage of embryonic development, the eggs are kept at 26°C, the gonads will develop into testes and the embryos will become male; at 31°C, the gonads will develop into ovaries and the embryos will become female. At intermediate temperatures, there will be different proportions of males and females (Yao *et al.* 2004).

Another rather fascinating example is the blue-headed wrasse (*Thalassoma bifasciatum*), a colourful reef fish. If an immature specimen arrives in an area of the reef where there are many females, and if the area is already home to a territorial adult male, it will develop into a female; otherwise, it will develop into a male. Not only that, but if the territorial male dies, one of the females will develop testes and become a male (Gilbert and Epel 2008, p. 5).

The case of sex determination is particularly striking, but the causal influence of the environment on development is ubiquitous: pressure, gravity, temperature, the presence or absence of conspecifics or predators, food quality and quantity (think of bees: whether a larva becomes a fertile queen rather than a sterile worker depends almost entirely on whether it is fed royal jelly, a protein-rich food) are all factors that help to determine phenotypes. Admittedly, these cases may seem bizarre and extreme to us, but phenotypic plasticity, already known to embryologists at the end of the 19th century, is part of the normal development of organisms: not everything needed to produce the phenotype is contained in the genes.

Attention to phenotypic plasticity has increased greatly in recent years, and it is not difficult to see why. Think of environmental sex determination: rising global temperatures are threatening animals whose sex is environmentally determined. If only female turtles are born in a given area, the shortage of males will lead to population decline and likely extinction (Blechschmidt *et al.* 2020). On the other hand, phenotypic plasticity may also prove to be an advantage (let us not forget that it has passed the test of natural selection!). For example, the ability of an organism to develop a phenotype capable of accessing a different type of resource than its ancestors, or to survive a different temperature, or to change sex when mates are scarce without waiting for evolutionary time, can make all the difference in a rapidly changing environment such as the present one.

2.6 Causes

Up to this point, we have talked about influence, determination, and causality in an intuitive way. Before going any further, however, it will be useful to clarify what exactly we mean when we say that there is a *causal relation* or *causation* between living things and the environment and to distinguish between linear causal relations and cyclic (also called "feedback" or "retroactive") causal relations. Recognising their coexistence allows for a richer and hopefully more accurate description of the relationship between living things and their environment.

The notion of a *cause* is as fundamental to our thinking and understanding of phenomena as it is resistant to conceptual treatment, so much so that Bertrand Russell (1872–1970) declared that there was no place for it in a scientific worldview and called for its expulsion from our philosophical vocabulary (Russell 1912–1913). Without claiming to deal with the problem of causality (to get an idea of the breadth of the debate, see Beebee *et al.* 2009), what interests us for the purposes of this volume is to distinguish and clarify as far as possible two different causal patterns that a philosophy of the environment must speak to: linear causation and cyclic causation. The examples in the preceding paragraphs will help us to do this.

2.6.1 *Linear causation*

Let us start with linear causation (Figure 2.2, a and b). When we say that a certain event C is the cause of another event E, it is because we have observed a certain regularity: when an event of type C *occurs*, an event of type E also occurs, and the former occurs *before* the latter. For example: if we observe that when turtle eggs are incubated at 26°C the hatchlings are all male, we will be inclined to recognise the existence of a relationship between the two

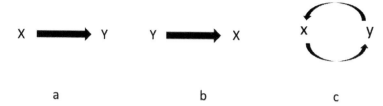

Figure 2.2 The causal relation between the surrounder (*x*) and the surrounded (*y*). (a) *x* exerts a causal influence on *y*, but not vice versa (what happens in the environment exerts a causal influence on the living beings that adapt to it); (b) *y* exerts a causal influence on *x*, but not vice versa (living beings actively modify the environment through ecosystem engineering); (c) *x* exerts a causal influence on *y* and *y* exerts a causal influence on *x*, which, modified by the causal influence of *y*, exerts a new, different causal influence on *y* (by modifying the environment, living beings influence their own evolution, as illustrated by niche construction theory).

events. We will refer to this relationship as causal and its terms (the *relata*) as cause and effect, respectively. Simplifying somewhat, we can say that in linear causation, the cause precedes the effect and that there is a unidirectional link from cause to effect. However, it is rare for the relationship between cause and effect to be direct, and this often complicates the identification of the relevant cause. In the case of sex determination in turtles, for example, temperature controls hormone production, and hormones determine gonad development and thus sex specification. To prove this, if we injected our turtle eggs with oestrogen synthesis inhibitors, their gonads would develop into testes even when incubated at the temperature at which they would normally develop into ovaries. We can therefore say that a certain temperature causes the production of a certain hormone, which causes the differentiation of the gonads and thus the development of ovaries or testes, in a kind of domino effect. Moreover, especially in the living world, an effect is rarely produced by a single cause. The emblematic example is gene expression: it is now widely accepted that most phenotypic traits are the result of the regulatory action of networks involving a large number of genes interacting with each other and with other substances in the cell (see Box 3.1).

There are two aspects of causality that are important to bear in mind. The first is that it is generally assumed – and I share this assumption – that *relata* in causal relations are events or processes (Varzi 2001, chapter 3; Sanford 2009): it is *having been incubated* at a certain temperature that caused the embryos *to develop* as males. In everyday life, however, we tend to formulate causal relations in terms of objects; in other words, although *relata* are things that happen, we often talk about them as if they were the objects to which these things happen. This is also true in the context we are dealing with in this volume. Consider, for example, the statement: "In some species, temperature determines sex." In this we seem to acknowledge the existence of causal relations between two objects: temperature and sex. However, it is clear that the statement could be formulated more precisely in terms of events, such as: "In some species, a certain molecular agitation of the medium determines the production of certain hormones involved in the maturation process of the gonads and their subsequent differentiation." An entire book written in this way, however, would be likely to frighten off even the most enthusiastic reader.

The second important aspect of causality is that we cannot perceive the causal relations as we perceive events; all we can detect is a regular succession between one kind of event and another. On a regularity view of causation, which has its origins in the thinking of David Hume (1711–1776), causality is nothing more than a relationship we imagine on the basis of the fact that, repeatedly, every time we see an event of type C, an event of type E follows.

However, a regular succession is not always an indication of a causal relation. In fact, we cannot exclude the possibility that the regular correspondence we have observed between several incubation events of eggs at a certain temperature and several birth events of, say, only males is a simple coincidence. So we need to test our hypothesis. For example, we will have to try to see if male-only spawning events occur at temperatures other than 26°C, or we can try to construct a counterfactual scenario by eliminating the cause to see if the effect still occurs. Once the hypothesis has been tested – that is, once it has been ascertained that the correlation in question is in fact indicative of a causal regularity – there is no way of ruling out the possibility of this causal link's failing to occur in the future, that is, following our example, of a scenario in which the incubation of eggs at 26°C *is not* followed by the birth of only male specimens. (Indeed, it is precisely on the possibility of such a result that the fate of many species threatened by climate change depends.) From a theoretical point of view, one way of dealing with this difficulty is to interpret regulatory theory in probabilistic rather than necessitarian terms. Instead of characterising the causal relation in terms of necessity (if incubation takes place at 26°C, then, necessarily, only male specimens will be born), it can be understood as a probabilistic dependency relation: to say that C causes (or influences or determines) E is to say that the occurrence of C increases the probability that E will occur (Laudisa 2012; Sanford 2009). For example, in claiming that air pollution in Manchester during the Industrial Revolution (a certain event) caused a change in the frequency of *Biston betularia* genotypes (another event, namely a process), we are claiming that the air pollution increased the probability of the dark variant's predominating over the pale variant. Similarly, in recognising that the presence of an adult male causes the blue-headed wrasse to develop as a female, we are claiming that the first event increases the likelihood of the second. Context plays a key role: if C increases the probability of E's occurring in one context, it may not necessarily do so in another. For example, if the predators of the peppered moth had based their recognition of prey not on vision but, say, on hearing, the dark variant would not have had an advantage over the light variant in

19th-century England. Similarly, we cannot rule out the possibility of a *T. bifasciatum*'s failing to develop into a female despite the presence of an adult male, as the causal influence of the adult male might be mitigated or nullified by other environmental factors.

It should be clear, even from these few examples, that the study of the relationship between a given organism and its environment is extremely complex, but it is precisely this complexity that must be addressed if we are to consider whether and how to intervene in environmental issues. The situation becomes even more complex when we look a little more closely at the types of causation that take place between living things and their environment. Up to this point, in fact, we have treated the relationship between the environment and living things as a relation of linear causation that proceeds from the surrounder (the environment) to the surrounded (species, populations, organisms) (Figure 2.2a). On closer inspection, however, causation also seems to proceed in the other direction, that is, from living things to the environment, in a more or less direct way (Figure 2.2b). Let us take the case of the peppered moth again. First of all, a change in the frequency of the variants is likely to have an effect on the environment: because the dark colouration reflects less light than the light one, for instance, a greater number of dark moths could increase the temperature of the population's immediate surroundings. Similarly, if the light variant has traits that the dark variant lacks and that make it suitable prey for a certain predator, that predator's food resources will change as the frequency of the variants changes.

A specific case of environmental modification that needs to be highlighted is ecosystem engineering, defined in ecology as that set of organismic activities that modulate the availability of resources for the organisms themselves and other species and thereby "modify, maintain and/or create habitats" (Jones, Lawton and Shachak 1994, p. 374). The classic example is the construction of dams by beavers. In the process, beavers alter hydrology and create wetlands that can last for centuries and occupy kilometres of land. The front of the largest beaver dam discovered to date, in Canada, is about 800 metres long, covers an area of about 70 square kilometres, and can be seen from space. The dams create pools of water that are deep enough to keep them from freezing in winter, providing beavers with a constant supply of food. The structures of the riparian zones are modified, the availability of nutrients changes, and, ultimately, the entire habitat is altered, along with the plant and animal communities that inhabit it.

Living things, endowed with a metabolism, often capable of movement and perception and sometimes endowed with self-awareness, have the tools to consciously or unconsciously *modify* their surroundings. *Allogenic* ecosystem engineers do this using biotic or abiotic materials: they build dams, nests, dens, and, as we shall see, cities. By contrast, *autogenic* ecosystem engineers, such as trees and earthworms, modify the environment through their own physical structures.

2.6.2 Cyclic causation

Ecosystem engineering is a form of linear causation that proceeds from the surrounded to the surrounder. However, the moment the surrounded modifies its surrounder, the causal action of the latter on the former can change. In other words, a living thing can carry out processes that modify the environment, and the environment, thus modified, will exert *new* pressures on the living thing that carried out those processes and on subsequent generations. The first beavers that built a dam created an environment for themselves whose selective pressures (resources, predators, shelters . . .) were different from those of the environment without the dam. The result was a new environment with a different causal influence than the previous one, determined by the actions of the beavers themselves. The beaver example, however striking, is but one of many. As we shall see, organisms are *active participants* – some consciously and deliberately, others less so – in their relationship with their environment and in their own evolution.

The linear pattern of causation does not seem sufficient to account for this different type of causal influence, which, as we will see, characterises niche construction processes. In such processes, the causality at work seems instead to be cyclic causality in the form of a feedback mechanism (Figure 2.2c). Feedback occurs when x exerts a causal influence on y and y, in turn, exerts a causal influence on x (or z, which in turn exerts a causal influence on x). In cyclic causality, unlike in linear causality, the beginning and the end of the causal process are not clearly identifiable: the *relata* appear to be both cause and effect, and the cause–effect temporal order, so well established in our cognitive system, is challenged. This different pattern of causation – explored primarily by systems science, cybernetics and, more recently, evolutionary biology – is presupposed by niche construction theory and is central to the biosphere theory and the Gaia hypothesis, to which we now turn.

2.7 Niche construction theory

In his last book, *The Formation of Vegetable Mould, through the Action of Worms* (1881), Darwin illustrates how worms are adapted to an environment that they modify through their own activities. If we were to examine the morphology of an earthworm without knowing anything about its environment, we would regard it as an aquatic animal because we would find few of the structural adaptations of terrestrial animals. But earthworms live in the soil. How is it possible for animals with a physiology that is adapted to an aquatic environment to live in a terrestrial one?

The answer lies in the active modifications that earthworms make to their environment, from building underground tunnels to altering soil chemistry. The modified environment is passed on from generation to generation (along with the ability to modify it), enabling earthworms to maintain their "aquatic" physiology. Earthworms, in other words, have kept their environment stable over evolutionary time: their physiology has not changed, because their environment has not changed. Living in a stable environment costs less in terms of energy expenditure and is safer because the organism knows how to move around in it.

While this constructivist aspect of Darwinian theory has not been emphasised by the view of adaptation proposed by the Modern Synthesis (for which, as we have seen, adaptation is mainly a unidirectional process prompted by the environment and realised through natural selection), it is present in Uexküll's *Umwelt* theory (presented in the previous chapter) and has been taken up forcefully by Lewontin, a Darwinian geneticist who is critical of certain aspects of the Modern Synthesis (Forestiero 2009; Barker and Odling-Smee 2014).

Uexküll, let us recall, explained the correspondence between organism and environment in terms of the transcendental construction of the latter by the former: each species constructs its *subjective* environment and is consequently adapted to it. Uexküll's construction, however, is transcendental, not material. It is nonetheless clear that the *Umwelt* is also the place where an organism can act materially (it is no coincidence that the only work by Darwin cited in *A Foray into the Worlds of Animals and Humans* is one on earthworms). That organisms are builders – transcendental and material – of their environments is central to Lewontin's perspective:

> First, organisms determine which elements of the external world are put together to make their environments and what the relations are among the elements that are relevant to them. . . . As a consequence of the properties of the animal's sense organs, nervous system, metabolism, and shape, there is a spatial and temporal juxtaposition of bits and pieces of the world that produces a surrounding for the organism. . . . A second facet of the relation between organism and environment that needs to be clarified is this: organisms not only determine what aspects of the outside world are relevant to them by peculiarities of their shape and metabolism, but actively construct, in the literal sense of the word, a world around themselves. . . . Third, organisms . . . are in a constant process of altering their environment.
>
> (Lewontin 2000, pp. 52–55)

Compared to Uexküll, Lewontin views the construction of the environment from an evolutionary perspective and goes one step further: it is not the environment that determines the organism, nor the organism that determines the environment. An organism and its environment are *co-determining* and thus *co-evolve*.

58 *Philosophy of the environment*

It is Lewontin's conception that inspired niche construction theory (NCT), proposed in the 1990s by John Odling-Smee, Kevin Laland, and Marcus Feldman. According to NCT, the relationship between organisms and their environment is not merely one of adaptation of the former to the latter, nor construction of the latter by the former. Instead of seeing organisms and the environment as two distinct poles of an asymmetrical relationship, one must see organisms and the environment as two poles of a dynamic relationship in which organisms play an active role in their own development and evolutionary destiny. In NCT, the relationship between the surrounder and the surrounded is understood not as a one-way causation but as a cyclic causation: input determines output, which determines a new input, and so on.

> Organisms, through their metabolism, their activities, and their choices, define, partly create, and partly destroy their own niches. We refer to these phenomena as "niche construction". We argue that niche construction regularly modifies both biotic and abiotic sources of natural selection in environments and, in so doing, generates a form of feedback in evolution.
>
> (Odling-Smee, Laland and Feldman 1996, p. 641)

Before proceeding, it is important to clarify the difference between ecosystem engineering and niche construction. Although they are closely related processes, they are not exactly the same thing. In fact, not every instance of ecosystem engineering is also a process of niche construction, because we can conceive of instances of ecosystem engineering that do not generate feedback in evolution. For example, suppose that one day a spider constructs a web that is slightly different from those of the other members of its species. If this particular web does not confer any fitness-related advantages or disadvantages on the spider relative to its peers, or if it does but the ability to construct it is not heritable, then this is a process of ecosystem engineering *but not* niche construction.

Niche construction takes place through the activities of organisms and their more or less conscious choices (trophic interactions, metabolic activities, physiological and behavioural activities; see Box 2.2) and can have positive or negative consequences for other species. In general, but not necessarily, niche construction increases the fitness of building organisms and reduces the selective pressures acting on them, as we saw in the case of earthworms.

2.7.1 *Example: The mole burrow*

The mole burrow (recall sentence 5 of Figure 2.1: "The mole moves easily in its environment despite being virtually blind") is an exemplary case of niche construction. Moles are small mammals that feed mainly on earthworms.

Understanding the environment 59

They can be severely short-sighted (but able to perceive light) and spend most of their life in complex underground tunnel systems that can be hundreds of metres long. Females build their nests from material found on the surface near the tunnels (grass, leaves, paper, wool, and, in recent years, plastic) and place them in special chambers next to the main tunnels so that the young can be removed quickly if predators arrive. This way of life is made possible by the physiological and behavioural characteristics of moles: the mole's squat, cylindrical body has front limbs equipped with strong claws for digging, which are turned outwards to sweep the earth away from the snout; its senses of smell, hearing, and touch are highly developed, and so on. The correspondence between moles and their environment is the result of evolution. According to NCT, the best way to explain this correspondence is to recognise that, in addition to natural selection – which retains adaptive variations – there is another process at work, namely niche construction, by which organisms modify, more or less consciously, the selective pressures on themselves, on subsequent generations, and on other organisms. By living underground, the mole gains access to certain resources, protects itself from predators, and reproduces more safely by building burrows. Moreover, just like earthworms, the mole will leave its descendants a modified environment. In fact, in addition to genetic inheritance, NCT must recognise at least a second form of inheritance, namely ecological inheritance (see Box 2.1): organisms pass on to their descendants not only their own genes but also the environment they have modified.

BOX 2.2 Types of niche construction

Based on the different types of ecosystem engineering, three types of niche construction can be distinguished: constitutive (autogenic engineering), relational (autogenic and allogenic engineering), and external (allogenic engineering) (Aaby and Ramsey 2022).

In constitutive construction, the process takes place through the organisms' own physical constitution. Trees alter hydrology, nutrient cycling, moisture, and soil stability, and it is to these environmental conditions – modified by their activity – that they are adapted. The phenomenon of phenotypic plasticity, that is, the ability of an organism to change its phenotype (usually in the early stages of development) as a result of environmental cues (see Section 2.3.2), can be included in autogenic construction. By changing itself, an organism also changes its environment: available resources change, as do prey and predators. For example, some plants may change their physiology in response to the vibrations caused by caterpillar chewing, increasing their chemical defences; others may change the shape of their leaves to capture more light, thereby changing the selective pressures to which they are subject.

Relational construction, on the other hand, is realised through the relationships that organisms maintain with one another and with abiotic factors. Emperor penguins, for example, are the only vertebrate species that can breed during the Antarctic winter, when temperatures can drop to −50°C. The trick is to huddle close together: in just two hours, the temperature around the group rises to −37°C. Bacteria, on the other hand, which normally live suspended in a medium, can attach themselves to a surface and "attract" other bacteria, even of different kinds, until they form three-dimensional structures called biofilms. Biofilms have a complex architecture, criss-crossed by channels that allow for the passage of nutrients and the removal of waste, and their components (the different bacteria) are able to communicate with each other through biochemical signals. The conditions within the biofilm (e.g. pH value and the availability of oxygen and micronutrients) are different from those in the external environment and are much more favourable, making certain bacterial biofilms, such as the plaque on our teeth, particularly difficult to eradicate.

The third type of niche construction is external construction, using materials that are present in the environment or produced by the organism itself, the paradigmatic case being the construction of dams by beavers. To this we can add, for example, nests, burrows, spider webs, pupal cocoons, and so on. Humans, as we will see in Chapter 3, are exceptional niche builders, capable of various types of construction.

In conclusion, it is important to emphasise that although niche construction processes are generally adaptive for the constructing species, as in the case of the mole or the other examples given in this section, this is not always the case. The process of *negative* niche construction actually decreases the fitness of the builders, threatening their survival and that of their descendants, and thus the persistence of the species. Consider, for example, plant bacterial pathogens. When a pathogen enters, say, the leaves of a plant, it triggers an infection process. As the pathogen multiplies, a combination of interactions takes place between the plant and the bacteria, as well as between the bacteria themselves. This combination of interactions modulates the host plant's defences and alters the environment of the bacteria. Interactions that successfully suppress host defences or increase the nutrients available to the bacteria can be considered a form of positive niche construction: the pathogens benefit from the niche construction activity, as do their offspring. On the other hand, interactions that induce host defence mechanisms, and thus limit pathogen growth, can be considered a form of negative niche construction, in which the fitness of the constructor decreases (Preston 2017).

This is the case not only for pathogenic bacteria but also for tumour cells and many viruses. It may also be the case for the human niche, as we will begin to see in the following paragraphs and in more detail in Chapter 3.

2.8 The Earth system

Let us now try to broaden our view, shifting from individual organisms and their populations and species to life as a whole – living matter in contrast to non-living matter. We can then ask ourselves about the relationship that exists between life as a whole and its environment, the biosphere. Here too, as with the organism–environment pair, a form of correspondence becomes apparent: life as we know it can only emerge and persist under certain conditions. Why certain conditions and not others? How does life as a whole interact with the external conditions that are its conditions of possibility? One possible answer is that life is adapted to its environment, the biosphere, because it has built it up and acts as a regulating factor for the entire Earth system, much like a thermostat (a rather controversial hypothesis, as we shall see).

2.8.1 *The biosphere theory*

According to the inventor of the modern concept of the biosphere, the Russian geochemist Vladimir Ivanovich Vernadsky (1863–1945), "[a]ll living matter can be regarded as a single entity in the mechanism of the biosphere" (Vernadsky 1998, p. 58). Although living matter is very different internally, it has special properties that are not found in non-living matter. In particular, living matter is able to self-regulate, as Claude Bernard argued, and to create new energy-rich chemical compounds. Because of this, in Vernadsky's view, life is a *geological force* that, from the moment it emerged, has gradually changed the chemical and physical properties of the Earth, thus changing its own environment. The altered environment has in turn "retroacted" on life, conditioning its evolution.

The example of the Great Oxidation will help to illustrate this (Blaustein 2016). The earliest forms of life were likely anaerobic organisms, that is, organisms able to live in the absence of oxygen. Around 2.5 billion years ago, however, the activity of photosynthetic cyanobacteria began to change the composition of the atmosphere, enriching it with free oxygen, that is, oxygen not combined with other elements, such as carbon dioxide (CO_2). At the same time, carbon dioxide levels dropped and anaerobic life forms became extinct or were restricted to less oxygenated areas of the planet. The presence of free oxygen radically changed the chemical composition of the Earth and allowed for the presence of new metabolisms, such as aerobic respiration. The new metabolisms increased the self-sustaining capacity of organisms and created the conditions for the evolution of multicellular life, in a feedback mechanism that can be seen as a process of niche construction on a global scale.

In Vernadsky's biosphere theory, life and its environment are co-determining (and co-evolving). This co-determination must be understood from a systemic perspective, ideally indebted to the thought of Humboldt on the one hand and Bernard on the other. As Vernadsky wrote in the preface to *Biosphere* (1926), one must "consider all empirical facts from the point of view of a *holistic mechanism* that combines all parts of the planet into an indivisible whole" (Vernadsky 1998, p. 40). Without going into the details of the theory, we can think of the different parts of the Earth system (the "envelopes" of the planet, the atmosphere, the hydrosphere, the biosphere, and the lithosphere . . .) as parts of an engine powered by solar energy. The different envelopes are traversed by a flow of energy and connected by exchanges of matter (in the form of biogeochemical cycles of carbon, oxygen, water, nitrogen, sulphur, phosphorus . . .), such that a change in one part has repercussions on the others and on the whole. In this system, the biosphere is a "region of transformation of cosmic energy" (Vernadsky 1998, p. 47), a kind of gigantic metabolic system, to speak metaphorically, capable of self-regulation.

Vernadsky's holistic view was transferred to ecology by the ecologist George Evelyn Hutchinson (1903–1991) and used to explain the functioning of ecosystems. With a little simplification, we can say that the smallest pool of water, with its microorganisms, functions just like the biosphere (which can therefore be considered the global ecosystem), that is, by recycling matter and transferring energy.

Ecosystems are dynamic complexes of plant, animal, and microorganism communities and their non-living environment, which interact as a functional unit.[8] The non-living component of the system includes the flow of energy, primarily from the sun, water, non-living nutrients, gases, and concentrations of organic and inorganic substances. The living component includes three broad categories of organisms, grouped in terms of their role in the energy flow. Primary producers (plants, algae, photosynthetic bacteria) are able to "fix" solar energy through photosynthesis and make it available to consumers (animals) in the form of chemical energy; dead organisms are then reconverted into inorganic material – for example nutrients for primary producers – by decomposers (mainly fungi, bacteria, and some invertebrates), which can decompose the biomass and convert organic molecules into inorganic ones. The interconnected processes by which the elemental components of organic matter circulate within ecosystems, between ecosystems, and in the biosphere are the biogeochemical cycles mentioned earlier.

Vernadsky's biosphere theory has long been unknown to most, as the 1988 preface to the English translation points out. However, its importance today is difficult to underestimate. For example, the Intergovernmental Panel on Climate Change (IPCC) refers to it (implicitly) when, in its glossary, it defines the biosphere as

> [t]he part of the Earth system comprising all ecosystems and living organisms, in the atmosphere, on land (terrestrial biosphere) or in the

oceans (marine biosphere), including derived dead organic matter, such as litter [the mixture of dead organic matter – branches, leaves, animals . . .], soil organic matter and oceanic detritus [dead organic material suspended in water that normally harbours colonies of microorganisms that decompose it].

(Möller *et al.* 2022, p. 2901)

2.8.2 The Gaia hypothesis

Ideally continuing the systemic and holistic vision inaugurated in ecology by Humboldt, promoted in physiology by Bernard, and articulated in biogeochemical terms by Vernadsky, in the 1970s chemist James Lovelock (1919–2022) proposed, and with microbiologist Lynn Margulis (1938–2011) later refined, the Gaia hypothesis, named after the primordial goddess of Greek mythology, the personification of the Earth and the origin of life (Lovelock 1972). As in Vernadsky's theory, in the Gaia hypothesis the atmosphere has a biogenic character and the biosphere is a system capable of self-regulation. Two elements in particular distinguish the Gaia hypothesis from the biosphere theory, making it more controversial, scientifically, but also more popular with the general public and parts of the environmental movement. The first is its finalistic (at least at first sight) explanation of homeostasis; the second is Lovelock's claim – not shared by Margulis – that Gaia is an organism (Levit and Krumbein 2000).

In formulating the Gaia hypothesis, Lovelock and Margulis start from the consideration of a seemingly bizarre fact: since the beginning of the formation of our solar system more than four billion years ago, the energy emitted by the sun has progressively increased, yet the temperature of the Earth's surface has remained roughly constant, *precisely at a value suitable for life as we know it*. What could be the reason for this correspondence (if we do not want to invoke theological explanations)? First, it can be noted that the Earth's atmosphere is currently very different from that of other known planets, such as Mars and Venus, and that life exists on Earth but not, as far as we know, on other planets. Therefore, Lovelock and Margulis suggest, it is reasonable to assume that life has exerted – and continues to exert – an influence on the Earth's atmosphere, just as Vernadsky anticipated (note that Lovelock and Margulis were unaware of Vernadsky's theory when they formulated the Gaia hypothesis, as pointed out in the preface to the English translation of *Biosphere*). On this view, the properties of the Earth's atmosphere are evidence of homeostasis on a planetary scale: the stability of the Earth system is necessary for the well-being of life, and life, in turn, helps to maintain this stability.

The hypothesis that Lovelock and Margulis put forward is that

> the total ensemble of living organisms which constitute the biosphere can act as a single entity to regulate chemical composition, surface pH

and possibly also climate. The notion of the biosphere as an active adaptive control system able to maintain the Earth in homeostasis we are calling the "Gaia" hypothesis. . . . Hence forward the word Gaia will be used to describe the biosphere and all of those parts of the Earth with which it actively interacts to form the hypothetical new entity with properties that could not be predicted from the sum of its parts.
(Lovelock and Margulis 1974, p. 3)

To understand what is meant by the statement that the biosphere is an adaptive control system capable of maintaining the Earth in homeostasis, consider the operation of a heating system controlled by a thermostat. The thermostat measures the ambient temperature (input) and turns the heating system on or off accordingly (output). However, the ambient temperature (and therefore the activation of the system) depends on the system itself, as the temperature will be higher after the system has been switched on, and vice versa. In other words, the input depends on the output, and it is in this way that the temperature is kept constant around a predetermined value (Érdi 2008, pp. 8–9; Onnis 2021, pp. 274ff.). On the Gaia hypothesis, the ensemble of living things (the biosphere in the preceding quotation) is like the thermostat of the Earth system, capable of keeping it in a stable state. The Earth thus falls into the class of so-called *cybernetic systems*, those systems capable of steering "an optimum course through changing conditions *towards a predetermined goal*" (Lovelock 1979, p. 48, emphasis added), through complex patterns of cyclic causation between the components, the components and the whole, and the external environment.

For example, we are able to stay upright when the surface beneath us is moving (such as when we are on a ship or a bus), or to stay cool when it is hot. Similarly, irons, electric ovens, and heating systems are able to maintain a chosen temperature. On the Gaia hypothesis, the Earth is a self-regulating system that tends towards a goal – homeostasis – and its main self-regulating system is life itself.

It is a short step from what has just been said to the idea that the Earth is a superorganism that actively and intentionally pursues an objective. For this reason, the Gaia hypothesis raised more than a few eyebrows in the scientific community when it was first proposed, and the book in which Lovelock presented it to the general public, *Gaia: A New Look at Life on Earth* (1979), received widespread acclaim but also a plethora of negative reviews from leading biologists of the time. For some it was simply considered unscientific, for others a mere metaphor not to be confused with a mechanism, while still others branded it an "evil religion" (cf. Ruse 2013). Today, however, the hypothesis is at the centre of renewed interest, both for the systemic vision it proposes and for the pioneering role it has played in climate modelling with the Daisyworld model (Box 2.3). It is only by understanding how the Earth system works that we can try to predict, for example, how resilient it is to anthropogenic perturbations or understand which parts of the system it would be most effective to intervene in, and when. Let us therefore consider whether the scientific community's original scepticism toward the Gaia hypothesis was well founded. Does self-regulation necessarily imply intentionality and purpose? Is the idea that the Earth is a superorganism scientifically acceptable? While the first question can be answered in the negative, the idea that the Earth can be considered a superorganism faces objections that are difficult to overcome.

That self-regulation can occur without intention and without teleology – that is, without the collective planning of a goal to be achieved by organisms – was shown by Lovelock with the model of a simplified world, Daisyworld, developed with his student Andrew Watson (Ruse 2013; Lenton 1998). In fact, the model shows how temperature regulation on a global scale can be the result of feedback processes between organisms and the environment that do not involve any form of intentionality or finality (Box 2.3).

BOX 2.3   The Daisyworld model

Daisyworld is a model of a simplified, flat, cloudless Earth where there are only two species of organisms: white daisies and black daisies. Like Earth, Daisyworld is heated by a sun that gets brighter over time: the temperature is bound to rise. At the origin of Daisyworld, when the temperature is cooler, black daisies thrive. The black daisies indeed heat up more: they absorb more sunlight and, in doing so, also heat up the surrounding medium, promoting their own growth by means of a positive feedback mechanism (i.e. amplifying the effect of the input, in this case sunlight). The black daisies thus create an optimal environment for their own survival and reproduction.

As they spread, the black daisies warm the planet to the point where white daisies (which thrive at higher temperatures, since they reflect more light) also begin to flourish. As the temperature continues to rise, the white daisies replace the black ones, until the population is made up entirely of white daisies. By reflecting the light, the white daisies "correct" the rising heat from the sun by means of negative feedback (which dampens the effect of the input). With only white daisies – or at least a majority of them – the temperature is stable and life on Daisyworld is guaranteed (at least until the sun's heat rises to the point where it can no longer be corrected and the world ends). As should be clear, there is no intentionality involved in this process: the self-regulation of Daisyworld can take place without teleology.

Of course, in reality things are much more complex than in Daisyworld: the environment is not homogeneous; the number of variables – biotic and abiotic – and types of feedback that can occur is enormous. But even

> on Earth, the correspondence that takes place at the level of individuals, populations, or species (organisms construct their own niches by modifying their environments) affects the correspondence at the global level: "In the real world, coupling between life and its environment occurs at all scales, beginning with localised niche construction and with ecosystems emerging as integrated systems between the individual and the global levels" (Lenton 1998, p. 445).

Let us now turn to the idea that the Earth is a superorganism. As a preliminary remark, it should be noted that this claim was not present in the original formulation of the hypothesis (Lovelock 1972; Lovelock and Margulis 1974), where Gaia was understood as a *system of control* that the biosphere exerts over the atmosphere. The Gaia hypothesis as we have presented it in this context (as well as its validity or otherwise) is therefore not dependent on the ontological claim that the Earth is a superorganism.

In recounting – almost 20 years later – his moment of inspiration for formulating the Gaia hypothesis, Lovelock writes:

> Suddenly, the image of the Earth as a living organism able to regulate its temperature and chemistry at a comfortable steady state emerged in my mind. At such moments, there is no time or place for such niceties as the qualification "of course it is not alive – it merely behaves as if it were".
>
> (Lovelock 2000, pp. 253–254, quoted in Ruse 2013, p. 5)

There are two ways of interpreting this statement: the first – more ontologically innocent – is that it is a metaphor, the appropriateness and heuristic value of which can be debated. The second is that the Earth system not only *behaves like* an organism but *is* an organism, and this interpretation is ontologically more challenging and controversial.

It is to the ontological reading that the criticism levelled by Richard Dawkins in *The Extended Phenotype* (1982) is directed. According to Dawkins, Lovelock is right to regard homeostatic self-regulation as one of the characteristic activities of living organisms. However, the presence of homeostatic self-regulation is not sufficient to render an entity a living organism: if it were, we would have to include electric ovens among organisms. Thus the Earth could be a cybernetic system *but not* an organism. In order for the Earth to be an organism, other conditions would have to be met.

Firstly, Dawkins notes that homeostasis in organisms is the result of evolution: once it appeared, it turned out to be an adaptive mechanism that increased the fitness of its bearers compared to those organisms that did not have it and was consequently conserved by natural selection. In order to attribute the status of "organism" to the Earth, we would have to show that its homeostasis is the result of evolution by natural selection: there would have to be a series of "competing" Earths, that is, other planets with their own biospheres, and among these, those that did not happen to develop an efficient mechanism for the homeostatic regulation of their planetary atmosphere would have to be extinguished. Today, the universe would be full of dead planets whose homeostatic regulation systems were not selected because they were not sufficiently efficient. As far as we know, however, this is not the case. Moreover, the Earth seems to lack another of the essential properties that characterise living organisms: to be an organism, the Earth would have to be able to reproduce, giving rise to other Earths. In this, Dawkins offers a powerful argument. That the Earth is a superorganism remains, at best, a potentially useful metaphor to help us understand, at least in part, how it works.

Beyond the partly justified criticism and scepticism regarding the Gaia hypothesis, it has generated "a new way of thinking about the Earth" (Steffen *et al.* 2020, p. 56) by challenging a purely geophysical conception of the planet and emphasising the influence of life on the global environment and the Earth system, along with the importance of the interconnections and feedback between the main components of the Earth system. This new way of thinking – which has antecedents, it is worth repeating, in Humboldtian science and Vernadsky's theory – is the foundation of Earth system science, a transdisciplinary enterprise (in which different disciplines work together for a common purpose) that began in the context of the Cold War[9] and was institutionalised in 1983, along with the establishment of the NASA Earth System Science Committee.

Earth system science, which aims to understand the structure and functioning of the Earth as a single, complex, adaptive system driven by interactions between energy, non-living matter, and organisms, is now confronted with questions of particular importance and urgency: How stable and resilient is the Earth system?[10] Are there critical thresholds beyond which the whole system could enter a state that threatens human well-being? How do human social dynamics contribute to the functioning of the system? Although I have neither the space nor the competence to answer questions of this magnitude here, we will return to some of them in the final chapter.

Notes

1 Consider, for example, Pope Francis's second encyclical, *Laudato si'* of 2015, addressed to the environmental question in its inseparability from the social one, and the concomitant institution of the World Day of Prayer for the Care of Creation.
2 The distinction between the extremely broad and the broad sense is not without complications – just think of the case of viruses mentioned in the previous chapter, note 2.
3 Environmental studies is an academic field that emerged in the 1950s and 1960s in the United States. It constitutes a multidisciplinary field encompassing both

physical and biological sciences and the humanities and addresses the study of the environment and, more specifically, the impact of human activities on the environment.
4 The term "biosphere" was introduced by the Austrian geologist Eduard Suess (1831–1914), alongside the already existing "atmosphere".
5 This is what the evolutionary biologist John B.S. Haldane (1892–1964) called it. In the 1920s, Haldane and the Soviet biochemist Alexander Oparin (1894–1980) independently proposed abiogenesis, or the heterotrophic theory of the origin of life, according to which organic compounds are synthesised under certain prebiotic conditions, as illustrated by the example of the ampoule. The latter is a simplification of the experiment carried out by Stanley Miller and Harold Urey in 1953 to test the abiogenesis hypothesis, which proved that organic molecules could have formed from inorganic molecules in the Earth's primitive atmosphere.
6 According to Brandon, although the two environments – selective and developmental – can be considered in isolation for ease of analysis, the distinction would only hold in the real world if phenotypes were static entities, that is, the end result of development. But this is not the case: phenotypes are dynamic and temporal entities. For example, in some circumstances the selectively relevant differences may be differences in the time it takes for a particular morphology to develop, rather than differences in the final morphology. An example is tadpoles that develop in temporary ponds. When the pond dries up, those that have developed an adult morphology can jump away, while those that develop more slowly will die (Brandon 1990, pp. 50ff.).
7 When phenotypic plasticity is observed in the larval or embryonic stages of animals and plants, it is generally referred to as "developmental plasticity" (Gilbert and Epel 2008, p. 7). Partly to avoid complicating matters, and partly because it is not always clear when a developmental process can be considered complete, I will simply speak of phenotypic plasticity.
8 Like many of the terms we deal with in environmental philosophy, the concept of an ecosystem – introduced by the ecologist Arthur Tansley in the 1930s (Tansley 1935) – is difficult to define unambiguously, so much so that the philosopher of science Sahotra Sarkar (2002) has branded it one of the worst-defined terms in the ecological literature. The definition quoted earlier is that contained in the aforementioned Convention on Biological Diversity (CBD 1992).
9 During the Cold War, environmental sciences and Earth sciences saw unprecedented growth thanks to military funding. Contrary to the working hypothesis pursued in this volume, according to some authors it is in this context that the modern idea of the environment emerged (Warde *et al.* 2018).
10 In Earth system science, "resilience" is defined as "the capacity of a system, be it an individual, a forest, a city or an economy, to deal with change and continue to develop", as can be read on the Stockholm Resilience Centre website. This meaning is only partially consistent with the original meaning – proposed by the ecologist Crawford Stanley Holling (1973) – which, for example, refers not to the concept of development but to the more neutral and ontologically less demanding concept of persistence.

References

Aaby, B.H. and Ramsey, G. (2022) 'Three kinds of niche construction', *British Journal for the Philosophy of Science*, 73(2), pp. 351–372.
Barker, G. and Odling-Smee, J. (2014) 'Integrating ecology and evolution: Niche construction and ecological engineering', in Barker, G., Desjardins, E. and Pearce, T.

(eds.) *Entangled Life: Organism and Environment in the Biological and Social Sciences*. Springer: Dordrecht, pp. 187–211.
Beebee, H., Hitchcock, C. and Menzies, P. (eds.) (2009) *The Oxford Handbook of Causation*. Oxford: Oxford University Press.
Blaustein, R. (2016) 'The great oxidation event', *BioScience*, 66(3), pp. 189–195.
Blechschmidt, J., Wittmann, M.J. and Blüml, C. (2020) 'Climate change and green sea turtle sex ratio-preventing possible extinction', *Genes (Basel)*, 25 May, 11(5): 588. https://doi.org/10.3390/genes11050588. PMID: 32466335; PMCID: PMC7288305.
Brandon, R.N. (1990) *Adaptation and Environment*. Princeton: Princeton University Press.
Brandon, R.N. (2012) 'The concept of environment in evolutionary theory', in Kabasenche, W.P., O'Rourke, M. and Slater, M.H. (eds.) *The Environment: Philosophy, Science, and Ethics*. Cambridge MA: MIT Press, pp. 19–35.
CBD (1992) *Convention on Biological Diversity*. Available at: www.cbd.int/doc/legal/cbd-en.pdf (Accessed 14 June 2024).
Darwin, C. (1881) *The Formation of Vegetable Mould, through the Action of Worms, with Observations on their Habits*. London: John Murray.
Dawkins, R. (1976) *The Selfish Gene*. Oxford: Oxford University Press.
Dawkins, R. (1982) *The Extended Phenotype*. Oxford: Oxford University Press.
Díaz, S. et al. (eds.) (2019) *Summary for Policymakers of the Global Assessment Report on Biodiversity and Ecosystem Services of the Intergovernmental Science-Policy Platform on Biodiversity and Ecosystem Services*. Bonn, Germany: IPBES Secretariat.
Dobzhansky, T. (1937/1951) *Genetics and the Origin of Species*. New York: Columbia University Press.
Eldredge, N. (1995) *Reinventing Darwin: The Great Debate at the High Table of Evolutionary Theory*. New York: Wiley.
Érdi, P. (2008) *Complexity Explained*. Berlin: Springer.
Forestiero, S. (2009) 'Ambiente, adattamento e costruzione della nicchia', in Casellato, S., Burighel, P. and Minelli, A. (eds.) *Life and Time: The Evolution of Life and Its History*. Padova: Cleup, pp. 253–283.
Gilbert, S.F. (2001) 'Ecological developmental biology: Developmental biology meets the real world', *Developmental Biology*, 233, pp. 1–12.
Gilbert, S.F., Bosch, T.C. and Ledón-Rettig, C. (2015) 'Eco-Evo-Devo: Developmental symbiosis and developmental plasticity as evolutionary agents', *Nature Reviews: Genetics*, 16(10), pp. 611–622.
Gilbert, S.F. and Epel, D. (2008) *Ecological Developmental Biology*. Sunderland, MA: Sinauer Associates Inc.
Hall, B.K. (1999) *Evolutionary Developmental Biology*, 2nd edition. Dordrecht: Springer.
Holling, C.S. (1973) 'Resilience and stability of ecological systems', *Annual Review of Ecology and Systematics*, 4, pp. 1–23.
Huneman, P. (2019) 'How the modern synthesis came to ecology', *Journal of the History of Biology*, 52, pp. 635–686.
Jablonka, E. and Lamb, M.J. (2005) *Evolution in Four Dimensions: Genetic, Epigenetic, Behavioral, and Symbolic Variation in the History of Life*. Cambridge, MA: MIT Press.
Jax, K. (2023) *Conservation Concepts: Rethinking Human–Nature Relationships*. London: Routledge.
Jones, C.G., Lawton, J.H. and Shachak, M. (1994) 'Organisms as ecosystem engineers', *Oikos*, 69(3), pp. 373–386.

Laland, K.N., Odling-Smee, J. and Gilbert, S.F. (2008) 'EvoDevo and niche construction: Building bridges', *Journal of Experimental Zoology (Mol. Dev. Evol.)*, 310B, pp. 549–566.
Laudisa, F. (2012) 'Causalità', *APhEx*, 5, pp. 121–145.
Lenton, T.M. (1998) 'Gaia and natural selection', *Nature*, 394, pp. 439–447.
Levit, G.S. and Krumbein, W.E. (2000) 'The biosphere theory of V.I. Vernadsky and the Gaia theory of James Lovelock: A comparative analysis of the two theories and traditions', *Zhurnal Obshchei Biologii*, 61(2), pp. 133–144.
Lewontin, R.C. (1983/1985) 'Organism as the subject and object of evolution', in Levins, R. and Lewontin, R.C. (eds.) *The Dialectical Biologist*. Cambridge, MA: Harvard University Press.
Lewontin, R.C. (2000) *The Triple Helix: Gene, Organism, and Environment*. Cambridge, MA: Harvard University Press.
Lovelock, J.E. (1972) 'Gaia as seen through the atmosphere', *Atmospheric Environment*, 6, pp. 579–580.
Lovelock, J.E. (1979) *Gaia: A New Look at Life on Earth*. Oxford: Oxford University Press.
Lovelock, J.E. (2000) *Homage to Gaia*. Oxford: Oxford University Press.
Lovelock, J.E. and Margulis, L. (1974) 'Atmospheric homeostasis by and for the biosphere: The Gaia hypothesis', *Tellus: Series A*. Stockholm: International Meteorological Institute, 26(1–2), pp. 2–10.
Merino, N. *et al.* (2019) 'Living at the extremes: Extremophiles and the limits of life in a planetary context', *Frontiers in Microbiology*, 10, art. n. 780.
Minelli, A. (2007) *Forme del divenire. Evo-devo: la biologia evoluzionistica dello sviluppo*. Torino: Einaudi.
Möller, V. *et al.* (eds.) (2022) 'IPCC, 2022: Annex II: Glossary', in Pörtner, H.-O *et al.* (eds.) *Climate Change 2022: Impacts, Adaptation and Vulnerability. Contribution of Working Group II to the Sixth Assessment Report of the Intergovernmental Panel on Climate Change*. Cambridge and New York, NY: Cambridge University Press, pp. 2897–2930. https://doi.org/10.1017/9781009325844.029.
Odling-Smee, F.J. and Laland, K.N. (2011) 'Ecological inheritance and cultural inheritance: What are they and how do they differ?', *Biological Theory*, 6, pp. 220–230.
Odling-Smee, F.J., Laland, K.N. and Feldman, M.W. (1996) 'Niche construction', *The American Naturalist*, 147(4), pp. 641–648.
O'Hanlon, S.J. *et al.* (2018) 'Recent Asian origin of chytrid fungi causing global amphibian declines', *Science*, 360, pp. 621–627.
Onnis, E. (2021) *Metafisica dell'emergenza*. Torino: Rosenberg & Sellier.
Park, C. (2001) *The Environment: Principles and Applications*, 2nd edition. London and New York: Routledge.
Pievani, T. (2005) *Introduzione alla filosofia della biologia*. Roma-Bari: Laterza.
Pigliucci, M. and Müller, G.B. (2010) *Evolution: The Extended Synthesis*. Cambridge, MA: MIT Press.
Preston, G.M. (2017) 'Profiling the extended phenotype of plant pathogens: Challenges in bacterial molecular plant pathology', *Molecular Plant Pathology*, 18(3), pp. 443–456.
Rahel, F.J. and Olden, J.D. (2008) 'Assessing the effects of climate change on aquatic invasive species', *Conservation Biology*, 22(2), pp. 5212–533.
Ricklefs, R.E. (1990) *Ecology*, 3rd edition. New York: W.H. Freeman and Company.
Ruse, M. (2013) *The Gaia Hypothesis: Science on a Pagan Planet*. Chicago and London: University of Chicago Press.
Russell, B. (1912–1913) 'On the notion of cause', *Proceedings of the Aristotelian Society*, n.s., 13, pp. 1–26.

Sanford, D.H. (2009) 'Causation', in Kim, J., Sosa, E. and Rosenkrantz, G.S. (eds.) *A Companion to Metaphysics*, 2nd edition. Hoboken, NJ: Wiley-Blackwell.

Sarkar, S. (2002) 'Defining "biodiversity"; assessing biodiversity', *The Monist*, 85(1), pp. 131–155.

Steffen, W. *et al.* (2020) 'The emergence and evolution of earth system science', *Nature Reviews Earth & Environment*, 1, pp. 54–63.

Tansley, A.G. (1935) 'The use and abuse of vegetational concepts and terms', *Ecology*, 16, pp. 284–307. https://doi.org/10.2307/1930070.

Thompson, J.N., Thompson, M.B. and Gates, D.M. (2024) 'Biosphere', in *Encyclopedia Britannica*. Available at: https://www.britannica.com/science/biosphere (Accessed 23 September 2024).

Varzi, A.C. (2001) *Parole, oggetti, eventi e altri argomenti di metafisica*. Roma: Carocci.

Vernadsky, V. (1998) *The Biosphere*. Translated by D.B. Langmuir. New York: Copernicus.

Waddington, C.H. (1975) *The Evolution of an Evolutionist*. Ithaca, NY: Cornell University Press.

Warde, P., Robin, L. and Sörlin, S. (2018) *The Environment: A History of the Idea*. Baltimore, MD: John Hopkins University Press.

West-Eberhard, M.J. (2003) *Developmental Plasticity and Evolution*. Oxford: Oxford University Press.

Yao, H.H., DiNapoli, L. and Capel, B. (2004) 'Cellular mechanisms of sex determination in the red-eared slider turtle, *Trachemys scripta*', *Mechanisms of Development*, 121(11), pp. 1393–1401.

3 Building the human environment

Both this chapter and the next are devoted to the environment in the narrow sense, that is, the human environment, to which sentences 7, 8, and 9 in the list proposed at the beginning of Chapter 2 refer, and which are repeated in Figure 3.1 for convenience.

Looking at these sentences, one thing stands out: while it is clear that sentences 7 and 8 refer to the environment of human beings – of the Amazon tribes and of humanity as a whole, respectively – sentence 9 seems to speak of a *specific kind* of environment, that is, the natural environment, somehow suggesting that there is also a non-natural environment.

And this is precisely how the human environment was conceived of at the Stockholm Conference, the United Nations Conference on the Human Environment held from 5 to 16 June 1972: as a natural and hand-made environment. This was the first global environmental conference and the first attempt both to take stock of the impact of human activities and to forge a common approach to the challenge of environmental conservation (Handl 2012). At the beginning of the declaration that emerged from the conference, we read:

> Man is both creature and moulder of his environment, which gives him physical sustenance and affords him the opportunity for intellectual, moral, social and spiritual growth. In the long and tortuous evolution of the human race on this planet a stage has been reached when, through the rapid acceleration of science and technology, man has acquired the power to transform his environment in countless ways and on an unprecedented scale. Both aspects of man's environment, the natural and the man-made, are essential to his well-being and to the enjoyment of basic human rights, even the right to life itself.
>
> (United Nations 1972, p. 70)

In line with the Stockholm Declaration, in what follows we will consider the human environment in terms of its two components, the artificial (Chapter 3) and the natural (Chapter 4), but it should be noted from the outset that the distinction is both difficult to maintain and likely not well founded.

DOI: 10.4324/9781003479642-4

Building the human environment 73

> 7. The environment of the Amazon tribes is in danger of disappearing due to deforestation.
> 8. "An increase of 2°C compared to the temperature in pre-industrial times is associated with ... a much higher risk that dangerous and possibly catastrophic changes in the global environment will occur."
> 9. "A healthy natural environment can also provide us solutions ... [for] some of the impacts of climate change."

Figure 3.1 Uses of the narrow sense of the term "environment" in which the surrounded is *Homo sapiens*.

Starting from the assumption that *Homo sapiens* is one species among others, this chapter proceeds along the same theoretical lines as Chapter 2. It illustrates how the environment has played, and continues to play, a crucial role in both the evolution of the species and the development of the human organism, in a process in which humans are not only the fruit but also the moulders of their environment. In other words, it shows that the correspondence between humans and their environment is the result of both adaptation by natural selection and human construction (Sections 3.1 and 3.2). It then explores the hypothesis that anthropogenic climate change can be explained as a monumental process of niche construction (Section 3.3).

3.1 Creatures of their environment

Chapter 2 highlighted how *some* of the physical, chemical, and biological factors that more or less closely surround an organism exert a causal influence on it. Indeed, the ecological environment influences the health and development of organisms and, consequently, their ability to survive and, possibly, to reproduce. Humans are not exempt from this effect. Their response, like that of other organisms, is to adapt during their development and lifetime (e.g. through phenotypic plasticity and ecosystem engineering) or in intergenerational time, through evolution by natural selection and the process of niche construction. The end result, although always provisional in an ever-changing environment, is that correlation between living things and their surroundings that characterises the modern concept of the environment.

3.1.1 Big brains in big bodies

The genus *Homo* – of which our species is the sole survivor – has evolved ever-larger bodies and brains over time. It is estimated that over the last two million years the average body size of most *Homo* species has increased from about 50 to about 70 kilograms and that there has been an increase (particularly rapid between 800,000 and 200,000 years ago) in the relative and absolute size of the brain. Various explanations for this have been proposed, but they all revolve around the idea that over the course of their evolutionary history, humans encountered a number of challenges in their ecological environment and met them through adaptations in body and brain size. The main challenges have been extreme or unpredictable environmental conditions. The Pleistocene, the epoch in which our ancestors lived,[1] was characterised by repeated glacial cycles and severe extinctions: in order to survive, it was necessary not only to fight fierce and gigantic predators with little more than rocks but also to withstand extreme temperatures, in arid environments with scarce and fluctuating resources.

It is clear that, in the face of such challenges, the size of an organism is a fundamental biological trait: the ability to move, access to water and food, metabolism and resistance to fatigue and temperature, success in competing with other organisms, and the development of hunting strategies all depend on it. Some environmental challenges are temporary, while others play out over a longer, even an evolutionary, timescale. The former include challenges faced by our ancestors during their lifetime or over a few generations. The latter, on the other hand, have spanned millennia, resulting in the extinction of certain populations and the survival of others. Both have taken place (and continue to take place, albeit in different forms) in the ecological environment. Four hypotheses have been put forward and tested concerning the role of the environment in the evolution of human brain and body size (Will *et al.* 2021). The first two concern more short-term environmental conditions, while the latter two concern conditions that have played out on an evolutionary timescale.

If we define "stressful environmental conditions" as those conditions that lead to a strong reduction of fitness in populations, *the environmental stress hypothesis* suggests that greater cognitive or behavioural flexibility (related to brain size)[2] and greater mobility and reduced vulnerability to predation (related to body size) help to counteract conditions such as cold, dry, and nutrient-poor environments. In addition to the environmental stress hypothesis, there is *the environmental constraints hypothesis*: while it is true that larger bodies and brains are, in principle, an advantage, they are also more "expensive", requiring more resources to grow and maintain. Consequently, in environments with few resources, smaller bodies and brains may be favoured: fitness is a trade-off between the cost of the trait and its usefulness.

Let us now consider the evolutionary timescale. According to the *environmental variability hypothesis*, on an intergenerational scale, having a larger body and brain reduces the risk of extinction in the presence of unstable environmental conditions and habitat fragmentation. The environmental variability hypothesis is flanked by the *environmental consistency hypothesis*, the evolutionary-scale version of the first two hypotheses: in stable environments on an intergenerational scale, larger brains and bodies will be found, because environmental stability will be able to guarantee the resources to maintain them from generation to generation. Conversely, in highly variable environments on an intergenerational scale, the variable availability of resources will limit body and brain size (phenotypes that consume too much energy will tend to disappear).

Using the conceptual tools developed in the previous chapter, and simplifying somewhat, we can attempt to construct a short historical sketch on the basis of the hypotheses just outlined. In the ecological environment of our ancestors, life used to take place in extreme and variable environmental conditions. Under such conditions, those who were endowed with a large body and a large brain were more likely to survive and reproduce than those who were not (recall the selective environment: certain characteristics of the ecological environment *differentially* influence the reproductive contributions of organisms). The "big body and brain" trait proved to be not only adaptive but also heritable, so much so that it spread over generations and changed the appearance of the lineage to which we belong: on average, we are bigger and have bigger brains than our ancestors.

There is an important piece missing from this story, however: the developmental environment. Provided that a certain genotype is inherited, it is not certain that a certain phenotype will follow *ipso facto* from a certain genotype. The environment, as we have outlined (Chapter 2, Section 2.3.2), intervenes not only a posteriori in the selection of phenotypes but also in their production (development) and maintenance. As developmental biologist Scott Gilbert (2012, p. 20) writes, "the environment plays instructive roles in development and selective roles in evolution". In other words, for a human being to have a large body and a large brain, it is not enough for this information to be present in the genotype; a number of other conditions, linked to the development of the organism, must also be fulfilled (cf. Box 3.1). Let us therefore put to the side the example used to illustrate the causal role of the environment in the evolution of our species and focus on the developmental environment, remembering that this, together with the selective environment, is part of the ecological environment and that the development of organisms is an integral part of the evolutionary process.

BOX 3.1 Gene expression

There is now some consensus that genes are not simple causal agents, that is, that *a* particular phenotypic trait does not simply result from *a* particular genetic trait. Rather, the idea is that phenotypic traits are causally linked to networks composed of tens or hundreds of genes together with their products (RNA, proteins, other types of molecules . . .) interacting with each other. In addition, gene expression (the complex process that begins with the transcription of DNA into an RNA copy and generally ends with the production of a protein) is very sensitive to environmental conditions and depends on the materials in the environment. Looking at this in more detail, developmental biology currently maintains that gene expression depends not only on the gene sequence but also on processes that are *external to* it (and therefore environmental processes), or "epigenetic processes". One of the best known of these, and the one that most clearly illustrates the role of the environment in gene expression, is DNA methylation.

It turns out that DNA can be methylated; that is, a small molecule can attach to some of its bases, often cytosine. Methylation does not change the role of the cytosine (*if* a gene codes for a protein, the protein will be the same, whether its cytosines are methylated or not), but it *does affect the probability that* the gene will code for the protein in question (recall the interpretation of the causal relation outlined in Chapter 2, Section 2.4, where causality is viewed as a probabilistic dependence relation rather than a necessary one); that is, it plays a causal role in determining whether or not a gene is transcribed. Generally (but not always – causality is here understood as a dependency relation in a probabilistic sense), genes in densely methylated regions are not transcribed. The example of methylation thus illustrates the extent to which a factor in the immediate surroundings of the DNA – the methylated groups that attach to cytosines – can influence gene transcription and the production of the relevant protein. Methylation patterns therefore determine the expression or non-expression of a gene. These patterns, moreover, can be passed on from mother cells to daughter cells; that is, they can be inherited. For this reason, many proponents of the Extended Evolutionary Synthesis – notably the biologists Eva Jablonka and Marion Lamb (2005) – argue that in addition to the genetic inheritance recognised by the Modern Synthesis, epigenetic inheritance, exemplified by the inheritance of methylation patterns, must also be recognised (see also Box 2.1).

3.1.2 Signals from the developmental environment

When we talk about the development of an embryo into an adult organism and say that it is conditioned by the environment, what environment are we talking about? Think of the genome of an embryo: it is contained within its cells. What is its environment? Is it the nucleus of the cell that surrounds it, or the planet on which the embryo is located? Or perhaps both? In the latter case, how can such things as temperature and certain substances in the mother's environment exert a causal influence on matter (the embryo's genome) without being in direct contact with it? This is ultimately the same problem of action at a distance that Newton tried to solve in *Opticks* through the concept of a fluid or medium, a concept later taken up by Lamarck (as we saw in Chapter 1). Having abandoned Newtonian aether and Lamarckian explanations, developmental biology now speaks of *environmental signals*. Let us recall the examples given in the previous chapter: temperature is a signal for the development of the turtle embryo, the presence of predators is a signal for the blue-headed wrasse, a certain type of food is a signal for the bee larva, and so on. In the presence of receivers capable of reacting to these signals and interpreting them, the environment contains information. It is by reading this information – environmental signals – that organisms, including humans, preadapt[3] to and develop within the environment in which they are born. Let us look at this in a little more detail and with the help of some examples.

When we think of our environment, we generally think of what is external to us, and the boundary is typically defined by our skin: when we go swimming we are in an aquatic environment, and the water is external to us and surrounds us. Similarly, when we go for a walk the environment is the air that surrounds us, together with the ground that supports us. But if we zoom out, the environment is also the park we are walking in, the city in which the park is located, the continent on which the city is located, the entire planet, and so on. We can also zoom in and discover that we are an environment for our internal organs, which are an environment for our cells, which are an environment for our genes. And we are also an environment for other organisms that inhabit our bodies: mites, bacteria (often organised in colonies), viruses, fungi, and so on. There are environments within environments and surrounders that are surrounded.[4]

A similar vertigo effect occurs when we think of a genome. Imagine that a certain section of the DNA of an embryo cell contains the information to produce the *large body* trait. This piece of DNA is part of a macromolecule, which is therefore its environment, with which it interacts. The macromolecule, however, will be both the surrounding and the surrounded. In fact, as we have said, in human beings the DNA is packaged into chromosomes within the nucleus of the cell; thus the chromosomes serve as the environment of the genes, the nucleus of the cell as the environment of the chromosomes, the cell of the nucleus, and so on, right down to what we consider to be the organism's external environment: the park in which I am taking a walk, the city in which I live, a region with a Mediterranean climate, on planet Earth.

In order to keep the vertigo effect under control, it may be useful – as is done in medicine, for example – to distinguish the *microenvironment*, that is, the immediate surroundings, from the (macro)environment. The microenvironment of a cell, for example, includes other cells, molecules, and structures (such as blood vessels) that surround and support it. Normally, when we talk about the microenvironment, the surrounded is represented by cells. However, the concept can be extended: for example, an animal's microenvironment will be the area that most closely surrounds it and with which it is in direct contact. Although it is likely impossible to make a clear-cut distinction between the microenvironment and the macroenvironment and their different causal contributions to the development of an organism, it seems reasonable to assume that some environmental influences will, on balance, be negligible (e.g. the relative position of Venus and Mercury), while others will clearly be relevant (e.g. the temperature of the microenvironment).

It is not a stretch to say that the concept of the microenvironment is the contemporary version of Lamarckian *milieux* (for Lamarck, recall, *milieux* are not only fluids in which organisms are immersed but also the most important of all living circumstances, because they can act *directly* on organisms). The microenvironment is in direct contact with the surrounded and can therefore exert mechanical effects on it and convey information from the macroenvironment in the form of electrical or chemical signals. The causal relationship between the microenvironment and its surrounded often takes the form of a feedback relationship. For example, the behaviour of cancer cells is determined not only by the cells themselves but also by their microenvironment, from which they obtain nutrients and oxygen and from which they receive signals for growth and development. As cancer cells replicate, however, they cause changes in the microenvironment, which in turn feed back to the cancer cells themselves and to healthy cells (Baghban *et al.* 2020).

To illustrate the relationship between the micro- and the macroenvironment, let us briefly consider the case of the meadow vole *Microtus pennsylvanicus*, a small rodent which is able to preadapt to the environment that awaits it at birth (of course, there is no intention or awareness involved in this process). In its mother's womb, the mouse develops a thick fur if its birth will occur in the autumn and a thin one if it will be born in the spring. This is thanks to a series of environmental cues that are transmitted and elicit responses from the organisms. Specifically, certain information about the macroenvironment (changes in the length of a day) is transmitted to the embryo through the microenvironment (the placenta). The embryo processes the information received and regulates itself accordingly through epigenetic mechanisms (see Box 3.1). More precisely, changes in the length of the day lead to changes in the mother's melatonin levels; these are transmitted through the placenta to the embryo, which develops one coat of fur rather than another (Gluckman, Hanson and Low 2019). Like the meadow vole, humans exhibit phenotypic plasticity and can develop different phenotypes depending on the environmental cues they receive, particularly in the early stages of their development (Nettle and Bateson 2015). For example, the foetus's exposure to a reduction in oxygen or food will typically induce an immediate adaptive response, that is, reduced foetal growth, which will help it to survive with limited resources until birth. In other words, the foetus receives signals from the mother's macroenvironment – via the microenvironment – and adjusts accordingly, producing a phenotype that is appropriate to the macroenvironment that awaits it.

In general, with Eco-Devo biology (Gilbert and Epel 2008, chapter 1), we can say that in the case of humans, as in the case of other organisms, the environment is a normal agent in the production of the phenotype: what we are depends to a very large extent on the environment in which we develop and in which we conduct our existence.

The immune system – which distinguishes self from non-self and generally prevents the latter from crossing the boundaries of an organism – shows that human beings are as much "creatures" of their environment as they are creatures of their genes. Genetically speaking, in fact, a human being can produce millions of different types of immune cells, but the number actually present in each individual is only a fraction of this potential number. This fraction depends on the environment, that is, the antigenic agents to which the individual has been exposed throughout its development (all those entities recognised by the immune system as foreign to the organism, including, for example, viruses and bacteria). The same applies to the digestive system, certain parts of which develop in response to the types of bacteria with which the gut is in symbiosis. The same goes for muscle formation. For example, many of the genes needed to build and maintain muscles are not expressed in microgravity: astronauts who live in microgravity for long periods suffer from severe muscle atrophy.

It is therefore clear that the environment exerts a causal effect on organisms, including humans. To this causal effect, organisms respond with phenotypic plasticity and evolutionary adaptations. But that's not all: as the previous chapter anticipated, humans are all-round ecosystem engineers and masters of niche construction. It is to these processes that we now turn.

3.2 Moulders of their environment

The ecological environment of *Homo sapiens* today is very different from that of the earliest *Homo* species: in the Pleistocene, when much of the water on the planet's surface was in the form of ice, the climate was colder and drier, and the dominant vegetation was an arid steppe. The population from which our species originated is estimated to have had 18,500 members of reproductive age and was probably structured in family groups of nomadic hunter-gatherers (Huff *et al.* 2010). Today, the world population exceeds eight billion, the majority of whom live in complex societies and inhabit cities: humans are born into a highly constructed environment and receive "an ecological inheritance that includes a legacy of houses, cities, cars, farms, nations, e-commerce and global warming" (Odling-Smee, Laland and Feldman 2003, p. 241). Recent studies suggest that – contrary to popular belief – the anthropogenic modification of the environment and the exploitation of natural resources are not modern phenomena. The species *Homo sapiens* was already a radical architect of its environment in the late Pleistocene, long before the industrial economy, the population explosion, and globalisation (Boivin *et al.* 2016).

80 *Philosophy of the environment*

The radical modification of the environment has certainly had positive consequences for the fitness of humans: those who live in cities in wealthy and peaceful parts of the world are much more likely to leave home in the morning and return safe and sound in the evening than our Pleistocene ancestors were. These changes have also come with negative consequences, however, as illustrated by the statements in Figure 3.1 and as the recent Covid-19 pandemic has shown. Indeed, if we consider the early stages of the epidemic, it is clear that the global spread of the new coronavirus and the disease it caused was largely determined by human mobility, and it has been hypothesised that densely populated cities may in general suffer more prolonged epidemics than less populated ones (Rader *et al.* 2020).

Niche construction theory offers a promising explanation of this tension. Indeed, it predicts that niche construction is generally advantageous for the constructing species but recognises that certain types of niche construction may, as anticipated (Chapter 2, Section 2.5), prove deleterious under certain circumstances.

3.2.1 *Cultural niche construction*

Niche construction, let us recall,

> [p]rovides a second evolutionary route to the dynamic match between organism and environment. Such matches need no longer be treated as products of a one-way process, exclusively involving the responses of organisms to environmentally imposed problems: instead they should be thought of as the dynamical products of a two-way process involving organisms both responding to their environments, and changing their environments through niche construction.
> (Odling-Smee, Laland and Feldman 2003, p. 240)

Many, if not all, species are engaged in niche construction processes. *Homo sapiens*, however, seem to be particularly enterprising in this sense. Between 50,000 and 70,000 years ago, our ancestors set out from East Africa to occupy the entire planet. What made this possible, in addition to phenotypic plasticity, was their incredible ability to materially modify the environments in which they found themselves. This is how they were able to survive in climates that were extreme for their physiology and to cope with resource scarcity when it occurred. Technology and culture – from fire control to the production of clothing and shelters, from agriculture to the domestication of animals – clearly played a key role.

According to niche construction theory, human evolution is primarily (but not solely) *cultural* niche construction, that is, based on information acquired and transmitted not genetically (or epigenetically; cf. Box 3.1) but culturally. This gives humans a peculiar ability to influence their own evolution, since, in our species, cultural processes generally operate more rapidly than natural evolution. In fact, such processes do not depend on the generally random occurrence of adaptive variations: cultural variations are usually produced intentionally, in response to an environmental need. If I want a particular musical instrument to produce a certain sound, I do not have to wait for a change to occur spontaneously in the material from which it is made: I can modify my instrument to produce the desired sound. If I discover that the flour I have combined with water has by chance produced beer rather than bread, I will not have to wait for this process to happen again by chance: I will be able to reproduce it and improve it over time, making gradual variations (in this sense, cultural evolution seems more Lamarckian than Darwinian).

Cultural variations, moreover, can be transmitted in many more ways than genetic ones. Whereas genetic transmission in humans is unidirectional (vertical, from parents to children) and takes at least two generations, cultural transmission – consisting of knowledge, behaviour, and technological skills – is continuous, passing from many people to many others, within and between generations, vertically (from parents to children) and horizontally (among peers), and through various modalities: imitation, teaching, and learning from parents, but also from (and among) siblings, friends, and other members of society.

The transmission of knowledge and skills contained in our brains is complemented by the availability of a vast external archive – recording devices and technical prostheses of various kinds such as books, photographs, films, and that vast shared and participatory archive that is the Web. It is to this archival dimension that some trace the uniqueness of our species. Philosopher Maurizio Ferraris speaks, in this regard, of recording as the ultimate foundation of society:

> The benefit of having hands is, on the one side, the possibility of having practical supplements, such as a stick; on the other side, the possibility, in perspective, of having symbolic supplements, such as language. . . . And whether humans develop all the social attitudes we know . . . depends on the fact that humans, thanks to the possibility of keeping track of knowledge and duty, are able to build complex societies.
>
> (Ferraris 2022, pp. 108–109)

Eva Jablonka and Marion Lamb (2005, chapter 6) focus instead on the mode of transmission of cultural variations. Indeed, although other animals also have symbolic systems – for example the "dance language" used by bees to communicate information to their mates about how far away food is and in which direction it can be found – only humans have rich, articulate, and flexible symbolic systems. Bee dance is a food-related symbolic system, and as far as we know it has never occurred to a bee to apply it to other areas. In humans, the same symbolic system can instead be applied to different domains (language is used to talk about anything), and the same idea can be expressed through different symbolic systems (a word, a song, a painting, a dance . . .).

Human niche construction therefore has a strong cultural component, and we can view cultural inheritance as part of ecological inheritance (see Box 2.1):

> Generations of humans also inherit culturally modified rural and urban environments – fields of crops, terraces, artificial lakes, canals, roads, schools, hospitals, factories, police forces, electricity grids, waste products and pollution. We also inherit a world of our own making, complete with dogs, wheat, dairy cows, nectarines and countless genetically modified types of grapes and without dodos, woolly mammoths, and the numerous other species left extinct by human activities. This is both our ecological and our cultural inheritance.
> (Odling-Smee and Laland 2011, p. 227)

It should be noted that according to NCT (niche construction theory), there are no substantial differences between human niche construction and that of other species. Niche construction occurs when a species or population alters its ecological environment in a way that alters its own selective environment (and often, indirectly, that of other populations or species), causing an evolutionary response, *whatever the mechanism by which the changes take place* – be it dietary interactions, metabolic and physiological activities, or behavioural and cultural factors. For NCT, therefore, culture is a mode of niche construction that the human species shares with other species. Quite simply, the cultural component plays a greater role for humans than for other species.

The predominance of the cultural component, however, results in a peculiarity of the human niche construction process. Rather than being niche constructors, human beings are cumulative and progressive niche *modifiers*. In fact, they continuously modify their environment, regardless of adaptive needs or selective pressures in the narrow, biological sense. Whereas Pleistocene human niche construction was likely driven primarily by the need to survive extreme and unpredictable environmental conditions and predators, for a large segment of our species today it is more a matter of *continuing to modify* an environment to which we are, after all, adapted. Unlike Darwin's earthworms, which stabilise their environment, human beings continue to modify it, with an enormous expenditure of energy.

Although the boundaries between construction and niche modification are blurred, at least one element that distinguishes the two processes can be emphasised. Construction tends to stabilise the environment since, from an evolutionary and ecological point of view, living in a stable environment is safer and requires less energy. Consequently, it is generally repetitive: beavers will build dams in much the same way as they always have; earthworms will modify the soil in much the same way as the earthworms of the previous generation, and so will their descendants. The process of niche modification, on the other hand, is characterised by highly innovative behaviour and does not necessarily tend to create a stable environment (Gluckman, Hanson and Low 2019).

3.2.2 The Capitalocene

The process of change is largely determined by cultural rather than biological factors, and these can be traced back not to a need to survive and reproduce but to a general and legitimate aspiration: the improvement of quality of life. However, not only do different individuals and groups have different ideas about what constitutes an improvement to quality of life, but improvements to quality of life for one group may come at the expense of the quality of life of other groups or other species, as some positions in environmental ethics point out.[5] This becomes clear when trying to account for statements such as sentence 7 in Figure 3.1: "The environment of Amazon tribes is in danger of disappearing due to deforestation."

The Amazon Rainforest is the largest rainforest on the planet and is home to an impressive number of species. Many, if not all, are busy building their niches. Among them are several groups of *Homo sapiens*. For some people, the diversity of species of the Amazon rainforest represents an enormous "natural capital", a "sprawling storehouse of riches and resources, awaiting development", or, to use one of the slogans of the Brazilian government's institutional campaigns in the 1970s, a "land without men for men without land" (McNeill and Engelke 2014, p. 58). Upon their arrival in the 16th century, the first European settlers began to appropriate resources (in particular the *Pau-Brasil*, a red wood from which a dye was made that was highly valued in Europe) that were part of the environment of other human groups, indigenous to the area. The latter were almost completely wiped out by influenza, measles, and smallpox, diseases brought by settlers with whom they had never been in contact, for which they therefore lacked immune defences. In more recent times, similar dynamics have been at play, albeit with different protagonists. Take, for example, the Brazilian government's development project in the second half of the last century, which promised to alleviate the misery of the country's arid northeast. The plan basically consisted of populating part of the forest, towards which the spontaneous migratory flows of the poorer strata of the population were directed. Within a few years the forest was criss-crossed by highways and millions of migrants were pouring into it, carrying out massive deforestation in order to obtain land for cultivation and grazing. We can read this environmental transformation as a process of niche construction or modification (as we have said, the boundaries are blurred in many cases, and this is one of them). With the construction of roads and the removal of trees for grazing and agriculture, the new tenants of an ecological environment that was inhospitable to them modified the selective pressures on them (alleviating them)[6] and on other groups of their own species (increasing them), altering the types of resources available to them and forcing the Indigenous inhabitants to move further inland into the forest. The Indigenous inhabitants of the area, for their part, also engaged in niche modification in the same region, aimed at reducing selective pressures and improving *their* quality of life (over a much longer period, estimated at 20,000 years or more – see Gruhn 2020).

While the migrants legitimately sought to improve their quality of life, this was to the detriment of the Indigenous inhabitants of the area. However, both groups sought to achieve, with varying levels of success, that correspondence to the environment in which adaptation consists. If the new inhabitants had abandoned their environment of roads and farms and entered the forest, their chances of survival would have decreased: The same can be said for the Indigenous inhabitants of the area: in the migrant environment, they would likely have come into contact with viruses and bacteria to which they had no immunity.

However, some actors are missing from this brief reconstruction, for example the Brazilian government. Then as now, the exploitation of the Amazon is presented as a solution to poverty. Yet, as the environmental historians John McNeill and Peter Engelke (2014, p. 56) note, the Brazilian government – a military regime – sought to alleviate the conditions of misery but also, on the one hand, to reduce the pressing demand for land reform and, on the other hand, to populate the border regions with loyal Brazilians. Moreover, economic interests were closely intertwined with politics: the Amazon is an immense region in which people harvest timber, raise animals for consumption in urban markets, and grow soya, sugar, and palm oil. And again, national policies can fit in with, or conflict with, global environmental policies and the views of the international community. In response to international (and particularly European) criticism, for example, former Brazilian President Jair Bolsonaro (under whose political leadership deforestation increased considerably) responded – as reported in the *Guardian* on 19 July 2019 – that while Brazilians "understand the importance of the Amazon for the world", "the Amazon is ours", citing the country's national sovereignty over environmental resources.[7]

At this point it is imperative to clarify the explanatory power of NCT. Let us recall that NCT was proposed in the field of evolutionary biology – more precisely, in the context of the Extended Synthesis (cf. Box 2.1) – to account for the evolutionary feedback between organisms and their environment. When cultural processes and variants are considered, NCT also becomes applicable to *Homo sapiens*. However, it would be naive to think that a theory of evolutionary biology alone is capable of accounting for all the implications that processes of the type just described entail. More generally, it is clear that NCT is an important, but certainly not sufficient, explanatory and predictive tool for the construction of the human environment.

According to environmental historian Jason Moore, to speak of human environmental construction as if the subject *Homo sapiens* were a uniform,

Building the human environment 85

undifferentiated species (or in our terms, to speak of human niche construction without distinguishing the different subjects involved) is to conceal what Moore calls the "dirty secret" of modern world history, namely the relationship between environmental construction and power dynamics. The term "Anthropocene" (introduced, as we shall see, to denote the role of human biogeophysical forces in shaping the dynamics of the biosphere) treats the human species as an undifferentiated whole – as Moore observes – whereas in fact responsibility for the transformation of the biosphere is not uniform across all human communities. Moore therefore proposes that we replace the concept of the *Anthropocene* with that of the *Capitalocene*, which, unlike the former, does not refer to the *anthropos* as an undifferentiated collective actor, attributing to it historical responsibilities that should instead be attributed to capitalism:

> The Anthropocene makes for an easy story. Easy, because it does not challenge the naturalised inequalities, alienation, and violence inscribed in modernity's strategic relations of power and production. It is an easy story to tell because it does not ask us to think about these relations at all. It reduces the mosaic of human activities in the web of life to an abstract, homogeneous humanity. It removes inequality, commodification, imperialism, patriarchy, and much more from the problem of humanity-in-nature. No inequality, commodification, imperialism, patriarchy and more.
>
> (Moore 2016, p. 82)

It is a fact that the human species has used natural resources unequally in its niche construction. A cursory glance through any textbook on environmental history will show that industrialised countries have built their fortunes by exploiting natural resources, taking land and raw materials first from colonies and then from developing countries. The use of the past tense here should not mislead the reader: the current prosperity of Western countries continues to be built on the exploitation of poorer countries (and those richer in natural resources).

The Niger Delta – where "for decades, tankers filled up on crude where centuries before wooden ships had loaded slaves" (McNeill and Engelke 2014, p. 18) – is but one example among many. This densely populated rainforest region of Nigeria is home to one of the world's largest swamps (an ecosystem that is particularly rich in biodiversity). In the 1950s, Shell and British Petroleum began extracting oil, setting up around 160 oil fields and 7,000 kilometres of pipelines, dredging canals, and destroying the mangrove forests, which were essential to the functioning of the ecosystems that sustained the local human populations. In addition to the direct damage to the marshy habitat inflicted during the extraction system installation process, oil extraction has had disastrous environmental consequences in the area, thanks in part to corner-cutting to maximise profits. Between 1976 and 2005,

86 *Philosophy of the environment*

an estimated three million barrels of crude oil were dispersed into the environment in the Niger Delta. This was due to a combination of ordinary accidents, acts of sabotage by local populations, and soil and atmospheric pollution. It is important to note that these estimates are from the Nigerian government and may be on the low side. In fact, the United Nations recognised the Niger Delta as the area of greatest ecological risk in the world in the early 1990s. The local populations have not benefitted from oil extraction. On the contrary, their living conditions have worsened due to environmental deterioration and the resulting scarcity of resources. The beneficiaries of oil extraction are the Nigerian government and the countries that purchase the oil. The cost of cheap energy for Western countries is actually very high in terms of the environmental and human impact.

Whether or not one agrees with Moore's proposal, it is important to emphasise that niche construction in the case of *Homo sapiens* is not operated by a single, undifferentiated subject. Building on Uexküll's insight (cf. Chapter 1, Section 1.4.2), it could be argued that when it comes to the (transcendental, but above all material) environmental construction in which *Homo sapiens* is engaged, intraspecific differences, both individual and group, may have a significance that they lack in the case of other species. This is true not only because humans have constructed tools that expand their perceptive capacities, as Uexküll has pointed out, but also because human environmental construction is intertwined with social, economic, and geopolitical dynamics, the interests of nations, and power relations. Many disciplines must contribute to providing a comprehensive understanding of the process: from environmental history to geopolitics, from bioeconomics to human geography, and from anthropology to ethics, to name but a few.

3.2.3 Of mice and men

Niche construction has significant effects on other species, altering habitats and resource availability. In the human environment, certain species may be favoured over others. However, it is important to note that the human environment is not created from scratch but rather on the basis of modifications to pre-existing habitats that were once the environments of other species. Before discussing the second case, which has become more evident and concerning in the current environmental crisis, let us examine examples of species that thrive in human environments such as cities and cultivated fields, the most important and widespread examples of human ecosystem engineering. This section focuses on animal species, but it should be clear that the construction of the human niche likely involves, in one way or another, all kinds of organisms, including plant species, algae, fungi, and microorganisms (see Chapter 4, Section 4.3).

Some species have a high capacity to adapt to the human environment by seizing the opportunities it offers, often through forms of commensalism, that is, forms of interaction between species in which one takes advantage of the resources produced by the other. The common mouse, *Mus musculus*, for example, began taking advantage of the human environment when humankind was still nomadic but already building grain stores (Lewontin 1970; Bonhomme, Boursot and Orth 2001). The construction of grain stores is an example of allogenic ecosystem engineering: the resources are transformed from a raw to an "engineered" state, where they are cleaned, sorted, and stored. This alteration affects their availability, allowing ecosystem engineers to utilise them even when they would not typically be accessible (for instance, during winter). However, by constructing barns humans also altered – certainly unintentionally – the availability of resources for *Mus musculus*, who, given access to ready-made food in every season of the year, must have found humankind an excellent species with whom to share its evolutionary fate. When the agricultural revolution began some 12,000 years ago, the mouse had no difficulty coping with the rapid environmental change it entailed, being fortuitously preadapted to it. Rather than facing extinction, the species spread globally, along with its human commensals and wheat itself – another species whose fate was dictated, along with thousands of others, by the construction of the human niche.

In general, the spread of agriculture has led to the decline, if not the extinction, of many wild species adapted to the habitats that cultivated fields have replaced (the disappearance or extreme fragmentation of the natural habitat of many species is the primary cause of their extinction). On the other hand, it has benefitted both cultivated species, such as wheat, rice, and maize, and species that are perhaps more plastic from a behavioural point of view and are now widespread globally, such as *Mus musculus*. The same argument applies to cities, in which over half of the world's population resides. The croton bug, *Blattella germanica*, is one of the most widespread and common species of cockroach. It evolved in Asia, likely appreciating the products of culinary techniques and the heating and cooling of the urban environment, and then spread globally through trade (Johnson and Munshi-South 2017). Again, human niche construction proved favourable for other species.

The preceding cases share the common characteristic of being unintentional. In other cases, humans intentionally have an impact on other species through their niche construction. Pigeons, cited by Darwin – who bred them – as an emblematic example of artificial selection, were domesticated between 5,000 and 10,000 years ago in southwestern Asia and have become a popular food in Europe and North America. Farm escapees have found ideal living conditions in urban and peri-urban areas due to the availability of nesting substrates in buildings and abundant food sources, as well as a lack of predators.

Dogs, cats, and budgies – more or less standard pets – all live comfortably alongside humans. Cities, the result par excellence of human ecosystem engineering, often offer excellent habitats as diversified spaces with various, year-round resources, few predators, and numerous structures. Nevertheless, it is evident that human niche construction also has negative consequences for other species. For instance, pastures and monocultures are simplified ecosystems (where the paucity of primary producer species supports few types of consumers) that require the continuous use of pesticides. Cities, in turn, are anomalous ecosystems in which more individuals live than would be permitted by the space and resource constraints of a less engineered environment. By concentrating more individuals within their limits than the environment can support, cities need to access resources beyond their boundaries, where they must also dispose of their waste. Urbanisation leads to radical environmental changes, so much so that cities have significantly higher air temperatures than their surrounding areas, making them global warming hotspots, to use the terminology of the IPCC report (Doblas-Reyes *et al.* 2021).

The conversion of a significant portion of the Earth's surface into agricultural land, pastures, and urban ecosystems has occurred at the expense of habitats populated by other species, many of which – unlike mice and pigeons – have been unable to adapt to their new environments. As Comte observed (see Chapter 1), life constantly presupposes the necessary correlation of the organism and its appropriate environment. Natural selection, phenotypic plasticity, ecosystem engineering, and niche construction are all ways in which this correlation is realised and maintained throughout organisms' lives and, eventually, across generations. This correlation may fail, however, and those species that fail to establish a new one are doomed to extinction or – if subject to environmental conservation practices – to *ex situ* conservation, with the hope of future reintroduction into their natural habitat. Some species, for example, display little plasticity and cannot adapt to rapid environmental changes. Others are extremely specialised: their correlation with their environment is so strict that a single change is enough to endanger them (think of the koala, which feeds exclusively on eucalyptus). Still others may be reduced to such a low population level due to excessive predation that recovery is no longer possible. Again, when considering adaptation over evolutionary timescales, mutations that would allow for survival in a certain environment, assuming they can arise, may not arise in time.

In the Americas, what we now call "charismatic megafauna"[8] – sabre-toothed tigers, mammoths, giant sloths – disappeared with the arrival of humans between 11,000 and 13,000 years ago. The same happened in Australia 30,000 years earlier. Large flightless birds are among the paradigmatic victims: the dodo in Mauritius, the moa in New Zealand, the elephant bird in Madagascar. The extinction of the megafauna in the late Pleistocene was most likely due to non-anthropogenic causes – the transition from a glacial to an interglacial climate – combined with excessive predation and habitat modification by humans. Human responsibility for modifying the habitats of other species undoubtedly increased during the Holocene, which was characterised by more stable climatic conditions than the previous epoch. From the destruction of tropical habitats by European colonialism to the surge in population growth and energy consumption after the Second World War, the evolutionary history of *Homo sapiens* – which is also the history of its niche construction – is punctuated by the disappearance of countless species.

Extinction is undoubtedly the most extreme and obvious negative effect of human niche construction on other species, but it is not the only one. Even when a species does not become extinct, sharing the environment with *Homo sapiens* is rarely a good deal: hunting, fishing, breeding, deforestation, and the pollution of the air, water, and soil have accompanied the construction of our niche, with negative effects on the health, development, and evolution of other species. Not only that: while niche construction usually increases the fitness of the niche-constructing species, it can also, as we have seen, result in a process of *negative* niche construction. In this case, the fitness of the niche-constructing species decreases.

3.2.4 A silent spring

Pollution – one of the most widely felt environmental issues, at least since the 1960s – is undoubtedly an exemplary case of how the construction of the human niche affects the health, development, and evolution of other species, as well as the human species itself. In this context, it is worth recalling an episode of particular significance for environmental history and the history of environmentalism: the exposure, by Rachel Carson, of the dire consequences of synthetic pesticides, in particular DDT. Her book, *Silent Spring*, published in 1962, was a pivotal means of bringing this issue to the attention of the general public.

During the course of the Second World War, the war industry developed a number of chemical agents, some of which turned out to be harmful to insects but apparently not to humans. As Carson explains in the third chapter of the book, these substances differed from those previously used as insecticides. The latter, in fact, were derived from naturally occurring plants and minerals: arsenic, copper, manganese, pyrethrum (obtained from dried chrysanthemum flowers), and nicotine sulphate. The newer chemicals, such as DDT (dichlorodiphenyltrichloroethane), first synthesised at the end of the 19th century, were made in the laboratory. Of course, natural pesticides are not per se less toxic than synthetic ones, as the Borgias, who are said to have used an arsenic-based poison for their crimes, were well aware. However, the toxicity of arsenic has always been immediately apparent; DDT, on the other hand, seemed completely harmless to humans, and mammals in general, and harmful only to insects when it was first introduced. It was therefore hailed and promoted as a miracle substance: by 1952 there were almost 10,000 different insecticides on the market – most of them DDT-based – and between 1950 and 1980 40,000 tonnes of DDT were sprayed each year (Nespor 2020, p. 17). In some respects, it actually seemed like a miracle substance: one of its first uses was during the war, when it was sprinkled on bodies or pulverised in rooms to control fleas and lice. In Italy, for example, it was used by the Allies to end a devastating typhus epidemic in Naples in 1944 and, shortly afterwards, to combat malaria in the Italian regions of Campania, Veneto, and Sardinia. Even today, DDT is used for disease vector control (Van den Berg, Manuweera and Konradsen 2017). In evolutionary terms, it can be said that DDT increased the fitness of humans, as it allowed them to counteract the selective pressures of parasites and diseases.

DDT played a particularly important role in the fight against malaria: by 1951, malaria had been eliminated in the United States, and the DDT-based Global Malaria Eradication Program promoted by the World Health Organisation in 1955 eradicated malaria in several countries in Europe, the Americas, and Asia (although most of Africa was excluded from the programme).[9] As Rachel Carson revealed in her book, however, the feverish enthusiasm of the 1950s was ultimately unjustified. To gain a sense of the prevailing attitude, one need only turn to the advertisements of the time, which presented DDT as "a benefactor of all humanity", thanks to which humans would have better meat, more milk and butter, more productive crops, and cleaner houses (Figure 3.2).

Rachel Carson was trained in marine biology and was an ecologist. She therefore had a clear understanding of how ecosystems and food chains work: if insects are removed, the functioning of ecosystems is threatened. Pollination, one of the most fundamental ecosystem services, depends on insects. Insects recycle nutrients, disperse seeds, and maintain soil fertility. They are also the main food for many species of birds, reptiles, and fish, which in turn are prey for other species, and so on. As such, in the "Fable for Tomorrow" that opens *Silent Spring*, the inhabitants of an ordinary North American town wake up one day to a strange stillness, a spring without the song of robins and jays.

Carson laid bare the far-reaching consequences of DDT: nature is not made up of watertight compartments, and when a body of water or soil is contaminated, the poison spreads enormous distances from where it was used, especially if its molecule is very stable and therefore persistent. Indeed, DDT is classified as a POP – a Persistent Organic Pollutant (the wording "organic", i.e. carbon-based, can be misleading, warns Carson: carbon is not necessarily a symbol of life). If clover is sprayed with DDT, the chickens that feed on it will lay eggs that contain it. The same is true when it becomes food for cows: their milk, and any butter made from that milk, will contain DDT. Because of its persistence, the poison becomes part of the cycle of matter in an ecosystem and travels up the food chain. As early as 1969, a study showed that, after a single application of DDT, pesticide residues remained present in the tissue of forest mammals for nine years (Dimond and Sherburne 1969).

It is clear that DDT, which is part of the construction of the human cultural niche, has a causal impact on insect fitness and an unintended and less direct impact on the fitness of other organisms and on the functioning of ecosystems in general. One example will suffice to illustrate the complexity

Building the human environment 91

Figure 3.2 Penn Salt DDT advertisement, which appeared in *Time* magazine on 30 June 1947. Courtesy of the Science History Institute.

and delicateness of relationships in ecosystem and population interactions and the extent to which human affairs are intertwined with those of other species. In the 1950s, in British Guiana, the *Anopheles* mosquito, the vector of malaria, was successfully exterminated with DDT. However, two other mosquito species, which did not normally feed on human blood, survived. At the same time, the reduction in the malaria rate led to a 70 per cent increase in the human population in just a few years. This was followed by a major increase in the amount of land used for rice cultivation and a decrease in the amount of land available for livestock. In the absence of livestock, one of the two surviving mosquito species changed its prey and began feeding on human blood, and malaria transmission resumed (O'Shaughnessy 2008).

Like other POPs, DDT, by becoming part of the environment shared by humans and other species, alters the population dynamics of the ecological environment (e.g. by altering predator–prey relationships, as the case of Guyana illustrates). As it is absorbed by organisms, it becomes part of their developmental environment. Birds produce eggs that are thinner and more easily broken when stepped on by other birds, the embryos are smaller and weaker, and fewer survive. The evolutionary dynamics change. Rats develop tumours and become sterile. Rat embryos no longer attach to the uterus, and the offspring have a higher mortality rate. In general, in mammals – including humans – DDT is passed from the mother's milk to the offspring and is able to cross the placental barrier, becoming part of the embryo's microenvironment. It is now classified as a probable carcinogen (along with many other synthetic herbicides and insecticides that, like radiation, are mutagenic agents that can lead to permanent changes to DNA sequences), and it has been suggested that it may induce the epigenetic inheritance (see Box 3.1) of obesity and associated kidney, testicular, and ovarian diseases in our species (Skinner *et al.* 2013).

Chemicals such as DDT, developed by humans as part of their niche construction, can cause mutations and affect gene expression, thus becoming part of the genetic and epigenetic inheritance of our own and other species. They also become part of our ecological inheritance because, as they persist over several generations, they become part of the environment that will be inherited by future generations (see Box 3.2). Finally, they are part of our cultural heritage: the chemical formula and instructions for synthesising DDT are transmitted horizontally, as a basic internet search will show. At the same time, however, an internet search for "DDT" will also reveal information about Rachel Carson and about how, despite the smear campaign launched against her by the major chemical industries, which accused her of communist sympathies and scientific unpreparedness, her exposure of the dangers of DDT contributed significantly to the creation of an environmental public opinion movement capable of exerting pressure on institutions. In 1966, the use of DDT was banned on Long Island, where the insecticide had led to a serious decline in the osprey population. In 1972, it was banned in the United States altogether, and in 1978 it was partially banned for agricultural use in Europe.

BOX 3.2 Intergenerational responsibility

The second chapter of Rachel Carson's *Silent Spring* is entitled "The Obligation to Endure", which can mean both the obligation to withstand pressures and the obligation to continue to exist, not only as individuals but as a species. In her book, Carson stresses that future generations are unlikely to forgive the recklessness of her generation, which allowed dangerous chemicals to be used without prior study of their long-term effects and without regard for the integrity of the natural world.

A defining characteristic of environmental problems (pollution, biodiversity loss, climate change, depletion of natural resources) is in fact that they threaten generations yet unborn. One of the first to recognise this, like Carson, was philosopher Hans Jonas in his 1979 book *The Imperative of Responsibility*. Jonas proclaims the need for a new ethics, specific to the "technological age": an ethics of responsibility, in which responsibility corresponds to the self-restraint of technology in order to protect both nature and present and future human beings. For Jonas, the new ethics should be based on the following imperative: act so that the effects of your actions are compatible with the permanence of genuine human life (Jonas 1984).

Recognising the dangers associated with new technologies and the need to reconcile economic growth and the environment, the 1987 Brundtland Report (a landmark document in the history of environmentalism, produced by the World Commission on Environment and Development) defines "sustainable development" as development that meets the needs of the present generations without compromising the ability of future generations to meet their own needs. It also specifies that the concept is based on both intragenerational social equity (environmental emergencies affect all countries equally, but poor countries have fewer resources to deal with them) and intergenerational social equity. Indeed, it was the first official international document to recognise that humanity must also care for the needs of future generations.

Since the Brundtland Report, the principle of intergenerational equity in environmental protection and management has been affirmed. This can broadly be formulated as follows: the planet must be handed over to future generations in no worse a state than we inherited it. Article 3 of the 1992 United Nations Framework Convention on Climate Change states that

> [t]he Parties should protect the climate system for the benefit of present and future generations of humankind, on the basis of equity and in accordance with their common but differentiated

responsibilities and respective capabilities. Accordingly, the developed country Parties should take the lead in combating climate change and the adverse effects thereof.

(United Nations 1992, p. 9)

This principle has gradually been incorporated, in different forms and ways, into the constitutions of many countries, including Brazil, Argentina, Norway, the Dominican Republic and, most recently, Italy. On 8 February 2022, the revision of Articles 9 and 41 of the Italian Constitution was approved. In particular, the following paragraph was added to Article 9, aimed at protecting the country's landscape and historical and artistic heritage: "[The Republic] protects the environment, biodiversity and ecosystems, also in the interest of future generations."

However, the principle of intergenerational equity raises important ethical and metaphysical questions. The costs incurred *today* by policies aimed at mitigating the effects of climate change, for example, will bear fruit that will be enjoyed by *future* generations. In other words, current generations will be paying for actions taken by past generations (for which they have no recourse) for the benefit of future generations (who do not yet exist). This makes such costs difficult to calculate and to accept: is it right, for example, to limit the potential economic growth of poor countries or to reduce the quality of life of people who *currently exist* in order to improve the quality of life of people *who do not (yet) exist*? (For possible answers, see Meyer 2021; Pellegrino 2012.) In addition to this question, there is an even more fundamental one: is it possible, and if so how, for certain actions to be addressed to "non-existent" entities? From an ontological point of view, those who have yet to be conceived have an existence that is not too dissimilar to that of unicorns. And yet, according to the philosopher Tiziana Andina (2022), although they are a fictional subject, the result of an imaginative act, they seem to have an agent-like property, because people and institutions behave *as if* future generations existed.

3.3 A global biogeophysical force

In the previous chapter, having considered the niche construction process of a single species, we moved to the global level and suggested that life *as a whole* may be the protagonist of a kind of niche construction process. It is life in its totality that, in the biosphere theory and the Gaia hypothesis, interacts with non-living matter, determining the conditions of the biosphere and contributing to the functioning of the Earth system. We will now explore the extent to which humans are a part of "living matter", to use Vernadsky's expression, and therefore participate, for better or for worse, in the functioning of the Earth system.

3.3.1 The Anthropocene

As stated in sentence 8 in Figure 3.1: "An increase of 2°C compared to the temperature in pre-industrial times is associated with . . . a much higher risk that dangerous and possibly catastrophic changes in the global environment will occur." Why 2°C? References to the two-degree limit first appeared in working papers published by the environmental economist William Nordhaus in the mid-1970s, as part of what can be called the "natural range argument". Nordhaus argued that the climatic effects of the concentration of carbon dioxide in the atmosphere should be kept within the *normal range* of long-term climate variation (i.e. the maximum of the average variation observed so far). Exceeding the temperature of the pre-industrial era by two degrees would take us out of this range, that is, beyond the average temperature that, as far as we know, has characterised the planet over the last few hundred thousand years. Nordhaus offered no data to support his claim, which was not central to his writings. He identified this threshold by instead appealing to reason and prudence: exceeding it would lead us into unknown and unpredictable territory (Nordhaus 1977; Jaeger and Jaeger 2010). The two-degree limit has now become part of climate policy,[10] albeit in a slightly different form: it is now framed within a "climate catastrophe view" that identifies such a temperature rise with the threshold separating a safe state from a state of catastrophe (Jaeger and Jaeger 2010). For example, in the 1990 report of the Greenhouse Gas Consultation Group, we read that "[a]n absolute temperature limit of 2.0°C can be viewed as an upper limit beyond which the risks of grave damage to ecosystems, and of non-linear responses, are expected to increase rapidly" (Rijsberman and Swart 1990, p. ix). Whether one agrees with the catastrophe view or not, the point is that the human species has been able to change the composition of the atmosphere, increasing the concentration of carbon dioxide and consequently altering the planet's climate. In addition, the human species is the first multicellular species to likely be the cause of a new mass extinction. Human activity on the planet, in other words, can perhaps be equated with that of cyanobacteria and asteroids.

Cyanobacteria. The red bands that can be found in very old rocks testify to the fact that, around 2.5 billion years ago, something unusual happened on Earth: oxygen began to oxidise iron (as occurs in the formation of rust) in a world that, up to that point, had had very little oxygen. Cyanobacteria, through their photosynthetic activity, had begun to indirectly pump more oxygen into the atmosphere than had previously been the case, initiating what would prove to be the greatest epochal change – along with the emergence of life – the Earth had ever witnessed: the Great Oxidation (cf. Section 2.6).

Asteroids. A wide range of animal and plant fossils, which abound in rock layers dating back more than 65 million years, are completely absent in more recent rock layers. It is thought that this can be attributed to an enormous asteroid that struck the waters off Yucatan, with devastating consequences: fires, tsunamis, the release of dust and sulphur into the atmosphere, the cooling of the planet, and changes to ecosystems. Between 50 and 70 per cent of all species in existence at the time became extinct. This was the most recent of the so-called Big Five, the five mass extinctions that have punctuated the history of life on Earth.

Humans. In the late Pleistocene, human overkill contributed to the extinction of the megafauna. Predation was accompanied, over time, by urbanisation, agriculture, and deforestation. The movement of *Homo sapiens* across the length and breadth of the planet has also favoured the spread of invasive species, viruses, and bacteria. Today, the extinction rate is much higher than that witnessed by the fossils, to the point that, according to some palaeontologists, we are confronting the sixth mass extinction (Barnosky *et al.* 2011), the first caused by a single multicellular species. Moreover, since the industrial revolution, humans have switched from an organic energy regime (based on muscle power for mechanical energy and wood or other biomass for heat production) to an energy regime based on fossil fuels – first coal and then oil and natural gas. Human activity has thus begun to massively alter the composition of the atmosphere, increasing the level of carbon dioxide with wide-ranging consequences for the Earth system.

Will a hypothetical geologist of the future, looking at the layers of rocks corresponding to our era, find traces of an epochal transition? Are humans the new cyanobacteria and asteroids? A positive answer to these questions is the basis of the popularisation, in the early 2000s, of the term "Anthropocene" by atmospheric chemist Paul Crutzen and biologist Eugene Stoermer (Crutzen and Stoermer 2000), who were joined by chemist and climatologist Will Steffen and environmental historian John McNeill, among others:

> The term *Anthropocene* . . . suggests that the Earth has now left its natural geological epoch, the present interglacial state called the Holocene. Human activities have become so pervasive and profound that they rival the great forces of Nature and are pushing the Earth into planetary *terra incognita*. The Earth is rapidly moving into a less biologically diverse, less forested, much warmer, and probably wetter and stormier state.
>
> (Steffen, Crutzen and McNeill 2007, p. 614)[11]

Condemnation of the Anthropocene is, for its proponents, a call to individual and collective action and a declaration of confidence in technical and scientific progress. Given that – unless some global catastrophe wipes out our species – humans will continue to be a decisive environmental force for many millennia, science and technology have "the daunting task ... to guide society towards environmentally sustainable management during the era of the Anthropocene" (Crutzen 2002, p. 23). This will require both a change in human behaviour and the use of large-scale climate geoengineering. We will return to these issues in Chapter 5. First, though, in the next section, we will try to answer the question of *how* our species was able to become, in the words of biologist Carol Boggs (2016), a global "biogeophysical force", capable of altering the cycles of the biosphere and, with them, the environment of living beings itself.

3.3.2 A monumental process of niche construction

Recent studies have articulated in detail an intuition held by the proponents of NCT, namely that human-induced climate change "is perhaps the greatest example of monumental niche modification produced by one species alone" (Meneganzin, Pievani and Caserini 2020, p. 37; see also Boggs 2016; Boivin *et al.* 2016). Let us recall that, by modifying the biotic and abiotic factors at work in natural selection, niche construction generates a type of feedback within evolution. Therefore, in order for a process to count as niche construction, three criteria must be met. First, the organism in question must significantly alter its environmental conditions. Second, these changes must influence selective pressures. Finally, there must be an evolutionary response to these changes (Matthews *et al.* 2014).

There is little doubt that, in the case of humans, the first criterion has been met: human activities have caused the planet's surface temperature to rise by about 1°C compared to pre-industrial levels. Some of the consequences associated with this change are already known: rising sea levels, changes in marine and terrestrial ecosystems, retreating glaciers, and loss of biodiversity.

To determine whether the second criterion has also been met, we must consider whether climate change is affecting selective pressures. That this is indeed the case is illustrated by the examples of sex determination discussed in the previous chapter. More generally, temperature serves as an environmental signal for the developmental stages of numerous organisms. According to the website of the European Environment Agency, many species in Europe have accelerated important events in their life cycles: some frogs have been laying their eggs earlier, certain birds have fast-tracked nest building, and butterflies and migratory birds have expedited their arrival. The reproduction period of several thermophilic insects, including butterflies, dragonflies, and bark beetles, has lengthened. This extension allows them to produce more generations per year, leading to changes in predator–prey relationships and, more generally, in population dynamics. The same changes can be seen in vegetation: the pollen season in Europe now starts ten days earlier on average than it did in the 1960s and lasts longer. Furthermore, as should be clear by now, the different components of an ecosystem are interconnected. What happens, for instance, if pollen is available but pollinators are absent? This is known as a "phenological mismatch",[12] which arises when the phases of the life cycles of species in antagonistic (e.g. prey–predator) or mutualistic (in which all participants benefit, as in pollination) relationships change at different rates, misaligning. The species that fail to change their behaviour or form new relationships face a lack of resources and reduced reproductive success; namely, their fitness decreases. While behavioural flexibility and phenotypic plasticity can help organisms to cope with rapid environmental changes, such as those caused by human niche construction, organisms may sometimes respond to changes inadequately, falling into what are called "evolutionary traps". We will discuss this aspect further in the final chapter; for now, it suffices to point out that climate change imposes new selective pressures that affect organisms' physiologies and life cycles.

This leads us to the third criterion: there must be an evolutionary response caused by the changes in question. This criterion seems to have been met as well. Faced with changes in the environment, organisms must adapt to the new situation (which, it should be noted, may not necessarily be negative; for example, thermophilic species may benefit from it). Adaptation, as we have seen, can take place through various strategies. Some species are migrating to more favourable habitats (although habitat fragmentation caused by human activities makes this process difficult). Species that are unable to migrate face, roughly, the following alternatives to extinction: adaptation through phenotypic plasticity or behavioural flexibility, or adaptation through evolution by natural selection. Plasticity and behavioural flexibility are likely the most effective adaptive strategies for responding to rapid environmental change as they do not rely on genetic variation, which, let us remember, is not directed by the environment, which means that the needed variation may not arise (or may not arise in time). However, numerous studies suggest that in recent years, climate change has led to the emergence of heritable genetic variations in various animal populations, including birds, squirrels, and mosquitoes (see e.g. Bradshaw and Holzapfel 2006).

It is time to consider the consequences of the extensive process of human niche construction and modification *for the constructor species itself*. In general, as already mentioned, niche construction benefits the constructor species, and *Homo sapiens* is no exception. It is thanks to niche construction that our "unlikely species", as the philosopher of biology Telmo Pievani (2002, p. 165) calls it, has avoided extinction and spread globally. According to John McNeill and Peter Engelke (2014), the period from 1945 to the present was significant in the process of planetary spread, earning the name the "Great Acceleration".

During the Great Acceleration, the world's population tripled due to a decrease in mortality rates, an increase in average lifespan, and a post–World War II population boom resulting from human niche construction and modification. The demands of the war facilitated the development of new technologies and justified massive public health interventions, such as the construction of hospitals, the administration of vaccines and antibiotics, malaria control, and an overall improvement in hygiene. Additionally, technological advancements and the use of new fertilisers and pesticides enhanced agricultural production, providing more resources and reducing poverty.[13] In evolutionary terms, it can be said that during this period the fitness of humans increased, on average, compared to the previous historical period.

However, the construction of the human niche requires an impressive amount of energy. This energy is supplied mainly by fossil fuels, the use of which releases greenhouse gases such as carbon dioxide, altering the carbon cycle and changing the composition of the atmosphere. The rise in greenhouse gases in the atmosphere is the primary cause of both local and global climate change. Furthermore, the construction of the human niche has impacted and continues to increasingly impact the water cycle (e.g. through changes to the hydrological systems that supply water to cities and agricultural areas), the phosphorus cycle, and the nitrogen cycle, which are the main components of most fertilisers used in agriculture. Although they receive less media attention, these effects are highly concerning. As Carson illustrated in his assessment of the risks associated with POPs, the planet is not compartmentalised, and changes in one part will have consequences – often difficult to predict – for others and for the entire system. For instance, the outflow of water from fertilised agricultural land can significantly affect nitrogen and phosphorus levels in rivers. When rivers meet the ocean, a layer of fresh water forms on top of the salt water, preventing the latter from coming into contact with oxygen from the air. The nitrogen and phosphorous present in the freshwater layer promote the growth of algae. As the algae die, they sink to the bottom, and their decomposition leads to a further reduction in oxygen levels. As a result, the oxygen present is no longer sufficient to sustain life; fish and other marine life either emigrate or die, resulting in the formation of "dead zones", which are now widely found along the coasts of the Americas, Europe, and Asia (Boggs 2016).

It is therefore through the colossal process of niche construction and modification that humans have begun to have a *major* causal influence on the cycles of the biosphere, and it is for this reason that the construction and modification of the human niche may turn out to be a *negative* niche construction process: one that reduces the fitness of the constructing species. Among the most serious threats faced by our species are an increase in infectious diseases and a decrease in the availability of food and water. Concerning the former, climate change will increase the growth and survival rates of vectors such as *Anopheles* mosquitoes, which depend on temperature and humidity. As a result, we can expect an increase in these diseases and their appearance in new geographical areas (Kulkarni, Duguay and Ost 2022). An IPCC press release issued on 28 February 2022 offers a concise but effective illustration of the second point:

> Increased heatwaves, droughts and floods are already exceeding plants' and animals' tolerance thresholds, driving mass mortalities in species such as trees and corals. These weather extremes are occurring simultaneously, causing cascading impacts that are increasingly difficult to manage. They have exposed millions of people to acute food and water insecurity, especially in Africa, Asia, Central and South America, on Small Islands and in the Arctic.
> (IPCC Press Release 2022, p. 1)

There is no guarantee that we will overcome this genuine evolutionary challenge. As philosophers of biology Andra Meneganzin and Telmo Pievani, and environmental engineer Stefano Caserini point out:

> As typical of any recursive interaction, like the constructor organism–environment interplay in NC [niche construction] processes, we are the driver of change, but this does not imply that the whole process is under our control. We *Homo sapiens*, experienced niche constructors and major evolutionary drivers of the ongoing sixth mass-extinction, are now threatening the survival of our own civilization.
> (Meneganzin, Pievani and Caserini 2020, p. 38)

Like all other species, humans possess adaptive strategies, which will be discussed in the final chapter. One of them, highlighted in bold in the IPCC press release mentioned earlier, is worth mentioning now: "Safeguarding and strengthening nature is key to securing a liveable future" (IPCC Press Release 2022, p. 2). This brings us to the topic of nature conservation, which is the focus of Chapter 4.

Notes

1 The Pleistocene is the geological epoch that lasted from approximately 2.5 million to 11,700 years ago. It is estimated that the line of descent that led to *Homo sapiens* evolved between 550,000 and 750,000 years ago and that the first *sapiens* specimens may date back some 300,000 years.
2 Establishing the relationship between brain size and cognitive abilities is one of the great challenges of evolutionary biology and palaeontology. It is generally believed that species with relatively large brains in relation to their bodies have greater behavioural flexibility (they are more able than others to change their behaviour in the face of environmental contingencies) and a greater ability to find solutions to novel problems. A recent study (Benson-Amram *et al.* 2016) has experimentally documented the existence of a correlation between relative brain size and problem-solving abilities in some mammalian species.

3 I understand "preadaptation" as the possession of the properties necessary to enable an organism to transition to a new niche, habitat, or environment.
4 This peculiarity of the environment is emphasised by Aristotle in Book IV of the *Physics*, where he writes that all things that are, are somewhere and that this somewhere, for material bodies, is not an object but *a place*. Since more than one thing can be said to surround a material body x, Aristotle distinguishes between the common place of all things (the whole universe) and the specific place of x, that is, the smallest surrounder of x, which is included not only in the universe but also in every other intermediate surrounder of x: "We say that a thing is in the world, in the sense of in place, because it is in the air, and the air is in the world; and when we say it is in the air, we do not mean it is in every part of the air, but that it is in the air because of the surface of the air which surrounds it" (Aristotle 1991, IV, 211a24–28).
5 According to the Deep Ecology movement promoted by Arne Naess (1912–2009), for example, there is a need to move away from a "shallow ecology" – which fights pollution and resource depletion with the wealth of rich countries as a goal – towards a "deep ecology", which recognises every organism as a node in the biospheric web, of equal value and in possession of the same right to life (Naess 1973). Although deep ecology has enjoyed some success in environmental activism, it is not without its critics: see, for example, Guha (1989). Peter Singer, on the other hand, has become a reference point for animal activism by denouncing "speciesism", that is, the anthropocentric prejudice of valuing the interests of one's own species over those of other species (Singer 1975). In turn, Val Plumwood (1939–2008), an exponent of ecofeminism, has emphasised the parallelism between different forms of oppression, which reinforce each other. Indeed, the oppressor (the white man) has positioned himself variously as the oppressor of women (as a man), of Black people (as white), and of other animals (as human) (see e.g. Plumwood 1993).
6 The results were short-lived, however: in most of the region, the cleared land was poor in nutrients and unsuitable for agriculture and livestock, and the farmers soon found that after a few years they had to move to other areas and clear more trees (McNeil and Engelke 2014, p. 58).
7 https://www.theguardian.com/world/2019/jul/19/jair-bolsonaro-brazil-amazon-rainforest-deforestation.
8 Certain species are thought to possess a "non-human charisma" that makes them not only more loved but also more worthy of conservation – at least from the perspective of the everyday human being. Factors that confer charisma on species include rarity and distinctiveness (i.e. fame), the way they are viewed within a society (reputation), and aesthetic factors, on a scale ranging from the "cuddliness" of the panda to the feral royalty of the big cats (Ducarme, Luque and Courchamp 2013). In any case, it should be noted that charisma is a historically and culturally determined property: honey bees, for example, have recently acquired charisma thanks to massive campaigns aimed at their conservation, and the charismatic megafauna that fascinate us today were likely not viewed as such by our ancestors.
9 It should be noted, however, that the programme was discontinued in 1969, largely because it had become clear (especially after the resurgence of malaria in Sri Lanka) that no single strategy could prove truly effective in malaria control and prevention (Nasir *et al.* 2020).
10 The 2°C limit was officially adopted as climate policy by the Council of the European Union in 1996 and recognised globally with the Copenhagen Accord in 2009 (the outcome of COP15, the 15th Session of the Conference of the Parties to the United Nations Framework Convention on Climate Change; see the introduction to this volume). Although it adopts the 2°C limit, the text of the Copenhagen Accord also acknowledges that this could prove insufficient and that a more stringent 1.5°C limit should be adopted in the future, as would be confirmed by the 2015 Paris Agreement.

11 The term "Anthropocene" has not been formally recognised as designating a geological epoch; see Chapter 5.
12 Phenology is the branch of ecology that studies the relationship between factors such as temperature, humidity, and the duration of daily illumination and the phases of plant (e.g. germination and flowering) and animal (e.g. migration, reproduction, hibernation) development.
13 It should be noted, however, that a decrease in poverty does not go hand in hand with a decrease in inequality. For instance, an estimated one billion people have been lifted out of hunger in the last two decades, but poverty has increased alarmingly in sub-Saharan Africa, where more than 40 per cent of the world's poor are concentrated (Mercadante 2019; Schoch and Lakner 2020).

References

Andina, T. (2022) *A Philosophy for Future Generations: The Structure and Dynamics of Transgenerationality*. Translated by A. Emmi. London and New York: Bloomsbury.

Aristotle (1991) 'Physics', in Barnes, J. (ed.) *The Complete Works of Aristotle, the Revised Oxford Translation, Vol. I*. Princeton: Princeton University Press.

Baghban, R. et al. (2020) 'Tumor microenvironment complexity and therapeutic implications at a glance', *Cell Communication and Signaling*, 18, art. n. 59.

Barnosky, A. et al. (2011) 'Has the earth's sixth mass extinction already arrived?', *Nature*, 471, pp. 51–57.

Benson-Amram, S. et al. (2016) 'Brain size predicts problem-solving ability in mammalian carnivores', *PNAS*, 113(9), pp. 2532–2537.

Boggs, C. (2016) 'Human niche construction and the Anthropocene', *RCC Perspectives*, 2, pp. 27–32.

Boivin, N.L. et al. (2016) 'Ecological consequences of human niche construction: Examining long-term anthropogenic shaping of global species distributions', *PNAS*, 113(23), pp. 6388–6396.

Bonhomme, F., Boursot, P. and Orth, A. (2001) 'Mus musculus', in Brenner, S. and Miller, J.H. (eds.) *Cambridge Encyclopedia of Genetics*. Cambridge, MA: Academic Press, pp. 1259–1261.

Bradshaw, W.E. and Holzapfel, C.M. (2006) 'Evolutionary response to rapid climate change', *Science*, 312, pp. 1477–1478.

Carson, R. (1962/2002) *Silent Spring*. Boston, MA: Houghton Mifflin Harcourt.

Crutzen, P. (2002) 'Geology of mankind', *Nature*, 415, p. 23. https://doi.org/10.1038/415023a.

Crutzen, P. and Stoermer, E.F. (2000) 'The "anthropocene"', *Global Change NewsLetter*, 41, pp. 17–18.

Dimond, J. and Sherburne, J. (1969) 'Persistence of DDT in wild populations of small mammals', *Nature*, 221, pp. 486–487.

Doblas-Reyes, F.J. et al. (2021) 'Linking global to regional climate change', in Masson-Delmotte, V. et al. (eds.) *Climate Change 2021: The Physical Science Basis: Contribution of Working Group I to the Sixth Assessment Report of the Intergovernmental Panel on Climate Change*. Cambridge and New York: Cambridge University Press, pp. 1363–1512. https://doi.org/10.1017/9781009157896.012.

Ducarme, F., Luque, G.M. and Courchamp, F. (2013) 'What are "charismatic species" for conservation biologists', *BioSciences Master Reviews*, 10, pp. 1–8.

Ferraris, M. (2022) *Doc-Humanity*. Translated by S. De Sanctis. Tübingen: Mohr Siebrek Ek.

Gilbert, S.F. (2012) 'Ecological developmental biology: Environmental signals for normal animal development', *Evolution & Development*, 14(1), pp. 20–28.

Gilbert, S.F. and Epel, D. (2008) *Ecological Developmental Biology*. Sunderland, MA: Sinauer Associates, Inc.

Gluckman, P.D., Hanson, M.A. and Low, F.M. (2019) 'Evolutionary and developmental mismatches are consequences of adaptive developmental plasticity in humans and have implications for later disease risk', *Philosophical Transactions of the Royal Society B: Biological Sciences*, 374, art. n. 20180109.

Gruhn, R. (2020) 'Evidence grows that peopling of the Americas began more than 20,000 years ago', *Nature*, 584, pp. 47–48.

Guha, R. (1989) 'Radical American environmentalism and wilderness preservation: A third world critique', *Environmental Ethics*, 11(1), pp. 71–83.

Handl, G. (2012) *Declaration of the United Nations Conference on the Human Environment (Stockholm Declaration), 1972 and the Rio Declaration on Environment and Development, 1992, United Nations Audiovisual Library of International Law*. Available at: www.un.org/law/av1.

Huff, C.D. et al. (2010) 'Mobile elements reveal small population size in the ancient ancestors of *Homo sapiens*', *Proceedings of the National Academy of Sciences*, 107(5), pp. 2147–2152.

IPCC Press Release (2022) *Climate Change: A Threat to Human Wellbeing and Health of the Planet: Taking Action Now Can Secure Our Future*, Berlin, 28 February. Available at: www.ipcc.ch/site/assets/uploads/2022/02/PR_WGII_AR6_english.pdf (Accessed 14 June 2024).

Jablonka, E. and Lamb, M.J. (2005) *Evolution in Four Dimensions: Genetic, Epigenetic, Behavioral, and Symbolic Variation in the History of Life*. Cambridge, MA: MIT Press.

Jaeger, C.C. and Jaeger, J. (2010) *ECF Working Paper; 2/2010*. Potsdam: European Climate Forum (ECF). Available at: https://publications.pik-potsdam.de/pubman/item/item_16141_1/component/file_16142/4466.pdf (Accessed 14 June 2024).

Johnson, M.T.J. and Munshi-South, J. (2017) 'Evolution of life in urban environments', *Science*, 358, art. n. 6363.

Jonas, H. (1984) *The Imperative of Responsibility: In Search of an Ethics for the Technological Age*. Translated by H. Jonas with the collaboration of D. Herr. Chicago and London: The University of Chicago Press.

Kulkarni, M.A., Duguay, C. and Ost, K. (2022) 'Charting the evidence for climate change impacts on the global spread of malaria and dengue and adaptive responses: A scoping review of reviews', *Global Health*, 18, art. n. 1. https://doi.org/10.1186/s12992-021-00793-2.

Lewontin, R.C. (1970) 'The units of selection', *Annual Review of Ecology and Systematics*, 1, pp. 1–18.

Matthews, B. et al. (2014) 'Under niche construction: An operational bridge between ecology, evolution and ecosystem science', *Ecological Monographs*, 84(2), pp. 245–263.

McNeill, J. and Engelke, P. (2014) *The Great Acceleration: An Environmental History of the Anthropocene since 1945*. Cambridge, MA: The Belknap Press of Harvard University Press.

Meneganzin, A., Pievani, T. and Caserini, S. (2020) 'Anthropogenic climate change as a monumental niche construction process: Background and philosophical aspects', *Biology & Philosophy*, 35, art. n. 38. https://doi.org/10.1007/s10539-020-09754-2.

Mercadante, F. (2019) 'Povertà, diminuisce ma per la maggior parte è creata artificialmente', in *Il Sole 24 Ore*, 2 December. Available at: www.econopoly.ilsole24ore.com/2019/12/02/poverta-nel-mondo/ (Accessed 14 June 2024).

Meyer, L. (2021) 'Intergenerational justice', in Zalta, E.N. (ed.) *The Stanford Encyclopedia of Philosophy*, Summer 2021 edition. Available at: https://plato.stanford.edu/archives/sum2021/entries/justice-intergenerational/ (Accessed 14 June 2024).

Moore, J.W. (2016) 'The rise of cheap nature', in Moore, J.W. (ed.) *Anthropocene or Capitalocene? Nature, History, and the Crisis of Capitalism*. Binghamton, NY: PM Press, pp. 78–115.

Naess, A. (1973) 'The shallow and the deep long-range ecology movement: A summary', *Inquiry*, 16, pp. 95–100.

Nasir, S.M.I. et al. (2020) 'Prevention of re-establishment of malaria: Historical perspective and future prospects', *Malar Journal*, 19, art. n. 452. https://doi.org/10.1186/s12936-020-03527-8.

Nespor, S. (2020) *La scoperta dell'ambiente. Una rivoluzione culturale*. Roma-Bari: Laterza.

Nettle, D. and Bateson, M. (2015) 'Adaptive developmental plasticity: What is it, how can we recognize it and when can it evolve?', *Proceedings of the Royal Society B: Biological Sciences*, 282, art. n. 20151005.

Nordhaus, W.D. (1977) *Strategies for the Control of Carbon Dioxide*. Connecticut: Cowles Foundation for Research in Economics at Yale University.

Odling-Smee, F.J. and Laland, K.N. (2011) 'Ecological inheritance and cultural inheritance: What are they and how do they differ?', *Biological Theory*, 6, pp. 220–230.

Odling-Smee, F.J., Laland, K.N. and Feldman, M.W. (2003) *Niche Construction: The Neglected Process in Evolution*. Princeton: Princeton University Press.

O'Shaughnessy, P.T. (2008) 'Parachuting cats and crushed eggs: The controversy over the use of DDT to control malaria', *American Journal of Public Health*, 98(11), pp. 1940–1948.

Pellegrino, G. (2012) 'Etica del cambiamento climatico', in Donatelli, P. (ed.) *Manuale di etica ambientale*. Firenze: Le Lettere, pp. 107–141.

Pievani, T. (2002) *H. sapiens e altre catastrofi*. Roma: Meltemi.

Plumwood, V. (1993) *Feminism and the Mastery of Nature*. London: Routledge.

Rader, B. et al. (2020) 'Crowding and the shape of COVID-19 epidemics', *Nature Medicine*, 26, pp. 1829–1834.

Rijsberman, F.R. and Swart, R.J. (eds.) (1990) 'Targets and indicators of climatic change: Report of working group II of the advisory group on greenhouse gases', in *Stockholm Environment Institute*. Draft version. p. 166. Available at: https://mediamanager.sei.org/documents/Publications/SEI-Report-TargetsAndIndicators-OfClimaticChange-1990.pdf (Accessed 14 June 2024).

Schoch, M. and Lakner, C. (2020) 'The number of poor people continues to rise in Sub-Saharan Africa, despite a slow decline in the poverty rate', *World Bank Blog*. Available at: https://blogs.worldbank.org/en/opendata/number-poor-people-continues-rise-sub-saharan-africa-despite-slow-decline-poverty-rate?cid=SHR_BlogSiteShare_EN_EXT (Accessed 23 September 2024).

Singer, P. (1975) *Animal Liberation: A New Ethics for Our Treatment of Animals*. New York: HarperCollins.

Skinner, M.K. et al. (2013) 'Ancestral dichlorodiphenyltrichloroethane (DDT) exposure promotes epigenetic transgenerational inheritance of obesity', *BMC Medicine*, 11, art. n. 228.

Steffen, W., Crutzen, P.J. and McNeill, J.R. (2007) 'The Anthropocene: Are humans now overwhelming the great forces of nature?', *Ambio*, 36(8), pp. 614–621.

United Nations (1972) *Report of the United Nations Conference on the Human Environment*. Available at: www.un.org/en/conferences/environment/stockholm1972 (Accessed 14 June 2024).

United Nations (1992) *United Nations Framework Convention on Climate Change*. Available at: https://unfccc.int/process-and-meetings/the-convention/history-of-the-convention/convention-documents (Accessed 14 June 2024).

Van den Berg, H., Manuweera, G. and Konradsen, F. (2017) 'Global trends in the production and use of DDT for control of malaria and other vector-borne diseases', *Malaria Journal*, 16, art. n. 401. https://doi.org/10.1186/s12936-017-2050-2.

Will, M. et al. (2021) 'Different environmental variables predict body and brain size evolution in *Homo*', *Nature Communication*, 12, art. n. 4116. https://doi.org/10.1038/s41467-021-24290-7.

4 Conserving nature

The last of the statements quoted in the second chapter to exemplify the various uses of the concept of the environment (Figure 2.1) claims that "[a] healthy natural environment can also provide us solutions ... [for] some of the impacts of climate change". This sentence is taken from the section devoted to "Nature protection and restoration" on the website of the European Environment Agency. A similar concept is expressed in the text of the EU Biodiversity Strategy for 2030, where we read the following:

> Climate change accelerates the destruction of the natural world through droughts, flooding and wildfires, while the loss and unsustainable use of nature are in turn key drivers of climate change. ... Nature is a vital ally in the fight against climate change.[1]

Commenting on this strategy, President of the European Commission Ursula von der Leyen argued that "[m]aking nature healthy again is key to our physical and mental wellbeing and is an ally in the fight against climate change and disease outbreaks".[2] Nature is also referred to in the Rio Declaration of 1992 (see Introduction in this volume) and in the already mentioned Stockholm Declaration of 1972, Principle 4 of which states that "[n]ature conservation, including wildlife, must therefore receive importance in planning for economic development", the natural environment being understood as one of the two components (natural and artificial) of the human environment. In these texts, alongside "nature", "natural environment", and "natural world", we also find expressions such as "natural resources", "natural disasters", and – specifically in the text of the Rio Declaration – "natural forests" (in contrast to "planted forests").

If we look at 50 years of global policies aimed at environmental protection and management, two considerations emerge with a certain clarity: that humans and their activities, on the one hand, and nature and its processes, on the other, seem to be viewed as belonging to two opposing realms and that human activities damage nature and the natural environment, which must be conserved or protected because they bring benefits – economic, physiological, and spiritual – to humans themselves.

DOI: 10.4324/9781003479642-5

What exactly is meant by "nature" and by the "natural environment"? The term "natural", both in common usage and in the environmental sciences and policy literature, is generally used to mean "neither made, changed, nor otherwise affected by humans" (Johnson et al. 1997, p. 582). This meaning, as we will see, is not without complications, despite its intuitiveness. In this chapter, after clarifying and critically discussing the distinction between natural and artificial that lies at the heart of Western thought (Sections 4.1 and 4.2), we consider the two main ways in which the natural environment is generally understood: as a set of natural resources and as wilderness (Section 4.3). We see that these two ways were co-present in the early instances of environmental protection (Section 4.4) before they diverged (Sections 4.5 and 4.6). Finally, we discuss a contemporary case of environmental protection (Section 4.7).

4.1 By nature and by other causes

Within Western thought, we find the first definition of "nature" in the work of Aristotle, particularly in Book II of the *Physics*. This definition has traversed millennia and has shaped our current conception of what nature is, how natural objects differ from artefacts, and the relationship between humans and *the rest* of nature. It would thus seem to be a good starting point for understanding whether there is indeed a categorical difference between a natural forest and a planted one and, more generally, between a natural and an artificial environment.

For Aristotle, nature is primarily a principle of change (and resistance to change), more precisely a principle of "motion and stationariness" (Box 4.1). Natural entities are those entities that possess such a principle and that, by virtue of it, are said to have a nature: entities – Aristotle specifies – such as animals and their parts, plants, and the simple bodies of which all things are composed (air, water, earth, and fire). Unnatural entities are entities that do not change or move, for example numbers and the prime mover, a supra-physical entity without which the natural world could not exist. Let us consider an example: for Aristotle, fire has a certain nature, a principle of change and movement that causes it to move upwards. Similarly, plants and animals possess a principle – a nature – according to which their development occurs and which determines their properties. Thus, for Aristotle, natural entities are first and foremost material objects. Precisely because of their materiality, they are subject to stasis or change, both of which are determined by a principle (a nature) that differs depending on the type of entity and determines what is natural for that type.

Among the natural entities thus understood, however, some have the principle of motion and stationariness *within themselves*, while others do not. Consider an acorn: no external intervention is necessary for it to become an oak tree, as the principle of necessary change is internal to the acorn itself. Now consider a wooden bed: for a tree to become a bed, an external intervention is needed to shape the material into a certain form, and this form is not in the wood but in the mind of the maker. Put differently, within the acorn there is a principle of change that causes the acorn to become an oak tree, but within the oak tree there is no principle of change that causes it to become a bed.

The principle of change also determines whether a certain change is natural or not: the development of the acorn into an oak tree is a natural change – or a change in accordance with nature – because it occurs according to a principle that is intrinsic to the acorn. Wood does not become a bed by virtue of a principle of change that is intrinsic to the wood (the same wood could become a table, for example). Things like acorns and things like beds belong to two different categories. The former exist *by nature*: they are natural objects. The latter are constituted not by nature but by other causes, like the art of the artisan. Accordingly, they have no innate impulse to change; their change is derivative of the (natural) materials of which they are made (Phys. II 192b12–192b23).[3]

Box 4.1 Aristotle's view on change

What characterises our world, for Aristotle, is becoming. Material bodies come into being through the composition of elements (water, air, earth, fire) and cease to be with their dissociation, when the elements recombine to form new composite bodies (such as living tissues and organs). In this sense, artefacts and natural objects are not very different.

For there to be change, according to Aristotle, three elements or principles are necessary: something that persists (the substrate, the matter) and two contraries, namely the absence of what is acquired (lack or privation of form) and what is acquired (form). Change is the passage from one state (privation) to a different state (form) of a persisting substrate. This passage is the transition from potentiality to actuality. Let us compare the statue the *Charioteer of Delphi* (an artefact) and the horse Bucephalus (an organism). If we were to melt the statue, the matter, the bronze, would remain, but the form – the image of the charioteer – would be lost. Indeed, when the *Charioteer of Delphi* was made from a piece of bronze, the matter was already present; it was the form that was acquired. The same goes for the embryo of the horse: in it, for Aristotle, the form is only potentially present, and it is precisely in the acquisition of the form that the process leading from the embryo to Bucephalus, the adult organism, consists, where the form, namely a specific arrangement of material parts, is fully realised (Berti 2011). Both a portion of bronze and an embryo have the form potentially: the bronze is potentially a statue, just as the embryo is potentially a horse.

> Without the realisation of the form, however, they would not become the *Charioteer of Delphi* and Bucephalus, respectively.
>
> Substrate, privation, and form are the principles of change (the necessary conditions, we might say) and are the same for both natural objects and artefacts. But they are not sufficient to explain it: for example, they do not tell us who or what initiates the process, nor what its end is. To answer these questions, we need to move from the level of principles to that of causes. Matter is the material cause (it answers the question "What is x made of?" or "What is the substrate of the change of x?"); form is the formal cause (it answers the question "What is x?"); the efficient cause answers the question "Who or what initiated the process and therefore produced x?"; and finally, the final cause answers the question "What is the purpose of the compound of form and matter?" While from the perspective of the material cause there is no difference between natural productions and artificial productions (both are made of matter), when it comes to the other causes the discourse changes: in the case of artefacts these causes are external, while in the case of natural objects they are internal to the objects. The formal cause and the final cause of an artefact are in the soul of the maker (the image, the model of the *Charioteer of Delphi*), while in natural objects they are found in the matter itself (the form of the horse – the soul – is already potentially present in the embryo). The efficient cause of the statue consists in the art of melting the bronze: without it, indeed, the substrate would not acquire its form. The process leading to the adult horse, by contrast, is internal to the organism; it does not need to be initiated and completed by an external maker (Code 1987).

4.2 The beaver dam

With Aristotle, both the view of nature as independent of an artificer and the consequent categorical distinction between natural objects and artefacts – as well as the foundations of the normative reading of nature that was destined to characterise Western thought thereafter – are outlined. If we consider the current use of the terms "nature" and "natural", we can distinguish at least three different meanings, all traceable to Aristotelian theory and illustratable through three pairs of oppositions.

First meaning: natural versus supernatural. When we speak of *natural sciences* such as physics, chemistry, and biology, we are referring to the opposition between natural (i.e. physical) and supernatural (i.e. supra-physical), or between natural and abstract (i.e. extra-physical). Deities and miracles (supernatural entities and events) are in fact the subject not of the natural sciences but of religious disciplines such as theology or human sciences like anthropology. The same goes for numbers and theorems, namely abstract entities that are the subject not of the natural sciences but of other specific disciplines. For this first meaning, therefore, nature is the set of entities and processes of the physical world, from quarks to galaxies. The derivation of this meaning from Aristotle's definition of nature as the principle of movement and rest is clear: generation and corruption, the acquisition and loss of properties, are characteristics of our world. It is precisely the ability to change that distinguishes material things from abstract and supernatural entities, which are outside of time and space and are not subject to change.

Second meaning: natural versus artificial. When we argue that *it is necessary to protect the natural environment*, or when we read that there is evidence suggesting that contact with nature brings physiological and psychological benefits to human health, we are referring to the opposition, inaugurated by Aristotle, between "natural" and "artificial". As we have seen, for Aristotle, nature and art are two ways in which entities undergo changes: natural objects develop thanks to nature, a principle intrinsic to them; artefacts do not possess this principle within themselves and receive their form from outside. There is no overlap between the set of natural objects and the set of artefacts: for Aristotle, an entity belongs to either one set or the other.

Third meaning: natural versus unnatural. When we claim that *it is natural for a cat to hunt mice*, or that it is unnatural or against nature for a bird to be in a cage, or again, that it is natural for an organism to reproduce, we are referring to the Aristotelian conception according to which the nature of a certain thing is also the principle that determines which change or behaviour is *natural* for that thing. This is the most controversial meaning of "natural" insofar as it attributes a normative value to nature, understood as an internal principle: cats have an *internal* principle (their nature) which, among other things, causes them to hunt mice. Those cats that do not hunt mice therefore act against nature.

4.2.1 Against nature

It is clear that while the idea of a feline conscientious objector may make us smile, to understand the potential risks associated with the normative meaning of "natural" it is sufficient to look at the various forms of discrimination that have dotted, and continue to dot, human history based on the idea that certain behaviours are unnatural or against nature (Mill 1874/2009; Pollo 2008; Tripodi 2015). Think of discrimination against gay and lesbian people or the exclusion of women from jobs considered foreign to their "feminine nature". Or think of those whose development has not followed the "natural" trajectory of members of our species, such as intersex individuals, who exhibit a combination of male and female sexual traits. It should now be clear that phenotypes are complex entities and that their relationship with any possible "internal principle" (the genotype is undoubtedly the most favoured candidate) not only is non-linear but cannot be considered in abstraction from the environment: what is the normal development of an organism if the achievable phenotypes are numerous, as shown by phenotypic plasticity? Furthermore, and above all, attributing normative value to the facts of the world is unfounded: in the natural world, things happen, and it is the task of the natural sciences to describe them and to understand their functioning. Whether these things are good or bad, right or wrong, is an entirely different matter. In describing, understanding, and predicting the facts of the world – the objective of scientific practice – science aims to be as independent as possible from the sphere of values, which are instead attributed by the observer and whose study is the subject of ethics. What has been called "Hume's Law", introduced by David Hume (1711–1776) in section 3.1.1 of his *A Treatise of Human Nature* (1739–1740), which aims to guarantee the autonomy of ethics, establishes that one cannot derive a "should" from a mere "is". From the proposition "Cats hunt mice" there is no way to derive the proposition "It is right that cats hunt mice" unless some evaluative content is already present in the first proposition, perhaps implicitly.

Following the philosopher of science Elliott Sober (1986), one can argue that the concept of naturalness is abused in a similar way to that of normalcy. The adjective "normal" can mean both *usual* and *desirable*. However, it is clear that the second does not follow from the first: the fact that we usually catch colds in winter does not make it desirable. A similar argument applies to "natural". The term is indeed used both to mean *not made by humans* (for example when it is said that propolis is a natural antibiotic) and to mean *good* or *right*. For example, the expression "natural ingredients" may seem to be a guarantee of goodness, but arsenic and lead are also perfectly natural. As for normalcy, the possession of the first property (naturalness as independence from human activity) does not entail the second (naturalness as goodness or rightness). Indeed, it is clear that rightness does not necessarily accompany naturalness – parasitism is perfectly natural, but it is not a behaviour that we consider praiseworthy – just as it does not follow from the possible naturalness of the reproductive process that it is right for a woman who does not desire a child to reproduce. As John Stuart Mill (1806–1873) argued, if we were to consider nature a standard of morality, on the one hand, we would have to recognise actions such as killing and torture as right, since nature is filled with such actions; on the other hand, every alteration of nature would be immoral, including alleviating suffering. I therefore agree with Mill's conclusion that "[c]onformity to nature, has no connection whatever with right and wrong" (1874/2009, p. 102).

To refrain from recognising naturalness as a moral standard is in no way to diminish or deny the seriousness of certain environmental issues (as well as other issues, such as the right to abortion or discrimination). Indeed, the opposite is likely the case. As Sober also observes, in equating what is natural with what is good,

> we hope to read our ethics directly from what happens in nature, and this gives us the illusion of needing to make no moral decisions for ourselves. This moral buck-passing is incoherent. What happens in nature is simply everything that happens. . . . It is no more a part of human nature to be healthy than to be diseased. Both kinds of phenotypes are to be found. . . . If we prefer one and wish to create environments in which it is encouraged, let us say so.
> (Sober 2006, pp. 351–352)

4.2.2 *The question of exceptionalism*

With the risk of understanding naturalness as a moral standard attended to, let us now focus on the first two meanings. In a broader sense, what is natural is opposed to what is "outside of nature", be it the supernatural or the abstract; in a narrower sense, what is natural is opposed to the artificial, where "artificial" is understood as what is constructed, modified, or influenced by humans. According to some, there are no compelling reasons to believe that human action gives rise to entities that, while not supernatural or abstract, are non-natural. For the philosopher Maurizio Ferraris, for example,

> [o]n one hand, it's hard to see why a termite mound or a dam built by beavers would be "natural", while the same artifacts, if made by human hands, would be "artificial". On the other hand, if we think about it for a moment, what underlies the alternative between natural and artificial is actually the alternative between natural and *supernatural*. . . . But let's not forget that even the plastic island in the Pacific is also natural, its elementary components are the remains of dinosaurs we have replaced.
> (Ferraris 2022, p. 248)[4]

According to Ferraris, viewing human artefacts as non-natural stems from a confusion between the first and second meanings of "natural": we believe that human productions belong to a different category than those of other organisms because, ultimately, we do not accept that humans are entirely natural, that they do not enjoy a special status, a certain *exceptionality* compared to other living beings.

Val Plumwood (2007) defines *exceptionalism* as the idea that the human species is radically different and separate from the rest of nature and other animals. In religious narratives, human exceptionalism generally derives from a peculiar relationship with a supernatural being: consider the first chapter of *Genesis*, for example, where we are told that God created humans in his image and gave them dominion over other living beings. In secular narratives, human exceptionalism is usually grounded in the supposed special status of the human mind – one that is "superior" to that of other animals. To cite just two illustrious examples: in *De Anima* Aristotle explains that humans – like all other organisms – are composed of matter and form (where form can be identified with the soul). Humans, however, are the only ones to possess a rational soul or mind. Moreover, a part of the human soul, the intellect, consists of the passive intellect (material) and the active intellect, which is separable from matter (and therefore not subject to change), deathless, and everlasting, just like the unmoved mover. For Descartes (1596–1650), on the other hand, both humans and other animals are machines, but humans – unlike other animals – possess reason, which is precisely what makes them human and distinguishes them from the other animals (Descartes 1637, Part V).

If we accept the theory of evolution by natural selection, however, the assumptions of human exceptionalism, both religious and secular, are brought into crisis. In fact, the presence of humans on Earth can be explained without resorting to a creator, and the human mind turns out to be nothing but the product of millions of years of natural selection that has preserved random adaptive mutations. From the perspective of evolutionary biology, all species – including *Homo sapiens* – are nothing but different branches of a tree with a single root.

If we exclude religious narratives (which are not the focus of this volume), then from a biological standpoint human exceptionality can be understood, at most, as a peculiarity. We are not the only species to possess technology, or to modify our environment, or to process signals and exchange information, or, likely, to formulate thoughts and have representations. Every species creates artefacts or, more generally, constructs its environment, each according to its needs and evolutionary path. Termites build termite mounds; humans build condominiums and cities. All living beings modify their environment, and many are engaged in niche construction processes. In this sense, the construction of the human niche is nothing exceptional. It is certainly peculiar: for example, the cultural element plays a more pervasive role and, to date, seems to have resulted in the continuous modification (rather than stabilisation) of the environment (cf. Section 3.2.1). Every species possesses modes of signal transmission and reception: some process those signals in ways that are not all that different from our own signal processing; others likely process them without any self-awareness. Uexküll's tick perceives butyric acid and drops itself onto the mammal (cf. Section 1.4). In a bacterial biofilm, systems of intercellular communication, namely different kinds of molecular signals and receptors, can "sense" population density and, when it reaches a certain point, trigger dispersal mechanisms (cf. Box 2.2). An insect "knows" when it is time to pollinate; a tree knows when it is time to sprout. Humans have minds and consciousness, and octopuses have minds that are equally peculiar, as illustrated by the philosopher of biology Peter Godfrey-Smith in his book *Other Minds* (2016). Whether the minds of octopuses are thought of as "less advanced" or "less complex" – or whatever expression one wishes to use to indicate an alleged human exceptionality – is clearly decided based on human standards.

It is in an anti-exceptionalist spirit that environmental ethicist Baird Callicott asserts the following:

> We are animals ourselves, large omnivorous primates, very precocious to be sure, but just big monkeys, nevertheless. We are therefore a part of nature, not set apart from it. Chicago is no less a phenomenon of nature than the Great Barrier Reef.
>
> (Callicott 1992, p. 18)

Similarly, Elliott Sober reiterates that, from a biological standpoint, if we accept that we are just one species among others, then we cannot find any foundation for the distinction between natural and artificial:

> Environmentalists often express regret that we human beings find it so hard to remember that we are part of nature – one species among many others – rather than something standing outside of nature . . . [but] seeing us as part of nature rules out the environmentalist's use of the distinction between artificial-domesticated and natural-wild. . . . *If we are part of nature, then everything we do is part of nature, and it is natural in that primary sense.*
>
> (Sober 1986, p. 180)

If exceptionalism is abandoned, it seems difficult to find a non-conventional foundation for the distinction between natural and artificial: if we fully acknowledge that *Homo sapiens* is just one species among others, relinquishing its special ontological status, then we must also view its productions as perfectly natural. A dam built by beavers and one built by humans would belong to the same set of entities, that of natural objects.

If even plastic is natural, however, what meaning can we give to the expression "natural environment"? If Chicago and the Great Barrier Reef are both natural, why is the latter subject to environmental restoration practices while the former is not?[5] If we abandon exceptionalism, statements like "Climate change accelerates the destruction of the natural world" seem to lose their meaning, and the European Biodiversity Strategy for 2030 risks becoming a lost battle even before it begins, as there is nothing to restore and protect. On the other hand, the claim that *Homo sapiens* is exceptional would seem to be unfounded – at least from the perspective of evolutionary biology.

4.2.3 Overcoming the impasse

At least two possibilities suggest themselves for overcoming the impasse that arises when one seeks to simultaneously recognise the naturalness of humans and the artificiality of their productions. The first is inspired by Aristotle and involves rejecting the assumption that the naturalness of the maker *ipso facto* implies the naturalness of the product. The second, a view that goes back to John Stuart Mill, involves grounding the natural/artificial distinction not in science but in common sense.

Pursuing the first possibility requires admitting that all productions, regardless of the maker, are artefacts. In fact, upon closer inspection, recognising *Homo sapiens* as part of nature and as one species among others while simultaneously acknowledging the artificiality of its productions seems to be a perfectly legitimate position if we are willing to recognise the productions of other organisms as artefacts as well. In other words, the artificiality of certain entities depends not on *the identity* of the artisan but on their *being produced* by an artisan. Aristotle's conception of nature allows us to recognise that the beaver dam is an artefact just as human-made dams are (Hennig 2009).

Indeed, according to the Aristotelian view, what a beaver does when it builds a dam is perfectly natural, both dictated by and in line with its internal principle and specific nature (and physiology). If a cat were to build a dam, by contrast, it would be doing something unnatural. Affirming that it is not in the nature of cats to build dams is, in this case, another way of saying that it is not within the physiological and behavioural capabilities of a cat to build dams. Note that the risk of falling into the normative interpretation of "natural" (illustrated in Section 4.2.1) can be averted – at least in principle – because what falls within the physiological and behavioural capabilities of a certain organism is nothing more than what, in fact, that organism does. If there are cats that do not hunt mice, this means that it is in the nature of cats both to hunt mice and not to hunt mice. If we plant maize in different conditions and discover that both tall and short plants result, then we should recognise that it is in the nature of maize to take the form of both tall and short plants, and so on.

Now even if the *construction* of the beaver dam is a natural process, on this view the resulting dams ought to be classified as artefacts regardless of who builds them. As with the bed in the Aristotelian example, if the wood of which the dam is made were to sprout, what would grow from that sprout would be a tree, not a dam. The beaver dam is an artefact since the material of which it is made (felled trees) would have had its own developmental trajectory had it not been made into a dam. Similarly, the materials of which the human-made dam is built would have had a different destiny had they not been used to build a dam.

The preceding outlined solution allows us to reconcile anti-exceptionalism with the intuition that artefacts are different from the products of nature. It has a downside, however, for if we apply it to the discourse concerning the environmental crisis, rather counterintuitive consequences arise. Excluded from the category of the natural environment, for example, would be not only cities but also beaver dams and various human and non-human artefacts (nests, termite mounds, and anthills, and likely even planted and restored forests), which would instead be recognised as part of the artificial environment. Therefore, although this solution is logically coherent, accepting it would require us to be prepared to recognise that the expression "natural environment" is commonly misused in environmental policies and practices. Perhaps this is too high a price to pay.

One could, of course, introduce a finer-grained distinction and acknowledge that *some* but not all human activities and products are natural. According to some proposals, any activity that "goes beyond our biological and evolutionary capacities" (cf. Katz 1995, p. 95; see also Brennan 1988) would not be considered natural. For example, giving birth spontaneously, without the intervention of medical technologies, would count as a natural process not because it is independent of human action but because it is independent of *a certain type* of human action, which exceeds our biological and evolutionary capacities (in this case, medical technology). However, an argument of this kind seems to bring in exceptionalism through the back door. In fact, it would seem to imply that while for non-human species their culture is part of their biology and evolution, this is not the case for *Homo sapiens*. But how can we do something that is not within our evolutionary capacity? Unless we are supernatural beings, the only sensible answer is that we cannot.

The second way to try to escape the theoretical impasse faced by those who want to acknowledge human non-exceptionalism and the natural/artificial distinction simultaneously starts from the distinction, outlined by John Stuart Mill in his essay "Nature" (1874), between a scientific and a common-sense meaning of "nature". In the scientific sense, "nature" means "the sum of all phenomena, together with the causes which produce them" (Mill 1874/2009, p. 66). In this sense – which Mill considers "the true scientific sense" of the term – "Art is as much Nature as anything else; and everything which is artificial is natural", since art does not have powers of its own and is simply

> the employment of the powers of Nature for an end. Phenomena produced by human agency, no less than those which as far as we are concerned are spontaneous, depend on the properties of the elementary forces, or of the elementary substances and their compounds. The united powers of the whole human race could not create a new property of matter.
> (Mill 1874/2009, p. 67)

In this sense, even the Great Pacific Garbage Patch is natural, as Ferraris claims, as is Chicago, as Callicott affirms.

However, Mill continues, since this use of "nature" does not account for one of the ways in which the term is commonly employed, namely in opposition to artefacts, it is necessary to admit a second meaning. In a non-technical sense – that is, one that belongs not to scientific language but to "the common form of speech" – "nature" means everything that happens "without the agency, or without the voluntary and intentional agency, of man" (Mill 1874/2009, pp. 67–68).

In fact, the natural/artificial distinction as formulated by Mill is part of everyday thinking and of practices and policies for managing the human environment. Data from experimental psychology would seem to suggest that while we consider ourselves part of nature, people view the natural environment as one that completely excludes humans, tending to identify it with uninhabited, wild spaces and viewing the non-natural environment as populated mainly by human artefacts. The suggested reasons for this are varied, ranging from urban life's promotion of a disconnection from nature to the possibility that the human/nature relationship is not conceptualised as a dichotomous one (Vining, Merrick and Price 2008).

Handing over the natural/artificial distinction to common sense rather than science has its own consequences, the desirability of which needs to be evaluated. For example, it is by no means certain that we all recognise the same things as natural, and it is not even certain that an individual person's conception of what is natural will remain constant throughout their life. In addition to the clear cultural differences that exist between human groups living in different environments, even an individual's perception can change, and it is possible that one day they may feel more a part of nature than another, or that at a certain time in their life they may recognise as natural something they will not view as such at a later time (Frantz et al. 2005). Naturalness thus risks becoming a subjective, volatile property that changes depending on the place and the time. With that said, this aspect may not be a flaw, at least under certain conditions. For example, greater understanding of the fact that different subjects – whether individual or social – and cultures view different entities and processes as natural[6] could promote the recognition, within environmental protection and management practices, of perspectives other than the Western one. Furthermore, it would allow us to account for the fact that different values have been attributed to naturalness over time. To give just one example, consider that in the 1950s naturalness was much less appreciated than it is today, while plastic, an emblem of artificiality, was viewed as a desirable material. At the time, some preferred plastic flowers to fresh cut flowers in their homes; after all, if the value of naturalness is excluded, artificial flowers are preferable: they require no maintenance, last longer, and can also be very beautiful. In fact, almost paradoxically, plastic was initially invented to address environmental problems. Elephants were at risk of extinction due to the demand for ivory (used, for example, in piano keys and billiard balls), and the same was happening to certain species of turtle, whose shells were sought after for combs (Freinkel 2011). At the time, plastic seemed like a good solution. (This does not mean, of course, that microplastics are not a form of pollution that ought to be eliminated[7] or that the "use-and-throw-away" mode is not a contradiction in terms when applied to a material that takes an extremely long time to decompose.)

The solution to the impasse based on the Millian distinction would seem to be a good one: if the natural/artificial distinction is grounded not in science but in common sense, then it is in principle compatible with renouncing human exceptionalism. Furthermore, the assertion that what is natural is what humans recognise as such is in agreement with the fact that, as far as we can observe from their behaviour, other organisms do not seem to recognise the natural/artificial distinction. We have seen that in building its nest the mole does not hesitate to use the plastic it finds in its environment; similarly, city birds use cigarette butts for anti-parasitic purposes, and coastal marine organisms take advantage of garbage patches to settle in the open ocean (cf., respectively, Kaplan 2012; Haram *et al.* 2021).

If we accept the solution just outlined, according to which "natural" environments are those environments that people recognise, perceive, feel, and conceptualise as natural, that is (at least in the West), environments devoid of humans and uninfluenced by human activity, two difficulties remain.

The first is that, as should now be clear, an environment without humans is not an empty environment. *Our* natural environment is (also) the environment *of* other living beings. Without discussing the ethical legitimacy of attributing to the human environment what is in fact the environment of others, it remains necessary to consider this when aiming to protect or restore the natural environment. Consider, for example, reforestation efforts (essential to containing greenhouse gas emissions in the atmosphere), which involve reintroducing tree and shrub species into areas where they were already present in the past. For these efforts to succeed, it will be necessary at the very least to consider that a forest must consist of plant species suited to the climate and soil of the area, that a certain composition of plant species will likely correspond to a certain composition of animal and microbial species, and so on.

The second difficulty with defining the natural environment as devoid of humans or uninfluenced by their activities is that the natural environment may simply no longer exist. This, for example, is the underlying thesis of the 1989 book *The End of Nature* by journalist and environmentalist Bill McKibben, to which we will return in the next chapter. First, however, let us focus on what is meant by the phrase "natural environment".

4.3 The natural environment

If a natural environment is one devoid of humans, then in what sense, according to the Stockholm Conference Declaration, is it part of the human environment? At this point, we can distinguish at least two different meanings of the expression "natural environment". In the first, the natural environment is the set of what are called "natural resources", that is, the part of our species' surrounder whose production (or reproduction) *does not depend* on our species and that constitutes a possible resource for it. In the second sense, the natural environment is that part of our species' surrounder that is least influenced by our activities: wild, pristine nature, *separate* from humans.

Depending on whether the natural environment is understood as a set of resources or as pristine nature, different environmental problems and approaches to managing the human environment will arise. In the former case, the main problem that needs addressing is the use of resources in a way that prevents their regeneration (in the case of renewable resources, such as forests or other resources from plant and animal species) or that causes their depletion (in the case of non-renewable resources within the timespan of human existence, such as fossil fuels). If, on the other hand, the natural environment is understood as wild nature, the problem is how to prevent the disappearance of "non-human" environments that humans can nevertheless experience, at least as spectators (that is, the problem of "protecting and restoring nature", in the words of the EU Biodiversity Strategy for 2030).

4.3.1 *Natural resources*

Every form of ecosystem engineering uses resources that can no longer be utilised, at least not in the same form and by the same species. When a forest is cleared and its wood is used as fuel, for example, that "resource" undergoes a state transition: living matter becomes non-living matter and is removed from the ecosystem, its chemical energy is transformed into thermal energy, and the process of photosynthesis is "reversed", so to speak (in photosynthesis, plants produce organic matter from solar energy and emit oxygen into the atmosphere, whereas combustion uses oxygen and emits energy). The removal of a forest from a larger ecosystem thus has consequences for nutrient cycles and energy flow, and hence for the biosphere as a whole (forests in particular act as carbon sinks, absorbing carbon dioxide). It is for this reason that the human environment cannot be considered in isolation from the environment of other living beings: many of the resources we use are also used by other organisms; many resources *are* other organisms, which in turn construct their environments and are moulded by them. Their construction, together with ours, contributes to that of the environment of living beings – the biosphere – determining the course of biogeochemical cycles.

We can define "natural resources" as that set of materials used by humans at a certain time, and potentially in the future, whose production and maintenance do not depend (or depend only to a limited extent) on human intervention. Note that natural resources – in accordance with the Millian solution discussed earlier – are relative. More precisely, what constitutes a resource – and what type of resource – varies depending on the time and society in question. In the 19th century, for example, the Arabian Peninsula was considered a region poor in natural resources, since oil had not yet become an energy source. In France, Italy, and Portugal, rabbit meat is consumed regularly, while in Anglo-Saxon countries rabbits are generally considered pets (which, it should be noted, does not preclude their being a resource, albeit perhaps a spiritual and aesthetic resource rather than a nutritive one).

As one can imagine, precisely defining what constitutes a resource and what does not is anything but simple (so much so that there is no shared definition), just as it is far from easy to define exactly what constitutes food and what does not (Kaplan 2019; Borghini and Piras 2021). The difficulty of defining *what* constitutes a resource, *for whom*, and *when* is compounded by the complication of specifying what counts as a *natural* resource and what does not. For example, it seems intuitively clear that the rabbit is a natural entity. However, it is also a domesticated animal: rabbit meat production typically occurs in farming, where the survival and reproduction of animals depends on humans. Rabbits also live in the wild, however, where their existence and reproduction do not depend on human intervention. Should we consider the latter, but not the former, a natural resource? More generally, what degree of human intervention is allowed for something to be considered natural? If one plant grows spontaneously in a forest, another is cultivated in that same forest, and still another is cultivated in a garage, are all three natural? In addressing questions like these, the metaphysician and food philosopher Andrea Borghini (2019) introduced the notion of the "edible environment" to describe that portion of the human environment that includes not only plants, animals, fungi, algae, and microorganisms that have been domesticated for human consumption but also the thousands of species that are regularly consumed by humans and are considered to some extent wild. Within it, as Borghini observes, the natural/artificial distinction is translated into the equally problematic distinction between "domesticated" and "wild" (see also Sober 1986; Siipi 2016). We will return to this topic in Section 5.3, where we will consider a proposal for revising the natural/artificial distinction.

The definition of a "natural resource" provided at the beginning of this section is clearly anthropocentric. However, viewing materials and other species found in the human environment as resources is not necessarily linked to an anthropocentric conception of the environment or to an imperial view of nature (cf. Section 1.5.2). That x is a resource does not imply that x must be *exploited* by humans or that resources exist only for humans. The plants found in botanical gardens, for example, are resources that are used – for scientific and recreational purposes – but not exploited. Grass is a resource for rabbits, just as dead organisms are a resource for saprophytic fungi. Indeed, if we could talk to the viruses and bacteria that populate our bodies, and if they possessed the concept of a *natural resource*, this is likely how they would define us: *their* environment, *their* natural resources.

If the human natural environment is understood as a set of resources, the main problem that must be addressed today, in light of the environmental crisis, is that the process of constructing the human niche has long been based on the unfounded belief that natural resources are inexhaustible. Traditionally, a distinction has been made between non-renewable and renewable resources. The former constitute a stock that cannot be replenished – at least not within a human lifetime. Oil, for example, which is classified as non-renewable, is actually renewable in principle (deriving from the decomposition of organic material), but it is believed that the process required for its generation typically takes millions of years.

Renewable resources, on the other hand, are those that usually regenerate within the span of human life. Yet they too are not inexhaustible. Their regeneration can be aided, slowed down or even prevented. Once a certain quantity of oil has been burned, there will be no way to regenerate it from the combustion residues. When, instead, a renewable resource is degraded – for example because it has been overused and is therefore unable to regenerate effectively – intervention is possible, provided certain thresholds have not been exceeded. For example, we know that below a certain population threshold (called the "minimum viable population"), a species is destined for extinction. The idea of sustainable resource use consists precisely in not exceeding the threshold beyond which renewable resources are unable to regenerate spontaneously. Establishing what this threshold is can clearly be difficult since it depends both on the type of resource and its environmental conditions. In general, the production of renewable resources is inseparable from ecosystem processes: it is likely that an ecosystem that is under excessive stress[8] will produce less of (or cease to produce) a certain resource (cf. also Section 5.1.1).

Let us conduct a thought experiment, taking what we have just said to the extreme. Imagine that, following a natural or anthropogenic planetary catastrophe, the conditions of the maximal ecosystem, the biosphere (temperature, humidity, water pH, salinity . . .), change to the point that they no longer contain the resources needed for the survival of current life forms, the result of billions of years of evolution. What scenarios can we reasonably imagine? We can envisage at least two: in the first, the new conditions – a new state of the system – would no longer be conducive to life, and thus we would have a nature devoid of biotic elements, meaning, simplifying a bit, devoid of organisms and their environments. In the second scenario, the biosphere could take on a new state, with conditions that are favourable to certain extant organisms but not to others. Imagine, for example, that these conditions do not support animal and plant life and only support bacteria and other organisms capable of surviving extreme conditions. In this second case, we would have an environment populated by life forms that are different from us and the life forms we know (perhaps hydrocarbon-eating bacteria, i.e. marine bacteria capable of surviving by feeding on hydrocarbons).

Putting aside this thought experiment, when it is claimed, as in the EU Biodiversity Strategy for 2030, that "climate change accelerates the destruction of the natural world through droughts, flooding and wildfires", the scenarios that are feared are not too distant from those just described. The phenomenon of coral bleaching caused by rising temperatures, for instance, is not a mere exercise of the imagination. Coral bleaching results when symbiotic algae (zooxanthellae) abandon the tissues of corals during periods of stress, such as when the temperature exceeds the colony's tolerance level (Glynn

1993). Since the photosynthetic pigments contained in the algae provide energy to the corals, the loss of zooxanthellae compromises their health and increases their mortality rate. Upon their death, corals may be replaced by other organisms, but this will entail a change in the entire trophic chain that depends on the corals, that is, a change in resources for other organisms.

In general, therefore, ongoing climate changes put stress on ecosystems, which then produce fewer natural resources than before, or natural resources that are different from those to which we are accustomed. As anticipated, however, there is another way to understand the term "natural environment". Coral reefs are not only a natural resource (among other things, for the tourism they generate and for their role as carbon sinks); together with tropical and boreal forests, for instance, they are also representatives of that pristine nature to which many humans attribute value, whether intrinsic or aesthetic, spiritual, and scientific.

4.3.2 Wilderness

Let us now explore the second main way in which the natural environment can be understood, namely as that part of our species' surrounder that is not influenced by its activities: wilderness, or uncontaminated nature (think of the majestic landscapes of Yellowstone Park, or of tropical islands, coral reefs, and pluvial forests).

Whereas understanding the natural environment as a set of resources involves interpreting the relationship between humans and the rest of nature especially in terms of the latter's *independence* from the former, understanding it as uncontaminated nature instead emphasises *separation*. In both senses, the natural environment is defined in relation to humans. Natural resources are defined in relation to humans because they are those parts of the surrounding environment that can be a resource for them. Similarly, uncontaminated nature is relative to humans because – at least in some of its modes, which we will now reconstruct – it is the result of a specific representation of nature. (Whether such a representation corresponds to an extra-mental reality is a matter of debate, as we will see.)

From the mid-20th century onwards, the idea of uncontaminated nature that emerged in the West has been that of the so-called *wilderness* (Callicott and Nelson 1998). The term "wilderness" conveys a specific vision of uncontaminated nature that originated in the United States and then spread to Europe. The key proponent of this vision is the philosophical movement known as transcendentalism, a North American version of European Romanticism which developed around the mid-19th century and whose major representatives are Ralph Waldo Emerson (1803–1882) and David Henry Thoreau (1817–1862).

Around the mid-19th century, the United States saw significant population growth and the construction of new cities, roads, and canals that facilitated the transport of goods. This was the era of the gold rush, railways, the first transatlantic crossings on steamboats, and gas lighting. What united the proponents of transcendentalism – an eclectic group of intellectuals, men and women who first arose among the liberal New England Congregationalists – was their criticism of the provincial, conservative, materialistic culture of the United States at the time (Myerson, Petrulionis and Walls 2010, introduction). In response to provincialism, they espoused cosmopolitanism, importing European and Asian literature into the United States – from post-Kantian philosophy to English and German Romanticism, from Persian poetry to Buddhist and Hindu scriptures. Against conservatism, they demanded social reform, from the abolition of slavery to the recognition of women's rights. To the materialistic culture of the time they responded with an exaltation of the human spiritual dimension, based on nature. For the transcendentalists, nature was animated and living, far from Cartesian mechanism and dualism and closer to the Romantic poetry of Coleridge and Wordsworth, for whom mountains were temples and icefalls as glorious as the gates of heaven.[9] Our relationship with such divinised nature is exemplified in Kant's conception of the natural sublime: unlike the reassuring beauty of a tidy garden with its harmonious proportions, mountain peaks are unsettling because of their power, which looms over us. Faced with the greatness and power of nature, the subject first loses himself, only to reaffirm his superiority to nature thanks to reason and moral sentiment (Kant 2000, §§ 23–29).

Even the choice of the name "transcendentalism" – which recalls Kantian transcendental idealism, opposed to the empiricism of John Locke (1632–1704) – is an exaltation of the human subject. By rejecting Locke's theory that the mind is a *tabula rasa* and all ideas (the material of knowledge) ultimately derive from experience, the transcendentalists, like Kant, acknowledged the existence of transcendental forms – such as space and time – residing in the mind. On their view, these make possible and shape human experience. In the transcription of a lecture Emerson delivered in 1842 titled "The Transcendentalist", we read:

> It is well known to most of my audience, that the Idealism of the present day acquired the name of Transcendental, from the use of that term by Immanuel Kant . . . who replied to the skeptical philosophy of Locke, which insisted that there was nothing in the intellect which was not previously in the experience of the senses, by showing that there was a very important class of ideas, or imperative forms, which did not come by experience, but through which experience was acquired; that these were intuitions of the mind itself; and he denominated them Transcendental forms.
>
> (Emerson 1842, pp. 101–102)

Nature's role in affirming humanity and – especially in Emerson – human spirituality as the supreme value (Coates 1998/2004, p. 136) can today be called, using the language of the Millennium Ecosystem Assessment,[10] an "ecosystem service" (see Box 1.2). More precisely, we can say that for Emerson and the transcendentalists in general, ecosystems not altered by humans offered spiritual and recreational benefits – that is, cultural ecosystem services.

The most interesting exponent of transcendentalism for contemporary environmental thought is likely Henry David Thoreau; it is therefore worth dedicating some space to him here. For Thoreau, the role of nature takes the form of cultural primitivism, the view that a "return" to a state of nature is an antidote to the ills of modernity (Box 4.2). Building himself a wooden cabin on a piece of land owned by Emerson on the shores of Walden Pond in Massachusetts, Thoreau lived away from the city for two years, renouncing comforts and superfluities. His was a rebellion against capitalism, against North American civilisation, whose greed and waste he deplored. At the same time, it was a quest for moral improvement: in the return to primitive, harsh, wild nature, a human being can understand what is truly essential in life, recognise the rest as superfluous, and abandon it. One can gain independence from material goods produced by society, and thus freedom. It is worth considering a passage from the second chapter of *Walden: Life in the Woods* (1854) – made famous by the film *Dead Poets Society* (1989) directed by Peter Weir – which exemplifies this concept:

> I went to the woods because I wished to live deliberately, to front only the essential facts of life, and see if I could not learn what it had to teach, and not, when I came to die, discover that I had not lived. . . . I wanted to live deep and suck out all the marrow of life, to live so sturdily and Spartan-like as to put to rout all that was not life. . . . Still we live meanly, like ants. . . . Our life is frittered away by detail. An honest man has hardly need to count more than his ten fingers, or in extreme cases he may add his ten toes, and lump the rest. . . . Simplify, simplify!
>
> (Thoreau 1854/1899, pp. 93–94)

For Thoreau, dedicating oneself to a hermit's life in the woods is not the only way to improve the human condition: even while living within civilisation, it is possible to renew contact with primal nature, to rediscover its wild force and its original vitality, as opposed to the decadence of civilisation. This can be achieved, for example, by alternating periods in civilisation with periods in nature, or by preserving portions of unspoiled nature within or near cities. "I think that each town", he writes,

> should have a park, or rather a primitive forest . . . where a stick should never be cut – nor for the navy, nor to make wagons, but to stand and decay for higher uses – a common possession forever, for instruction and recreation.
>
> (quoted in Callicott 1994, p. 11)

From our current perspective, his intuition was prophetic: on a planet where cities are increasingly expanding, efforts to conserve primitive forests[11] and, more generally, to create green spaces within urban places are multiplying. The case of Forest Park in Portland, Oregon, would seem to be a direct response to Thoreau's wish. Although only a few portions of the original forest remain, it still consists of about 20 square kilometres of protected urban forest, part of a system of parks and urban trails designed at the beginning of the 20th century by the Olmsted brothers, sons of the designer of Central Park in New York.

A few years after his Walden experience, Thoreau modified his purely experiential approach to nature, becoming a scientist *à la* Humboldt, whose work he admired. He began meticulously recording what he observed during his walks, compiling long lists of flowering and leaf-fall periods, contemplating the phenological relationships discussed in the previous chapter, and making detailed observations of vegetation and wildlife. His observations were so meticulous, writes historian Andrea Wulf (2015, chapter 19), that they can be used today to analyse the impact of climate change. By comparing the current flowering times of certain wild plants or leaf fall periods with those noted in Thoreau's journals, for example, it has been determined that many spring flowers around Walden Pond now bloom ten days earlier than they did in Thoreau's time.

From these observations of differences and recurrences, interrelations and connections, Thoreau arrived at the same conclusions as Humboldt: the components of nature are related, both to each other and to the whole. Nature is a living whole, knowledge of which requires not only science – its method, observations, measurements, and mathematical language – but also the senses, emotions, and artistic and poetic language. A crimson cloud suspended on the horizon is certainly "a mass of vapour absorbing all rays", but this explanation is incomplete insofar as that same cloud is also a "red vision [that] excites me, stirs my blood", as he writes in his journal (quoted in Wulf 2015, p. 258).

Box 4.2 Cultural primitivism

In *Leviathan*, Thomas Hobbes (1588–1679) describes the state of nature (a hypothetical human condition prior to the birth of society and institutions) as a state of war of all against all, the causes of which – competition, distrust, and the pursuit of glory – reside in human nature. In this condition, people do not work, as the fruits of their labour are uncertain; they do not engage in navigation or commerce, do not construct buildings or tools and machines, and do not cultivate culture or social relationships. As Hobbes writes, in this condition "the life of man [is] solitary, poore, nasty, brutish, and short" (Hobbes 1651/1909, p. 99), a state of continual fear and danger of violent death. As a contemporary example of this way of life, Hobbes cites "the savage people in many places of *America*", who, "except the government of small Families, the concord whereof dependeth on natural lust, have no government at all; and live at this day in that brutish manner" (Hobbes 1651/1909, p. 99). For Hobbes, nature is therefore a negative state from which to be redeemed through culture, that is, through the establishment of a form of government.

The French encyclopaedists – the editors of the *Encyclopédie*, led by Denis Diderot (1713–1784) and Jean-Baptiste Le Rond d'Alembert (1717–1783), among whom was Jean-Jacques Rousseau (1712–1778) – strongly opposed the Hobbesian vision, promoting the opposite idea, cultural primitivism, defined as "the conviction that happiness is greatest nearest to nature" (Coates 1998/2004, p. 128).

Cultural primitivism is characterised by two myths: the myth of the golden age and the myth of the noble savage. The myth of the golden age spans epochs and cultures (in the West, the earliest version is found in Hesiod's poem *Works and Days*) and essentially consists in the idea that civilisation is a form of corruption of an original state of nature in which people lived free and equal, in a condition of harmony and community. Like the negative state of nature imagined by Hobbes, the golden age is a mere fiction devised for argumentative purposes; just as Hobbes drew on the contemporary example of the "savage peoples of America", cultural primitivism drew on the contemporary example of the Indigenous peoples of the tropics, thus giving rise to the "myth of the Noble Savage", he who has not been corrupted – either physically or morally – by the vices of civilisation.

Jean-Jacques Rousseau's *Discourse on the Origin and Basis of Inequality Among Men* of 1755 is one of the works that best exemplify cultural primitivism and, in particular, the two myths at its heart. According to Rousseau, in depicting the state of nature as a condition of war and violence, Hobbes attributed to the state of nature and its inhabitants characteristics that were in fact proper to society and civilised humans (Douglass 2015, chapter 2; Menin 2021, pp. 40ff.). If one examines the "natural state of man", stripping it "of all the supernatural gifts he could have received and of all the artificial faculties he could only have acquired by long progress – considering him, in a word, as he must have come from the hands of nature" (Rousseau 1964, pp. 104–105) – one will discover, according to Rousseau, that the human being is nothing more than an animal that is slightly less physiologically endowed than others. Nevertheless, human beings are capable of imitating strategies and securing the resources they need in

> a land that, "abandoned to its natural fertility . . . and covered by immense forests never mutilated by the axe, offers at every step storehouses and shelters to animals of all species" (p. 105). Rousseau's is a benevolent nature, which nourishes and cares for its inhabitants and "treats all the animals abandoned to its care with a partiality that seems to show how jealous it is of this right" (p. 111). This is also why, on his view, "Negroes and savages trouble themselves so little about the wild beasts they may encounter in the woods": although they roam the forests naked and armed only with bow and arrow, "no one has ever heard that any of them were devoured by beasts" (p. 108). Nature, Rousseau argues, provides everything needed to survive, has destined us to be healthy and strong, and takes care of us. As he writes: "Most of our ills are our own work, and . . . we would have avoided almost all of them by preserving the simple, uniform, and solitary way of life prescribed to us by nature"; it is in "becoming domesticated" that the human being becomes "weak, fearful, servile, and his soft and effeminate way of life completes the enervation of both his strength and his courage" (pp. 110–111).

4.4 Deforesting Eden

Thus far, I have used the term "environmentalism" without defining it and without clarifying an underlying ambiguity that now needs to be addressed. In common speech, the term is often used to refer to an ideological position held by individuals and political movements. I prefer to call this ideological position "environmental activism" and will instead use the term "environmentalism" in a broader and less ideologically charged sense to refer to a set of policies, ethics, and practices aimed at the conservation and management of the natural environment. The remainder of this chapter is dedicated to this theme.

Concern for the natural environment has a long history. The Indian emperor Ashoka, for instance, who lived between 304 and 232 BCE, established forms of protection for forests and wildlife following his conversion to Buddhism, banning the use of fire in agriculture and hunting (Fisher 2018, chapter 4). Just as the concept of the environment is a relatively recent innovation (as discussed in the first chapter), so too is the phenomenon of environmentalism, which emerged and became institutionalised relatively recently and in a specific context, namely the colonial context. The birth of European environmentalism can be traced back to 18th-century French and British tropical colonies, whereas North American environmentalism emerged in the post-colonial United States between the 18th and the 19th centuries.

According to British historian and environmental activist Richard Grove (1955–2020), the need for environmental protection began to be felt in the context of the colonial exploitation of tropical lands around the mid-18th century. Simplifying an extremely complex scenario, it can be said that demands for environmental protection emerged as a consequence of the clash between the perspectives of two different social actors – governments and the scientific community – with regard to the same object, the tropics, from the Caribbean to Asia (Grove 1992, 1995). For the Dutch, British, and French governments, these were merely lands to be exploited for their natural resources (wood, minerals, game, and soil for agriculture). However, economic exploitation coincided with the rise of cultural primitivism (see Box 4.2) and what Grove calls "the Edenic island discourse": for many European intellectuals, artists, and even scientists, the tropics represented the tangible counterpart of idealised and symbolically rich landscapes; they were an earthly Eden, Arcadian utopias where humans and nature lived in harmony and simplicity. Plantations were destroying a long-sought and yearned-for paradise.

With that said, colonialism also facilitated the establishment of scientific communities in the "new" territories. The need to describe and catalogue flora, fauna, and geological formations – a completely unknown natural environment – pushed European trading companies to employ medical doctors and naturalists (i.e. individuals with scientific training), who communicated regularly, sharing information and discoveries, and who were often not subservient to the economic interests of their employers. Among these individuals, some were profoundly influenced by Humboldt's thought: for them, the relationship between deforestation, water use for irrigation, and the climate, as well as between environmental degradation, disease, and hunger, was evident. It was precisely from the scientific community that the first impulses for the protection of the natural environment and the first demands to governments in this regard emerged, marking the beginning of European environmentalism.

European environmentalism thus arose from an awareness within the scientific community established in the colonies of the consequences of certain human actions on the environment. The scientific community appreciated the connection between the excessive exploitation of resources (primarily deforestation and the seizure of water resources for plantation agriculture) and local environmental changes (soil erosion and drought) and threats to human health (diseases and famines).

One of the very first demands for environmental protection came from French scientists in Mauritius, who saw environmental management as a necessity motivated by aesthetic, moral, and economic considerations. They were successful in securing some protective measures from the French government: an ordinance in 1769 stipulated that to prevent soil erosion, 25 per cent of all land properties had to be maintained as forest, deforested areas had to be reforested, and forests within 200 metres of water had to be protected. Shortly thereafter, new laws were introduced to limit water pollution (caused by the effluents from indigo factories and sugar refineries) and to limit overfishing (Grove 1992).[12]

While the origins of European environmentalism can be traced to an understanding of the consequences of the unregulated use of tropical natural resources, it was progressive urbanisation, the expansion and mechanisation of agriculture, and the rapid growth of manufacturing that brought about similar concerns in the United States. As with European environmentalism, forests played a central role in this regard. A key event in the transformation of the modern American landscape was massive deforestation to make way for agricultural land, to obtain fuel for heating and manufacturing, and to build railways and cities: between 1850 and 1910, forests were being cut down at a rate of 35 square kilometres per day. It is in this context that North American environmentalism was born. *Man and Nature* (1864) by the scholar and politician George Perkins Marsh is likely the first book to explicitly and systematically address the human environment as it would be understood more than a century later at the Stockholm Conference, encompassing both its natural and its artificial components.

As Andrea Wulf (2015, chapter XXI) recounts, Marsh and his wife Caroline travelled for four years – from 1849 to 1853 – throughout the Middle East and Europe, gathering material and observations for the book (which Marsh completed in Italy, near Turin). During their travels, what struck them most was the contrast between their young, new world and a land shaped by thousands of years of human intervention. The landscape they saw in Egypt, for example, was the result of the transformation of the desert into cultivated fields through irrigation systems. Wild plants had been eradicated, and hills that had been terraced and cultivated for longer periods had become barren and desolate lands. The use of water for agriculture had enabled the creation of fertile fields in the short term but had impoverished lakes and large rivers in the long term, promoting desertification. This was the very phenomenon that had been denounced by Humboldt in the valley of Lake Valencia (see Section 1.2.2). For Marsh, a follower of Humboldt, the lesson was clear: nature is an interconnected whole of abiotic and biotic components, and human activities have effects that extend beyond what can be immediately observed. Furthermore, the fate of the natural environment is tied to human history: the Roman Empire fell because the Romans destroyed their forests and, with them, the very soil that fed them. This was also the message of *Man and Nature*, which was intended as a warning to the new world not to follow in the footsteps of the old.

The same processes that had led to the destruction of the natural environment in the Mediterranean (deforestation and the loss of wild fauna and flora, intensive agriculture and grazing, the alteration of hydrological systems through the construction of artificial lakes) were indeed underway in the

United States. However, Marsh argued that the manipulation of the environment is not inherently negative: on the contrary, human intervention generally improves nature by domesticating it, making it hospitable and productive for its human inhabitants. Marsh's exhortation was thus to reverse course and to interact with the natural environment with a better understanding of its processes, applying better techniques and a series of remedies: reforestation, controlled grazing and agriculture, the stabilisation of sand dunes, and the monitoring of environmental impacts.

The model of the relationship between humans and the natural environment promoted by *Man and Nature* is that of environmental stewardship inspired by a Linnaean view (see Section 1.5.2). As Marsh writes: "Man has too long forgotten that the earth was given to him for usufruct alone, not for consumption, still less for profligate waste" (Marsh 1864, p. 35). Far from primitivism and idyllic discourses, Marsh's environmentalism is interventionist: a manipulated and managed land is generally preferable to a state of nature. For Marsh, it is not about aspiring to return to a state of untouched nature but about better managing the natural environment, mitigating the human impact and repairing the damage done. The environment we inherited from our ancestors includes all the transformations that have been made to it throughout the history of our species (what we might call our "ecological inheritance", as we saw in Section 3.2.1), and we are merely temporary stewards, administrators who must manage a received asset in order to pass it on to our descendants (Lowenthal 2000). Yet just as our ancestors did, and as our heirs will do, we modify our environment, making it not just a simple asset to be protected or preserved but an integral part of our lives, a surrounding world to which we are adapted in part because we have built it in our image and which we will leave as a legacy to future generations.

This model of environmental stewardship includes both the preservation of pristine nature and the management of natural resources, encompassing the two ways of understanding the natural environment discussed at the beginning of the chapter. In the next section, we will examine two models of natural environment protection that, respectively, emphasise the preservation of wilderness (*preservationism*) and the conservation of natural resources (*resourcism*), as well as an attempt to reconcile them (the model of *ecological livelihood*).[13]

4.5 Preserving wilderness

The Scottish-born naturalist and engineer John Muir (1838–1914) is considered the founder of preservationism. Drawing inspiration from both transcendentalism and the model of environmental stewardship, Muir's vision is clearly religious-spiritual, in the Emersonian mould. It is through immersion in pristine nature that humans, ensnared in sinful civilisation, can return to

God. The conservation of nature is framed as a moral mission, a struggle between the good of spiritual pursuit and the evil of material greed:

> The battle we have fought, and are still fighting, for the forests is a part of the eternal conflict between right and wrong. . . . The smallest forest reserve, and the first I ever heard of, was in the Garden of Eden; and though its boundaries were drawn by the Lord, and embraced only one tree, yet even so moderate a reserve as this was attacked. And I doubt not, if only one of our grand trees in the Sierra were reserved as an example and type of all that is most noble and glorious in mountain trees, it would not be long before you would find a lumberman and a lawyer at the foot of it, eagerly proving by every law terrestrial and celestial that that tree must come down. So we must count on watching and striving for these trees, and should always be glad to find anything so surely good and noble to strive for.
> (Muir 1896, p. 276)

The reasons behind Muir's preservationism are thus primarily moral and spiritual: in line with transcendentalist philosophy, contact with untouched nature is seen as an antidote to consumerism, an experience that inspires imagination and elevates the soul, bringing humans into contact with the divine.

From the perspective of natural environment management practices, preservationism primarily translates to the establishment of nature reserves – regions of wilderness to be kept separate and, at least in appearance, untouched by human activity. Indeed, it was John Muir who contributed to the delineation of the new boundaries of Yosemite National Park in 1889, wrote the newspaper articles that promoted its establishment in 1890, and presided over the Sierra Club, an organisation originally dedicated to the preservation of the Sierra Nevada.

4.5.1 A conversation of the West

As J. Baird Callicott and Michael P. Nelson write (1998, p. 3), the concept of wilderness has been accused of being a "conversation of the West". In short, and simplifying somewhat, the charge is that wilderness is a representation of nature formed within a particular culture and within the confines of a specific social stratum, a Western environmental narrative "led by Euro-American men within the historical-cultural context of patriarchal colonialism" (Ward 2019, p. 34; cf. also Merchant 2003; Guha 1989; Cronon 1996; Plumwood 1998; Stano 2023). The idealisation of nature at the heart of transcendentalism – and adopted by preservationism – is, according to this criticism, the result of genocides that the idealisation neglects or even helps to mask. In the storyline of wilderness, one can read the history of European colonisation of the Americas. When European explorers arrived, tens of millions of people lived in North and Central America, with a long history of interaction with the land. One of the most significant effects of the colonisation of North America – the birthplace of the idea of wilderness – was the death of almost 90 per cent of the Indigenous population, mainly due to diseases against which their immune systems were powerless. As environmental philosopher Steven Vogel writes, "[a]rguably it was only because of this massive depopulation that it even became possible to view the North American continent as a pure wilderness: the land seemed unpopulated by humans simply because they had died" (Vogel 2015, p. 5).

The wilderness, however, was not at all viewed by its original inhabitants as a wild space devoid of humanity. Lakota Chief Luther Standing Bear (1863 or 1868–1939), for example, explains that the same lands that Europeans considered wilderness were not at all so for his people. These lands were their environment, to which they were adapted, a space they knew and had modified:

> We did not think of the great open plains, the beautiful rolling hills, and winding streams with tangled growth, as "wild". Only to the white man was nature a "wilderness" and only to him was the land "infested" with "wild" animals and "savage" people. To us it was tame.
> (Standing Bear 1933/2006, p. 38)

For European colonists, wilderness was not something to be preserved (it would only become so thanks to intellectual movements like transcendentalism and the interests of the scientific community); rather, it was something to be replaced with a copy of the European environment and kept away from farms and cities. Even its human inhabitants, the "savages", were to be domesticated and civilised. Standing Bear's attempt to make his contemporaries understand the cultural complexity and moral richness of his society by providing a precise and detailed ethnographic description in his book *Land of the Spotted Eagle* (quoted earlier) did little to change this view.

One might then ask whether there is anything real that corresponds to the idea of pristine nature. According to the ecologist Christian Lévêque (2014), the answer is no: pristine nature is – at least today – an imaginary, virtual phenomenon, an idea originally present in various forms in many religions (the Edenic myth), reinterpreted by European Romanticism, popularised as wilderness by transcendentalism in the United States, and recently returned to Europe.[14] And in fact, when we think of the ultimate symbol of pristine nature, the Amazon rainforest, we have to admit that it is no longer pristine at all. Some studies suggest that modern tree communities in the Amazon have been significantly shaped by a long history of plant domestication by Indigenous peoples (Levis *et al.* 2017). The implausibility of claiming that such areas are untouched becomes even more apparent when one takes a walk through a European forest: intuitively, there is no doubt that one is immersed in nature, but that nature is the result of thousands of years of human intervention (Delort and Walter 2001). Indeed, the land has been anthropised for much longer in Europe than it has in the United States, so much so that the establishment of parks and reserves has generally been less rigidly conceived, and nature conservation has often been combined with the preservation of cultural heritage. For example, Article 1 of Italy's first nature conservation law (Law No. 778 of 1922) states that "[t]he immovables whose preservation is of significant public interest because of their natural beauty or their special relationship to civil and literary history are declared to be subject to special protection. Scenic beauties are also protected by this law". It is important to note that the contrast between wilderness preservationism and resourcism is stronger in the United States than in Europe, where the idea of *cultural landscapes*[15] – that is, areas resulting from a long history of interaction between humans and nature, where the interaction between nature and culture is seen as producing harmonious units worthy of protection – was one of the major starting points of conservation and still plays an important role today (Jax 2023, pp. 22ff.).

4.5.2 *An ontological paradox*

In the United States, the idea of nature promoted by transcendentalism and adopted by preservationism was concretised with the law known as the Wilderness Act of 1964. As it states:

> A wilderness, in contrast with those areas where man and his works dominate the landscape, is hereby recognized as an area where the earth and its community of life are untrammeled by man, where man himself is a visitor who does not remain.

According to the law, an area must meet the following criteria to qualify as wilderness:

> (1) generally appears to have been affected primarily by the forces of nature, with the imprint of man's work substantially unnoticeable; (2) has outstanding opportunities for solitude or a primitive and unconfined type of recreation; (3) has at least five thousand acres of land or is of sufficient size as to make practicable its preservation and use in an unimpaired condition; and (4) may also contain ecological, geological, or other features of scientific, educational, scenic, or historical value.

The Wilderness Act established a system aimed at protecting unspoiled nature, which initially comprised 54 areas across 13 states and now includes more than 750 areas distributed across the majority of states. Ontologically, the Wilderness Act has consequences that are, at least on the surface, paradoxical. Let's see why.

The criteria contained in the law allow for certain areas to be delineated from others, by drawing boundaries. Boundaries created in this manner are called *de dicto*, or artificial, because they are the result of a collective decision-making process that results in a law. By contrast, *bona fide* or natural boundaries are independent of human action, like the boundaries of a lake: they do not seem to depend on any human social agreement; they exist in themselves and are what they are regardless of our intervention (Smith and Varzi 2000).

The paradox arises when we accept that wilderness areas came into existence the moment the law delineated their boundaries and would never have existed had those boundaries not been drawn. Those parts of the world that, since the Wilderness Act, are called "wilderness" therefore owe their existence to human action. If this is the case, wilderness areas should be considered artificial objects rather than natural ones. This conclusion aligns with the argument that wilderness areas are the material reification of a human idea, but it has counterintuitive – if not paradoxical – consequences for practices aimed at conserving *natural* environments: by establishing areas of pristine nature, we are increasing the number of artificial objects in the world.

It is important to make a clarification: recognising that wilderness areas are artificial because they are ontologically dependent on artificial boundaries in no way implies that the species communities and underlying ecosystems with which they at least partially coincide are also artificial. Unlike nature reserves, whose boundaries have been drawn with a ruler, the boundaries of ecosystems and species communities, with which wilderness areas partially overlap, seem to be less dependent on human intervention. What constitutes part of an ecosystem or a species community depends on the causal relationships between the parts of the system.[16] According to some authors (Chapman 2006; Prior and Brady 2017; Ward 2019), a relational and autonomous character can be attributed to wild areas, thus replacing the concept of *wilderness* with that of *wildness*, a related yet separate notion that focuses on the *autonomy* of non-human entities rather than their *separation*.

Let us return to the ontological paradox. A critique like the one just set out can be levelled against reforestation practices implemented to combat climate change and desertification and to preserve biodiversity. Reforestation involves planting a forest anew. Certainly, in Aristotelian terms, the matter is natural, but the form of the forest (e.g. its composition in terms of plant species) is, at least in part, dependent on us, as is its efficient cause (cf. Box 4.1): it is the human being, with the ability to select suitable species to compose the desired forest and grow saplings, who initiates and directs the process. Should we then say that the new forest is an artefact? And if so, what is the point of our environmental restoration efforts in general, given that their implementation would lead to the production not of natural objects but of new artefacts? Objections of this kind have been raised, for example, by environmental philosophers Eric Katz (1992), for whom the "human restoration of nature" is nothing but "a big lie" (Katz 1992), and Robert Elliot (1982), who describes restoration practices as a way to "fake nature". In the next chapter, a revision of the traditional natural/artificial distinction is proposed that may help us to respond to this type of criticism. For the moment, a different kind of consideration can be made in this regard.

In principle, recognising natural areas with *fiat* boundaries as artefacts in no way diminishes their importance or the need to preserve them, just as cultural landscapes are preserved even though they are precisely *cultural*. Rather, it means acknowledging that the reasons behind this need have to do with human interests and motives – for example, scientific or aesthetic interests and motives. The former are the same interests that drove scientific communities in tropical colonies to oppose the destruction of the natural environment. Wild ecosystems harbour species and processes that are not present in urban ones or other ecosystems heavily modified by humans. The increasing anthropisation of the environment means that wild ecosystems acquire inestimable value from a scientific point of view, if only because they could disappear entirely, and the only way to preserve less anthropised ecosystems may be to make them part of protected areas (i.e. artefacts).

Another reason to preserve wild areas is their aesthetic or recreational role: in this case, wild areas are also natural resources in the sense (and with the difficulties highlighted concerning the *natural* label) illustrated in Section 3.1.

When we watch a film, if a particular frame fascinates us we can press the pause button and watch it again; when we listen to a symphony, we can rewind and savour a passage over and over again. Similarly, we want to preserve the coral reef and the rainforest because our aesthetic experience of them evokes positive emotions in us. This thesis has been defended in particular by Elliott Sober (1986), who has drawn analogies between natural objects and artistic objects. With both natural objects and works of art, for example, we generally consider an original to be more valuable than a copy, even if we cannot tell the difference. If someone were to offer us a free visit to a perfect replica of Botticelli's *Birth of Venus*, we would likely decline, preferring to pay the ticket and queue at the Uffizi. The same seems to apply to a forest: given the choice between taking a walk in a primaeval forest and walking in a reforested forest, we would likely choose the former. We also believe that context is important for both works of art and natural objects. When acid rain threatened the Acropolis, some artefacts were moved indoors. But when given the choice between viewing a sculpture on the Acropolis and viewing the same sculpture in a museum, we are likely to prefer the former. The same goes for the snow leopard: between leaving it in its natural habitat, with all the risks that entails when a species is endangered, and keeping the remaining specimens in a zoo, both ordinary citizens and conservation scientists prefer the first option. Finally, both ordinary citizens and conservation scientists tend to attribute a positive value to rarity:

in general, priority is given to the conservation of rare species or ecosystems, just as a work of art is often considered more valuable the fewer the works produced by the artist.

4.6 Using resources, managing ecosystems

The preservationist model outlined in the previous sections historically contrasts with the resourcist model, the founder of which is considered to be Gifford Pinchot (1865–1946), governor of Pennsylvania from 1931 to 1935 and head of the United States Forest Service, established by President Roosevelt to counter the exploitation of forests by the large industrial monopolies of the time.

Pinchot was trained in the United States but within the German tradition of forest management. (At the time, Germany had the most advanced forest management knowledge and techniques: as mentioned earlier, Europe had a more intense and long-standing history of human impact compared to the United States.) Viewing forests as natural resources, Pinchot believed it was necessary to maximise productivity and minimise waste. Furthermore, he argued that resources should be used equitably and sustainably, that is, by everyone and over the long term.

In general, for resourcism (also somewhat misleadingly called "conservationism"), the natural environment equates to a set of resources available to humans, which they should avoid exhausting in order to continue being able to use them. "There are two things on this material earth", Pinchot (1947, p. 325) asserted, "people and natural resources", and the latter should be used to maximise the welfare of the former. Closer to a reductionist and mechanistic approach to nature compared to preservationism, the spirit of resourcism can be summarised by its utilitarian motto:[17] the greatest good for the greatest number of people for the longest time. Its two fundamental principles are thus the efficient use and maximisation of natural resources and the equitable distribution of the benefits derived from such use. For this reason, for Pinchot, the conservation of natural resources and economic development go hand in hand.

The natural environment, viewed by wilderness preservationism as the image of the divine, a source of spiritual enjoyment and moral fulfilment for human beings, is interpreted by resourcism in terms of "a collection of bits of matter, assembled into a hierarchy of independently existing chemical and organismic aggregates, that can be understood and manipulated by reductive methods" (Callicott 1994, p. 11) and that can be wisely managed in a well-regulated market.

This view was opposed by Aldo Leopold (1887–1948). Like Pinchot, Leopold was trained in the German tradition of forest management but later became a fierce critic of it. The goal of resource maximisation, according to Leopold, makes forest conservation a practice not too different from agriculture based on monocultures: the Germans, he wrote to a colleague, had taught the world to plant trees like cabbages (Guha 2000, p. 55). In other words, in Leopold's eyes, resourcism does not conserve forests but produces timber, and its scientific vision is outdated. Nature, as ecology teaches, is not a collection of separate, compartmentalised, reproducible pieces. Instead, it is an intricate system of tightly integrated processes of which humans are a part.

The conservation model proposed by Leopold in his 1949 book *A Sand County Almanac* attempts to bridge the gap between preservationism and resourcism (either you preserve nature or you exploit it – *tertium non datur*). According to Leopold, preserving nature does not necessarily entail a separation between humans and nature, just as land use is not inherently destructive. As Callicott (1994) argues, Leopold's conservation philosophy aligns with what is now understood as "sustainable development", the idea that human economic activities can occur without significantly compromising the health and integrity of ecosystems. However, Callicott acknowledges that the term "sustainable development" is vague and prone to misunderstandings, and thus he suggests that a better label for Leopold's conservation philosophy is *ecological livelihood*. Indeed, Leopold's proposal encompasses more than what is usually meant by *sustainable development*. It is not merely about producing goods with a lower environmental impact or reducing the ecological footprint of industrialised and developing societies; rather, it calls for a radical shift in how humans inhabit and use the natural environment. Specifically, humans must learn to recognise themselves as part of "the land community", the community of interdependent human and nonhuman animals, plants, soils, and waters, collectively understood (Millstein 2018). From this perspective, the importance of conserving unspoiled nature lies more in the preservation of habitats and species at risk of extinction than in its aesthetic and spiritual value. To this end, it is not always sufficient to segregate patches of nature in parks and reserves; sometimes a comprehensive ecosystem management approach will be necessary, that is, a planned and adaptive series of human interventions, which can be significant and long term (for example controlling or eradicating invasive species). Regarding natural resources, Leopold's perspective does not deny that the natural environment is also a collection of resources, but the production of goods must be subordinate to the health and integrity of the land community and should be pursued only if compatible with it.

4.7 The giant panda and us

In this chapter, four different historical models of the conservation and management of the natural environment have been presented, namely Marsh's environmental stewardship, Muir's preservationism, Pinchot's resourcism, and Leopold's ecological livelihood model.

Turning to the present, as environmental ethicist Jennifer Welchman (2012) notes, despite being met with sharp criticism in the environmental ethics literature (in particular, the model has been accused of having originated in patriarchal, elitist, and anthropocentric systems and ideologies), the stewardship model remains the framework on which contemporary environmental management and conservation policies and practices are based. To give but one example, in the United Nations Millennium Declaration[18] governments explicitly stated their intention "to adopt in all our environmental actions a new ethic of conservation and stewardship".

Within this general framework, we may follow biologist and conservation scientist Georgina Mace (1953–2020) in identifying at least four framings of conservation. More precisely, according to Mace (2014), there are four distinct ways of understanding the relationship between people and nature, each of which is associated with a different conservation framing. While these framings have their origins (and have predominated) in different times, they are currently present together.

The first framing is *nature for itself*: the natural environment is defined by an absence of people and identified with pristine nature, with wilderness. This corresponds to the preservationist model, which was dominant in natural environment management before the 1960s and translated mainly to the establishment of protected areas, prioritising the conservation of habitats and ecosystems in their wildest possible state. Today, as already mentioned, the idea of wildness is likely increasingly replacing the idea of wilderness.

The second and third framings – *nature despite people* and *nature for people* – emphasise the existence of a relationship between humans and the natural environment. With reference to the reconstruction offered in this chapter, we can say that these correspond to two different interpretations of the sustainable development model, which can be traced back, at least in part, to resourcism (see Section 4.3.1 and Box 4.2).

Nature despite people highlights the fact that people use resources provided by nature and that it is necessary not to exceed certain usage thresholds. Only in this way can nature continue to "produce" *despite* the presence of humans. From a conservation perspective, this approach promotes the sustainable use of natural resources aimed at ensuring that the impact of human actions on habitats and species will not exceed certain thresholds, which are in principle measurable. Examples characteristic of sustainability-based conservation include the already mentioned concept of a minimum viable population and the sustainable use of wildlife, meaning the utilisation of wildlife (e.g. in hunting activities) at a rate that does not lead to a decline over time.

Nature for people, on the other hand, emphasises that the natural environment provides essential goods and services to humanity, without which people could not survive. From the perspective of conservation theories and practices, the focus shifts from resources to ecosystems and their functions, with the latter understood as *ecosystem services* (see Box 1.2), from nutrient cycling to soil formation, from provision services (food, drinking water, fuel, and raw materials) to climate regulation, and even to non-material services such as spiritual, recreational, and cultural benefits.

According to Mace, a new framing has been emerging with the new millennium, alongside those examined earlier, characterised by a more integrated consideration of nature and human beings, nature and culture, and by greater collaboration between natural sciences and the humanities. The central idea of this new vision is that to understand the behaviour of ecosystems, it is necessary to jointly consider the social and ecological components of the Earth system: humans are an integral part of ecosystems, and their actions interact with ecosystem processes, participating in the feedback loops that characterise their functioning. This vision, which Mace calls *people and nature*, is perhaps the closest to the spirit of Leopold's proposal illustrated in the previous section.

To conclude this chapter, let us look at a concrete example of natural environment management featuring one of the emblematic species of environmentalism (Liu *et al.* 2001). In 1975, the Wolong Nature Reserve was established in southwestern China, aimed at protecting the giant panda. Contrary to expectations, the loss and fragmentation of suitable panda habitat accelerated rather than decreasing following the establishment of the reserve, reaching or even exceeding the levels of the area outside it. This was due to socio-economic factors. Between 1975 and 1995, the human population within the reserve increased from 2,560 residents to 4,260 (the one-child policy, then in force, did not apply to ethnic minorities, who constituted the majority of the reserve's residents). The inhabitants of Wolong, especially the young and thus the "workforce", became the main factor in the destruction of the bamboo forests, the pandas' habitat. Most of the workers were farmers, and the main economic activities on the reserve were agriculture (with the consequent deforestation), timber collection, road construction, medicinal herb collection, and tourism. Once the more easily accessible forests were exhausted, the local population had to resort to those in more remote and higher areas, the preferred habitat for pandas. To prevent further degradation and to restore the animals' environment, from 2001 the Chinese government began implementing new conservation policies that jointly considered the needs of local residents and the pandas' habitat, which are proving effective.

This case study, one among many, helps to show the complexity of the relationship between humans and their environment, a relationship that is influenced by both global socio-economic factors and local specific biophysical and socio-economic conditions. Considering natural and social factors in isolation, although less complicated from a scientific and practical point of view, does not seem in many cases to be an effective solution. In other words, considering the human environment in abstraction from that of other species – and vice versa – is a simplification that risks nullifying or undermining our human environment management and natural environment conservation practices.

Notes

1 "Communication from the commission to the European Parliament, the council, the European economic and social committee and the committee of the regions. *EU Biodiversity Strategy for 2030. Bringing nature back into our lives*", Brussels 20.5.2020, available on the website of the European Environment Agency.
2 https://ec.europa.eu/newsroom/intpa/items/683634/en
3 Aristotle uses the term *technê*, usually translated as "craft" or "art", to mean a practice that is based on a theoretical understanding. Accordingly, it seems reasonable to see Aristotelian *technê* as an ancient precursor of *technology*, and Aristotle as a precursor of the modern philosophy of technology (Franssen, Lokhorst and van de Poel 2023).
4 So-called "plastic islands" or "garbage patches" are vast oceanic areas where, due to the action of currents, waste present in the water (mainly microplastics) aggregates to form patches that range from the surface to the bottom of the ocean. At present, five such islands are known: one in the Indian Ocean, two in the Atlantic, and two in the Pacific. Among these, the Great Pacific Garbage Patch, situated between Hawaii and California, is the most famous. Although determining its exact dimensions is complicated because the islands move with the ocean currents, it is estimated that the Great Pacific Garbage Patch has an area of 1.6 million square kilometres (Lebreton *et al.* 2018).
5 Except perhaps for some of its artistic components. The possible analogy between natural objects and artworks will be briefly discussed in Section 5.2.
6 Some Indigenous communities do not even have a word for "nature" (Jax 2023, pp. 176ff.).
7 Microplastics are plastic particles that are generally smaller than 5 millimetres in diameter and that result from the degradation of larger plastic objects or are present in human commercial products (such as microbeads in certain toothpastes or exfoliating cosmetics). Since the mid-2000s, many countries have begun to ban such microbeads, and there are mobile applications that allow shoppers to scan products to check for their presence. The impact of microplastics on aquatic organisms and ecosystems is particularly negative: if ingested they can, for example, block the gastrointestinal tract or induce a feeling of satiety, causing organisms to die from starvation.
8 Stress at the level of ecosystems can be defined as a harmful effect that occurs following a disturbance caused by biotic agents (e.g. an invasive species) or abiotic factors (e.g. a flood).
9 These references are, respectively, to the sixth book of Wordsworth's *Prelude* and Coleridge's *Hymn before Sun-rise, in the Vale of Chamouni*.
10 The Millennium Ecosystem Assessment, a colossal research project launched in 2001 with the support of the United Nations, aimed to assess the consequences of ecosystem changes for human well-being and to provide a scientific basis for the actions necessary to conserve and sustainably use them.
11 The limitations of the natural/artificial distinction highlighted throughout this chapter reflect the difficulty of providing clear definitions of the different types of forests that are the focus of environmental management practices. In very simplified terms, *planted forests* are forests that are established for timber production or other services, typically consisting of a few – sometimes even just one – species of trees and characterised by intensive management. *Primitive* or *primary* forests, on the other hand, are composed of native species and show no visible signs of human activity.

12 As in Mauritius, in the West Indies, the Caribbean, and India it was the scientific community – this time British – that gave a decisive boost to environmental protection. Again, scientists experimentally demonstrated the causal link between deforestation and rainfall and lobbied governments to protect forests. In 1764, "rain reserves" – areas of protected forest to counteract and prevent drought – were established on the island of Tobago; in 1791, similar measures were adopted on the island of St Vincent in the West Indies. The policies developed in Mauritius, Tobago, and Saint Vincent provided not only a theoretical basis but also a practical model for European (and Indian) environmentalism (see Grove 1992).
13 I borrow these three labels from Callicott 1994.
14 The need to conserve wilderness – following the North American model – was formalised for the first time in Europe only in 2009 with a resolution of the European Parliament approved on 3 February that recognises that "the effective protection and, where necessary, restoration of Europe's last wilderness areas are vital to halting the loss of biodiversity by 2010".
15 The concept of a cultural landscape (*Kulturlandschaft*) was first used by the German geographer Carl Ritter in the early 19th century.
16 This does not mean, of course, that it is always easy to identify such boundaries precisely; spatial contiguity is not always indicative of functional interaction, for example, and interactions between parts of an ecosystem can involve different spatial and temporal scales (Strayer *et al.* 2003).
17 Utilitarianism is a form of consequentialism, the theory that the moral value of an action depends solely on its outcomes. For classical utilitarianism – represented by Jeremy Bentham (1748–1832) and John Stuart Mill (1806–1873) – an action is morally right only if it maximises happiness (understood as pleasure or the absence of pain). More precisely, an individual action is morally right if its consequences lead to an increase in overall well-being (Tripodi 2020, pp. 106ff.). For an introduction to consequentialism, see Sinnott-Armstrong (2023).
18 The Millennium Declaration was drafted at United Nations Headquarters in New York from 6–8 September 2000. As stated in the declaration, at the dawn of the new millennium heads of state and government gathered to reaffirm their faith in the UN and their commitment to promoting the purposes and principles of its Charter. The text, from which these quotations are drawn, is available in the United Nations digital library.

References

Berti, E. (2011) 'L'ilemorfismo da Aristotele a oggi', *Rivista di Filosofia Neo-Scolastica*, 103(2), pp. 173–180.
Borghini, A. (2019) 'Ordinary biodiversity: The case of food', in Casetta, E., Marques da Silva, J. and Vecchi, D. (eds.) *From Assessing to Conserving Biodiversity, History, Philosophy and Theory of the Life Sciences*. Cham: Springer, pp. 415–434.
Borghini, A. and Piras, N. (2021) 'On interpreting something as food', *Food Ethics*, 6, art. n. 1. https://doi.org/10.1007/s41055-020-00082-5.
Brennan, A. (1988) *Thinking About Nature: An Investigation of Nature, Value, and Ecology*. Athens, GA: University of Georgia Press.
Callicott, J.B. (1992) 'La nature est morte, vive la nature!', *The Hastings Center Report*, 22(5), pp. 16–23.
Callicott, J.B. (1994) 'A brief history of American conservation philosophy', in Covington, W.W. and DeBano, L.F. (eds.) *Sustainable Ecological Systems: Implementing an Ecological Approach to Land Management*. Fort Collins, CO: USDA Forest Service, pp. 10–14.

Callicott, J.B. and Nelson, M.P. (eds.) (1998) *The Great New Wilderness Debate*. Athens, GA: University of Georgia Press.
Chapman, R.L. (2006) 'Ecological restoration restored', *Environmental Values*, 15(4), pp. 463–478.
Coates, P. (1998/2004) *Nature: Western Attitudes Since Ancient Times*. Berkeley, CA: University of California Press.
Code, A. (1987) 'Soul as efficient cause in Aristotle's embryology', *Philosophical Topics*, 15(2), pp. 51–59.
Cronon, W. (1996) 'The trouble with wilderness: Or getting back to the wrong *nature*', *Environmental History*, 1(1), pp. 7–28.
Delort, R. and Walter, F. (2001) *Histoire de l'environnement européen*. Paris: Presses Universitaires de France.
Descartes, R. (1637) *Discours de la méthode*. Leyde: Joannes Maire.
Douglass, R. (2015) *Rousseau and Hobbes: Nature, Free Will, and the Passions*. Oxford: Oxford Academic.
Elliot, R. (1982) 'Faking Nature', *Inquiry*, 25, pp. 81–93.
Emerson, R.W. (1842) 'The trascendentalist', in Poirier, R. (ed.) *Ralph Waldo Emerson* (The Oxford Authors). Oxford: Oxford University Press, 1990.
Ferraris, M. (2022) *Doc-Humanity*. Translated by S. De Sanctis. Tübingen: Mohr Siebrek Ek.
Fisher, M.H. (2018) *An Environmental History of India: From Earliest Times to the Twenty-First Century*. Cambridge, MA: Cambridge University Press.
Franssen, M., Lokhorst, G.J. and van de Poel, I. (2023) 'Philosophy of technology', in Zalta, E.N. and Nodelman, U. (eds.) *The Stanford Encyclopedia of Philosophy*, Spring 2023 edition. Available at: https://plato.stanford.edu/archives/spr2023/entries/technology/ (Accessed 14 June 2024).
Frantz, C. *et al.* (2005) 'There is no "I" in nature: The influence of self-awareness on connectedness to nature', *Journal of Environmental Psychology*, 25, pp. 427–436.
Freinkel, S. (2011) *Plastic: A Toxic Love Story*. Boston, MA: Houghton Mifflin Harcourt.
Glynn, P.W. (1993) 'Coral bleaching: Ecological perspective', *Coral Reefs*, 12, pp. 1–17.
Godfrey-Smith, P. (2016) *Other Minds: The Octopus, the Sea, and the Deep Origins of Consciousness*. Glasgow: William Collins.
Grove, R.H. (1992) 'Origins of Western environmentalism', *Scientific American*, 267(1), pp. 42–47.
Grove, R.H. (1995) *Green Imperialism: Colonial Expansion, Tropical Island Edens and the Origins of Environmentalism, 1600–1860*. Cambridge: Cambridge University Press.
Guha, R. (1989) 'Radical American environmentalism and wilderness preservation: A third world critique', *Environmental Ethics*, 11(1), pp. 71–83.
Guha, R. (2000) *Environmentalism: A Global History*. New York, NY: Longman.
Haram, L.E. *et al.* (2021) 'Emergence of a neopelagic community through the establishment of coastal species on the high seas', *Nature Communications*, 12, art. n. 6885.
Hennig, B. (2009) 'The four causes', *The Journal of Philosophy*, 106(3), pp. 137–160.
Hobbes, T. (1651/1909) *Leviathan*. Oxford: Oxford University Press.
Hume, D. (1739–40/2000) *A Treatise of Human Nature*. Edited by D.F. Norton and M.J. Norton. Oxford: Oxford University Press.
Jax, K. (2023) *Conservation Concepts: Rethinking Human–Nature Relationships*. London: Routledge.
Johnson, D.L. *et al.* (1997) 'Meaning of environmental terms', *Journal of Environmental Quality*, 26, pp. 581–589.

Kant, I. (2000) *Critique of Pure Reason*. Translated by P. Guyer and E. Matthews and edited by P. Guyer. Cambridge: Cambridge University Press.
Kaplan, D. (2019) *Food Philosophy*. New York: Columbia University Press.
Kaplan, M. (2012) 'City birds use cigarette butts to smoke out parasites', *Nature*. https://doi.org/10.1038/nature.2012.11952.
Katz, E. (1992) 'The big lie: Human restoration of nature', *Research in Philosophy and Technology*, 12, pp. 231–241.
Katz, E. (1995) 'Restoration and redesign: The ethical significance of human intervention in nature', *Restoration & Management Notes*, 9(2), pp. 90–96.
Lebreton, L. *et al.* (2018) 'Evidence that the great pacific garbage patch is rapidly accumulating plastic', *Scientific Reports*, 8, art. n. 4666.
Leopold, A. (1949) *A Sand County Almanac: And Sketches Here and There*. Oxford: Oxford University Press.
Lévêque, C. (2014) 'La biodiversité en Europe: cherchez le naturel?', *Paysans et Société*, 345, pp. 27–36.
Levis, C. *et al.* (2017) 'Persistent effects of pre-Columbian plant domestication on Amazonian Forest composition', *Science*, 355, pp. 925–931.
Liu, J. *et al.* (2001) 'Ecological degradation in protected areas: The case of Wolong nature reserve for giant pandas', *Science*, 292, pp. 98–101.
Lowenthal, D. (2000) 'Nature and morality from George Perkins Marsh to the Millennium', *Journal of Historical Geography*, 26(1), pp. 3–27.
Mace, G. (2014) 'Ecology: Whose conservation?', *Science*, 345, pp. 1558–1560.
Marsh, J.P. (1864) *Man and Nature; or, Physical Geography as Modified by Human Action*. New York: Charles Scribner.
McKibben, B. (1989/2022) *The End of Nature*. London: Penguin Books.
Menin, M. (2021) *Rousseau, un illuminista inquieto*. Roma: Carocci.
Merchant, C. (2003) *Reinventing Eden: The Fate of Nature in Western Culture*. New York and London: Routledge.
Mill, J.S. (1874) 'Nature', in Matz, L.J. (ed.) *Three Essays on Religion*. Peterborough, ON: Broadview Edition, 2009, pp. 65–104.
Millstein, R.L. (2018) 'Debunking myths about Aldo Leopold's land ethic', *Biological Conservation*, 217, pp. 391–396. https://doi.org/10.1016/j.biocon.2017.11.027.
Muir, J. (1896) 'Address on the Sierra Forest reservation', *Sierra Club Bulletin*, 1(7), pp. 275–277.
Myerson, J., Petrulionis, S.H. and Walls, L.D. (eds.) (2010) *The Oxford Handbook of Trascendentalism*. Oxford: Oxford University Press.
Pinchot, G. (1947) *Breaking New Ground*. New York: Harcourt, Brace and Co.
Plumwood, V. (1998) 'Wilderness skepticism and wilderness dualism', in Callicott, J.B. and Nelson, M.P. (eds.) *The Great New Wilderness Debate*. Athens, GA: University of Georgia Press, pp. 652–690.
Plumwood, V. (2007) '"Human exceptionalism" and the limitations of animals: A review of Raimond Gaita's *"The Philosopher's Dog"*', *Australian Humanities Review*, 42.
Pollo, S. (2008) *La morale della natura*. Roma-Bari: Laterza.
Prior, J. and Brady, E. (2017) 'Environmental aesthetics and rewilding', *Environmental Values*, 26(1), pp. 31–51.
Rousseau, J.J. (1964) 'The second discourse', in *The First and Second Discourses*. New York: St. Martin's Press.
Siipi, E. (2016) 'Unnatural kinds: Biodiversity and human modified entities', in Garson, J., Plutynski, A. and Sarkar, S. (eds.) *The Routledge Handbook of Philosophy of Biodiversity*. New York: Routledge, pp. 125–138.
Sinnott-Armstrong, W. (2023) 'Consequentialism', in Zalta, E.N. and Nodelman, U. (eds.) *The Stanford Encyclopedia of Philosophy*, Winter 2023 edition. Available at: https://plato.stanford.edu/archives/win2023/entries/consequentialism/ (Accessed 14 June 2024).

Smith, B. and Varzi, A.C. (2000) 'Fiat and bona fide boundaries', *Philosophy and Phenomenological Research*, 60(2), pp. 401–420.
Sober, E. (1986) 'Philosophical problems for environmentalism', in Norton, B.G. (ed.) *The Preservation of Species*. Princeton: Princeton University Press, pp. 173–194.
Sober, E. (2006) 'Evolution, population thinking, and essentialism', in *Id.* (ed.), *Conceptual Issues in Evolutionary Biology*. Cambridge, MA: MIT Press, pp. 329–359.
Standing Bear, L. (1933/2006) *Land of the Spotted Eagle*. Winnipeg, CA: Bison Book.
Stano, S. (2023) *Critique of Pure Nature*. Cham: Springer.
Strayer, D.L. et al. (2003) 'A classification of ecological boundaries', *BioScience*, 53(8), pp. 723–729.
Thoreau, H.D. (1854/1899) *Walden; or, Life in the Woods*. New York, NY: T.Y. Crowell & Company.
Tripodi, V. (2015) *Filosofie di genere. Differenza sessuale e ingiustizie sociali*. Roma: Carocci.
Tripodi, V. (2020) *Etiche delle tecniche. Una filosofia per progettare il futuro*. Milano: Mondadori.
Vining, J., Merrick, M.S. and Price, E.A. (2008) 'The distinction between humans and nature: human perceptions of connectedness to nature and elements of the natural and unnatural', *Human Ecology Review*, 15(1), pp. 1–11.
Vogel, S. (2015) *Thinking Like a Mall: Environmental Philosophy after the End of Nature*. Cambridge, MA: MIT Press.
Ward, K. (2019) 'For wilderness or wildness? Decolonising rewilding', in Pettorelli, N., Durant, S.M. and du Toit, J.T. (eds.) *Rewilding*. Cambridge: Cambridge University Press, pp. 34–54.
Welchman, J. (2012) 'A defence of environmental stewardship', *Environmental Values*, 21(3), pp. 297–316.
Wulf, A. (2015) *The Invention of Nature: Alexander von Humboldt's New World*. New York: Alfred A. Knopf.

5 Confronting the crisis

This concluding chapter briefly addresses three topics – environmental denialism, environmentalism, and the so-called end of nature – a full discussion of which would require much more space than we can provide here. The goal is not to offer an exhaustive or definitive exposition but to propose avenues for future reflection that the reader may take up and explore independently.

Despite the severity of the environmental crisis, I believe that a positive and constructive interpretation of the present time is not only possible but desirable. Of course, it is necessary to clarify what is meant by *positive* and *constructive*. That an environmental crisis (in the sense spelled out in Section 5.1) is underway is undeniable. Compared to even just 50 years ago, however, individual, collective, and institutional attention to environmental issues has changed. Compared to then, we are currently "staying with the trouble", to use the title of a book by philosopher and biologist Donna Haraway (2016). Although the Anthropocene has not been formally recognised as a geological epoch,[1] the success of the term testifies to the widespread sentiment that the current environmental crisis, and climate change in particular, marks a pivotal moment in human history – and perhaps in natural history. As often happens, a profound rethinking of established concepts and categories of thought is accompanying these perceived epochal transitions: among these are undoubtedly *environment*, *environmentalism*, and *nature*.

This entire book is dedicated to a reflection on the concept of the environment. This chapter presents possible directions for a future rethinking of environmentalism, on the one hand, and the concept of nature and the natural/artificial distinction, on the other. The chapter begins by explaining what is meant by the term *environmental crisis* and why it is difficult to accept that a crisis is indeed underway (Section 5.1). It then discusses the provocative claim that environmentalism has run its course and examines some of the proposals that have been put forward in an attempt to shape a new environmentalism (Section 5.2). Finally, it considers the proclamation of the "end of nature" and suggests lines along which a possible revision of the traditional conception of nature might be articulated (Section 5.3).

DOI: 10.4324/9781003479642-6

5.1 The environmental crisis

That an environmental crisis is underway is a statement on which there is substantial agreement within the scientific community, just as there is agreement that (i) this crisis is unprecedented in human history in terms of scale, severity, and speed, and (ii) it is caused by our species (Park 2001). But what is meant by "environmental crisis"? And why do some people refuse to accept the data and results on which the scientific community has reached agreement?

5.1.1 Substantial agreement

In the GEO-6 – the Global Environment Outlook, the most recent report by UNEP (the United Nations Environment Programme), we read the following:

> the overall condition of the global environment has continued to deteriorate since the first edition of GEO [of 1997], despite environmental policy efforts across all countries and regions. Environmental policy efforts are being hindered by a variety of factors, in particular unsustainable production and consumption patterns in most countries and climate change. GEO-6 concludes that unsustainable human activities globally have degraded the Earth's ecosystems, endangering the ecological foundations of society.
>
> (UN Environment 2019, p. 4)

The latest reports from the IPCC (Intergovernmental Panel on Climate Change) and the IPBES (Intergovernmental Science-Policy Platform on Biodiversity and Ecosystem Services) are no more reassuring. The IPCC has no doubts about the reality of global warming and human responsibility for it and suggests that some triggered trends may be irreversible.[2] According to the projections reported by the IPCC, even in an (implausible) scenario where emissions were completely ceased, the temperature would remain roughly constant – meaning it would not decrease – for many centuries. In sum,

> [h]uman-induced climate change, including more frequent and intense extreme events, has caused widespread adverse impacts and related losses and damages to nature and people, beyond natural climate variability. Some development and adaptation efforts have reduced vulnerability. Across sectors and regions the most vulnerable people and systems are observed to be disproportionately affected. The rise in weather and climate extremes has led to some irreversible impacts as natural and human systems are pushed beyond their ability to adapt.
>
> (Pörtner *et al.* 2022, p. 9)

The IPBES, for its part, states that the changes in the natural environment over the past 50 years are unprecedented in human history. The causes are multiple, some of which I have already mentioned. The expansion of agriculture and the growth of infrastructure and cities, driven by population increase and higher consumption, occur at the expense of biodiverse forests and wetlands (since 1992, the urban area of the planet has doubled). The overexploitation of non-human organisms for human consumption is causing the decline of many species (for instance, 33 per cent of fish stocks are now classified as overfished).

Changes related to global warming, such as the rise in average sea levels (between 16 and 21 centimetres since 1900), the increase in average temperatures (0.2°C per decade over the past 30 years), and the increased frequency of floods, fires, and droughts, have led to alterations in many aspects of biodiversity, from the structure and dynamics of biological communities to species phenology. These changes have impacted the development and evolution of organisms and the overall state of ecosystems.

Certain types of pollution have increased (marine plastic pollution has increased tenfold since 1980), as have invasions of exotic species (which have increased by 40 per cent since 1980). More broadly, IPBES has no doubt that these trends indicate a significant, human-driven transformation of the planet's natural systems:

> Nature across most of the globe has now been significantly altered by multiple human drivers, with the great majority of indicators of ecosystems and biodiversity showing rapid decline. . . . Humanity is a dominant global influence on life on earth, and has caused natural terrestrial, freshwater and marine ecosystems to decline. . . . The global rate of species extinction is already at least tens to hundreds of times higher than the average rate over the last 10 million years and is accelerating.
> (Díaz *et al.* 2019, pp. 11 and 24)

The reports from major intergovernmental groups regarding the overall state of the global environment, climate change, biodiversity, and ecosystems are based on the results of the scientific community. They show substantial agreement on the severity of the current environmental situation and the causal role of human activities. Is it then legitimate, in light of these facts, to speak of an environmental *crisis*?

To address this question, we can start by distinguishing two ways of understanding the term "environmental crisis": a broad sense and a narrow sense. In the broad sense, the term has been used by scientists since the 1970s to refer to a range of problems caused by human activities, such as air, soil, and sea pollution; tropical deforestation; biodiversity loss; the depletion of natural resources; soil degradation and desertification; freshwater scarcity; climate change; atmospheric ozone depletion; and, more recently, the increase in nitrogen levels in soil and water (Park 2001, pp. 4ff.). Currently, it is indisputable that an environmental crisis in this broad sense is underway.

In the narrow sense, a crisis is a more specific change. In medicine, a crisis is a *significant and sudden* change in the course of a disease (Jax 2023, Box 3.3). In economics, it is a *sudden shift* from a situation of prosperity to one of depression. Therefore, in this narrow sense, in order for a change to be defined as a crisis it must meet certain criteria. What these criteria are is not a straightforward question, however, and determining whether they have been met is often difficult.

To illustrate, let us consider a proposal from economics. Canadian environmental economist Michael Scott Taylor (2009, p. 1244) defines an environmental crisis as "a dramatic, unexpected, and irreversible worsening of the environment leading to significant welfare loss". According to Taylor,[3] crises are distinguished from other changes primarily insofar as they are *dramatic and rapid*: a gradual reduction in a natural resource would not constitute a crisis, for example. Additionally, the change must be *unexpected*, meaning there must be a low probability of its occurrence. In this sense, crises differ from "resource tragedies" – situations where the overuse of a certain natural resource continues for a long time and where the result (the depletion of the resource in question) is therefore not unexpected. Furthermore, the change – or some aspects of it – must be *irreversible*. If, for example, natural resources have relatively short regeneration times and the conditions for their regeneration are met, then the ongoing change is not a crisis. Finally, for it to be considered a crisis, the environmental change must result in a *significant loss of well-being* (health, happiness, material well-being), meaning its impact must be extensive.

Before proceeding, it is worth delving into the concept of the "tragedy of the commons". Taylor uses the term "tragedy" in reference to the classic article "The Tragedy of the Commons" by the ecologist Garrett Hardin (1915–2003). The thesis posited in the article is that, in situations of population growth, the collective management of environmental resources inevitably leads to their depletion (positions such as Hardin's can indeed be called "neo-Malthusian"). Imagine – the article suggests – that access to a limited resource, such as a pasture, is unregulated. Each shepherd will seek to graze as much livestock as possible, and their behaviour will be perfectly rational: while the benefit is individual (more animals from which to profit for the shepherd), the cost (the burden placed on the pasture due to the additional animals) will be shared among all of the shepherds. In the absence of factors limiting the number of shepherds and animals, however, "the inherent logic of the commons remorselessly generates tragedy" (Hardin 1968, p. 1244). The pasture will be overexploited, leading to resource depletion. How to avoid the tragedy? According to Hardin, the collective management of the commons can only succeed under conditions of low population density, necessitating a relinquishment of reproductive freedom. Hardin's model has faced considerable criticism. In particular, political scientist Elinor Ostrom (1933–2012), Nobel laureate in economics in 2009, showed – through numerous concrete examples – that many local communities are capable of self-regulation and managing common resources, establishing effective mechanisms for controlling free riders, that is, those who benefit from a public good without paying for it (Ostrom 1990).

Returning to Taylor's proposal: the label "environmental crisis" – in what I have called "the narrow sense" – will therefore apply to those environmental changes that meet the criteria outlined earlier. But how to know if an environmental crisis so defined is underway? What are the conditions that give rise to a crisis? There are three preconditions that must jointly be met in order for an environmental crisis to arise: poor governance, positive feedbacks arising from the interaction of economic activity and the environment, and the existence of tipping points or critical thresholds. In Taylor's words (2009, p. 1244):

> The mechanism I propose is simple. A shock hits the system (the precipitating event), and it is allowed to propagate because of weak governance. It is magnified by positive feedbacks, and by doing so it crosses a boundary related to the tipping point. The dynamics of the system change irrevocably, environmental quality is driven to its lowest possible level, and we have a crisis.

According to Taylor's "crisis model", climate change could be a crisis in the making, and the situation does not seem to have changed much since he proposed his model in 2009. First, it is difficult to deny that there is an ongoing governance problem. It is enough to recall that the United States, historically the largest emitter of greenhouse gases, did not adhere to the Kyoto Protocol adopted at the third COP (COP 3) in 1997. COP 28 – which took place in 2023 in Dubai – ended with a compromise agreement calling for a "transition away" from fossil fuels after the stronger term "phase out" was blocked by petrostates including Saudi Arabia (and supported by 130 of the 198 countries negotiating in Dubai). And yet, the scientific community agrees that "phasing out fossil fuels is not negotiable" (Nature Editorial 2023). In general, policies to reduce global emissions are not sufficient to keep the temperature below 2°C, let alone the more desirable 1.5°C target mentioned in the Paris Agreement (Fekete *et al.* 2021). Thus, the condition of being a governance problem seems to have been met, unlike the second condition, which does not seem to have been met at the moment (as an example of the fulfilment of the second condition, Taylor suggests an escalating standoff between the superpowers, with each refusing to reduce emissions due to concerns about economic and military disadvantages). Finally, the third condition would seem to have been met, as the climate system appears to be characterised by the presence of tipping points, critical thresholds at which even a small change or perturbation can lead to a significant and often irreversible shift in the state or dynamics of the system (Russill 2015; Padoa-Schioppa 2021, pp. 90ff.).

A possible turning point, for example, could be the melting of the Greenland ice sheet, which is predicted to occur if the increase in temperatures remains between 1°C and 3°C. It is assumed that this will result not only in a rise in sea levels by several metres but also a decrease in the Earth's ability to reflect solar radiation (ice is white, just like the daisies of Daisyworld – see Box 2.3). Moreover, the release of large quantities of fresh water into the oceans could accelerate changes in ocean circulation, which, in turn, could hasten the melting of the East Antarctic ice sheet.

Having clarified what is meant by "environmental crisis", we can now state that there is substantial agreement within the scientific community that an environmental crisis in the broad sense is underway. It is also possible that some of the phenomena associated with the environmental crisis in the broad sense – climate change being one of the most plausible candidates – could lead to environmental crises in the narrow sense outlined earlier. If this is the case, why do many people continue to deny or downplay climate change in particular, and the environmental crisis in general?

5.1.2 Environmental denialism

A "scientific denialist" can be defined as someone who stubbornly and unreasonably refuses to accept results on which the scientific community has reached substantial consensus based on a thorough, critical discussion of the relevant empirical evidence, gathered over the course of prolonged studies.[4]

In the case of the environmental crisis, denialism typically targets climate change (on climate denialism, see Mann 2021) and biodiversity loss (on extinction denialism, see Lees *et al.* 2020). For instance, climate deniers reject the assertion that global warming is occurring or that it is significantly caused by human activities. Similarly, extinction deniers deny that the current extinction rate is far higher than the average rate of the past 10 million years and is accelerating. Alternatively, they may accept the claim concerning the extinction rate but deny that human activities are responsible for it. Essentially, environmental denialism asserts the falsehood of claims found in reports by UNEP, the IPCC, and the IPBES, viewing the scientific consensus on these matters as a conspiracy concocted by the scientific community or politics.

To support their positions, environmental deniers present seemingly rational arguments, such as the idea that we should only accept scientific results that are *beyond all doubt* and *unanimously agreed upon* by the scientific community. However, such stringent standards are not necessary for the validity of scientific findings; disagreement is a normal part of research, alongside the fallibility of knowledge. What is required for a solid and credible result, as emphasised in the title of the preceding section, is substantial consensus based on thorough discussion of the relevant evidence.

For example, within the scientific community it is legitimate and normal to disagree on the applicability of the term "environmental crisis" in a strict sense to the current situation. Some may find the criteria and preconditions set forth by Taylor inadequate and prefer a different model, or they may agree with them but dissent on whether all conditions are currently met. Additionally, scholars like the French sociologist and anthropologist Bruno Latour (1947–2022) argue that the term "crisis" is misleading because "talking about a 'crisis' would be just another way of reassuring ourselves, saying that 'this too will pass', the crisis 'will soon be behind us'" (Latour 2017, p. 7). However, this in no way entails denying or challenging the underlying scientific results upon which it can reasonably be asserted that an environmental crisis (in a broad sense) is underway.

What are the reasons for environmental denialism? A plausible explanation is that the environmental denier is motivated by economic or political interests or is a victim of propaganda linked to economic or political interests. As noted by ecologist Emilio Padoa-Schioppa (2021, p. 107), the strategy of denying the environmental crisis is bolstered by strong economic interests. When climate change became scientifically evident, industries affected by the need to reduce emissions and potentially transition energy sources deployed the techniques of misinformation and obfuscation, akin to past tactics used by the tobacco lobby to cast doubt on scientific findings regarding the harms associated with smoking (Oreskes and Conway 2010). Environmental issues inherently involve broad regulatory interventions by governments, which are inevitably entwined with economic concerns and electoral needs.

Among the more renowned figures of environmental denialism are two political leaders: US President Donald Trump and former Brazilian President Jair Bolsonaro. Despite the United States' standing as the largest historical emitter of CO_2, Trump consistently denied the reality of climate change and sought to undermine scientific findings while in office, to the extent that the journal *Nature* dedicated an article to detailing the damage Trump caused to scientific research and the environment (Tollefson 2020). Bolsonaro famously reacted to satellite data from Brazil's National Institute for Space Research (INPE), which showed an 88 per cent increase in Amazon deforestation in June 2019 compared to the previous year, by dismissing the INPE's data as lies and accusing its director of being in the pockets of foreign NGOs.[5]

While economic interests can explain, at least in part, the denialism of figures like Bolsonaro and Trump, they do not fully explain the denialism among ordinary citizens who do not necessarily cater to one electorate over another. Nor do they explain the attitude of those whom Latour calls "climate quietists" (to distinguish them from standard deniers or "climate sceptics"), whom he characterises as follows:

> Climate quietists, like the others, live in a parallel universe, but, because they have disconnected all the alarms, no strident announcement forces them up from the soft pillow of doubt: "We'll wait and see. The climate has always varied. Humanity has always come through. We have other

things to worry about. The important thing is to wait, and above all not to panic."

(Latour 2017, p. 11)

In addition to economic explanations, at least two other explanations of denialism can be proposed (which jointly clarify various aspects and forms of the phenomenon). The first, which I will not delve into here, is that contemporary societies are characterised by increasing distrust in expertise and scientific competence (Nichols 2017). The second, which I will focus on in the next section, is that environmental denialism, especially climate quietism, is part of a broader category of maladaptive behaviours that our species is exhibiting in a rapidly changing environment (maladaptive behaviours occur when, faced with a range of possible behaviours to choose from, the choice does not result in maximising fitness). To illustrate this point, we need to broaden our perspective, set aside Trump and Bolsonaro, and place the human species among other species. Just like other organisms, *Homo sapiens* must adapt to ongoing changes, and it has various strategies for doing so at its disposal. Like other organisms, however, humans can make bad choices based on environmental signals that were once reliable but have since become unreliable.

5.1.3 It's a trap!

Imagine a bird that is choosing where to build its nest. Its choice will not be random; it will rely on environmental cues, anticipating conditions at the time of hatching, such as the availability of food and foliage for cover. Similarly, a certain plant will decide to bloom when the environment reaches a specific temperature threshold, and the meadow vole we encountered in Chapter 3 will decide whether to develop thick or thin fur based on its mother's melatonin levels (these decisions clearly do not require rationality or consciousness). Such decisions are typically adaptive because they use signals that have been reliable over evolutionary time. If environments change rapidly, however, a certain signal may no longer correspond to a certain outcome: by the time the eggs hatch, the leaves may already have fallen, and food may be scarce. If so, our bird will have fallen into an evolutionary trap. An evolutionary trap occurs when, in a suddenly altered environment, an organism makes non-adaptive decisions based on environmental cues that were once reliable, even though better alternatives exist (Schlaepfer, Runge and Sherman 2002).

Like other organisms, humans must also sometimes adapt to rapid environmental changes. In addition to adaptive strategies shared with other species – migration, behavioural flexibility, phenotypic plasticity, genetic evolution – humans can count on certain specific means of niche modification, such as scientific, technological, and institutional innovations. Just like other organisms, however, humans are making non-adaptive choices due to evolutionary mismatches. A classic example is the rise in obesity, particularly in nations experiencing socio-economic growth, where markets offer food and beverages that were previously unavailable or not easily accessible to all. Today's environment provides abundant high-energy-density foods that stimulate appetite (processed foods and high-fructose corn syrup are pillars of the Western diet). Human physiology, however, has not evolved to cope with such significant and rapid changes in nutrition. The increase in obesity cases can therefore be interpreted as an evolutionary mismatch: the choice of appetising, sugar-rich foods (which increased fitness in the Pleistocene, when humans were much more active than today) has proven maladaptive in the contemporary environment (Gluckman, Hanson and Low 2019).

Other maladaptive choices have broader implications. Despite scientific alarms and empirical evidence, international and global environmental agreements are rarely adhered to, and the data is not encouraging. Carbon dioxide emissions continue to rise (with the exception of the pandemic period: in April 2020, emissions decreased by nearly 20 per cent compared to April of the previous year; Le Quéré et al. 2020). Necessary changes to individual behaviours and productive, social, and institutional systems are slow to materialise.

These maladaptive choices – delaying effective measures – may partly stem from cognitive biases resulting from our own evolution. This is the evolutionary trap into which the species *Homo sapiens*, according to some interpretations, has fallen: those same mechanisms that increased fitness in different environmental conditions have now proven maladaptive in changed circumstances, yet they have not been abandoned (Meneganzin, Pievani and Caserini 2020).

Evolutionary psychology, supported by neuroscientific research, offers this kind of explanation: the fundamental reason why it is difficult to motivate action on environmental problems is that our brains are not wired to respond to large threats that move slowly (as is the case for many environmental issues that involve small, subtle changes that accumulate over time until they produce large-scale effects). The human brain, in fact, is thought to have evolved to respond most effectively to threats with certain properties. Among these is the intention to cause harm: consider the difference between how we would react to the news that, say, 500 people have died from the flu in our country this year and the news that the same number of people (or even just one person) died in a bioterrorism attack. Furthermore, we are more driven to react when threats are imminent and sudden and when the causes are simple and clear, without any ambiguity (in the Pleistocene, when our brains were evolving, the primary need was likely to escape predators and other immediate and direct physical dangers). Environmental threats generally do not possess any of these properties: there are no identifiable intentions, they are rarely imminent and sudden, and their causes form a complex web (Olson and Rejeski 2018). To use a term proposed by the philosopher Timothy Morton (2013), many environmental phenomena – first and foremost global warming – are *hyperobjects*, entities that are diffusely distributed across space and time and that, therefore, cannot be perceived directly.

The fact that the human brain has evolved in a certain way – assuming the hypothesis just presented is correct – does not mean that behaviours cannot be changed and biases corrected. On the contrary, the brain is an extremely plastic organ, and cognitive limitations, once recognised, can be overcome with appropriate measures. It is clear that the necessary changes will be extensive, however, affecting, at a collective level, the entire energy system (we will return to this shortly) and, at a personal level, well-established lifestyles and habits.

Let us now set aside denialism. More simply and reasonably, we can accept scientific results and recognise that the present time calls for a rethinking of theories and practices that, in their traditional form, are likely obsolete and therefore not well equipped to address the contemporary environmental crisis. The old environmentalism and the old concept of nature – some may argue – no longer have a *raison d'être* in the Anthropocene, and it is necessary to declare their demise.

5.2 Environmentalism is dead. Long live environmentalism!

In 2004, an essay titled *The Death of Environmentalism* was published on the internet and gained widespread attention. The message of the essay is clear: environmentalism, in its institutional form, is obsolete and must be abandoned; declaring its death is the only way to make room for the birth of something new. The essay primarily refers to the North American context, asserting that environmentalist politicians should acknowledge their failures and recognise that "modern environmentalism is no longer capable of dealing with the world's most serious ecological crisis" (Shellenberger and Nordhaus 2004, p. 6). What is lacking, the essay argues, is the ability to articulate a vision of the future that is commensurate with the severity of the crisis, and this in at least two respects: in the formulation of legislative proposals, which have thus far been inadequate, and in the formulation of reference concepts to replace the ones that may have become obsolete or, in any case, that are accepted uncritically and not discussed. Although these observations refer to the North American reality, they can stimulate broader reflection.

Let us start with environmentalist politics' inability to formulate legislative proposals commensurate with the scale of the crisis. According to *The Death of Environmentalism*, traditional solutions to environmental problems are not suitable for the current crisis, the scale of which is unprecedented in human history. For instance, the problem of acid rain (precipitation with a lower pH than normal, due to the emission of certain gases into the atmosphere) was successfully addressed in the 1990s with a cap-and-trade policy, that is, the establishment of an emissions market. In practice, a maximum emissions cap was set for each company, which was then allowed to purchase "pollution credits" from other companies that managed to keep their emissions below the cap.

Although both the European Union and the United States have been implementing cap-and-trade policies to tackle climate change for some time in an attempt to limit global CO_2 emissions, the results have been disappointing compared to the acid rain case. In Europe, for example, it seems that much more was achieved by the reduction in consumption due to the restrictions imposed by governments during the pandemic, as can be read on the European Environment Agency's website. The problem is that, while the acid rain crisis was identifiable, already subject to regulation, and limited to specific industrial plants, climate change is a phenomenon of a different magnitude. It involves the global environment, the environment of all living beings. It is not a problem that can be solved by amending an existing law or passing a new one; quite the contrary, solving it would seem to require completely "transform[ing] the world energy economy" (Shellenberger and Nordhaus 2004, p. 15). For this purpose – the essay argues – technical solutions such as hybrid cars and emissions markets are insufficient.

We thus come to the second limitation of traditional environmentalism. In the face of an unprecedented crisis, environmentalist politics must rethink not only the form of its solutions and strategies but its very assumptions about what it means by "environment". More specifically, the essay identifies two erroneous assumptions: considering the environment as a separate "thing", and considering humans as separate from, and superior to, the "natural world". Since they understand the environment in this way, many environmentalists think of the environment as something to protect and defend, recognising themselves as its representatives and defenders. This attitude has led the non-expert public to view environmentalism as a partisan interest, typical of a rich and liberal intellectual segment of society, opposed to the working class.[6]

The preceding considerations show that, in the face of the current environmental crisis, it is indeed necessary to rethink environmentalism from its basic assumptions. The non-exceptionalist and fundamentally relational conception of the environment that has been outlined in this book offers a step in this direction.

Nevertheless, reading *The Death of Environmentalism* may leave one slightly unsatisfied. Even if we grant that "modern environmentalism, with all its unspoken assumptions, obsolete concepts, and exhausted strategies, must die to let something new live" (Shellenberger and Nordhaus 2004, p. 10), what exactly could this "something new" be?

The "new" vision to which the essay refers is so-called "eco-modernism" or "eco-pragmatism", which claims that many scientists recognise that we have entered a new geological epoch, the Anthropocene, and that "knowledge and technology, applied with wisdom, might allow for a good, or even great, Anthropocene".[7] To this end, eco-modernism argues, it is necessary to decouple human development from environmental impact, and what makes this decoupling possible is technology. Indeed, technology is viewed as a means of "reducing humanity's dependence on nature", making humans increasingly independent of ecosystem services (cf. Box 1.2).[8]

Despite some immediate perplexities that reading the manifesto may raise (for example, in what sense would the proposed vision be different from the traditional one, in which humans are separate from the natural world?), its content expresses a vision that is shared by a large segment of humanity, namely that *there is* a solution to the environmental crisis and that it lies in technology and its ability to ensure that human well-being will depend less and less on natural resources (many of which are being depleted). To cite just one (albeit striking) example, consider the production of artificial or synthetic meat (Wurgaft 2020). This could – in principle – address the expected increase in meat consumption (between 73 per cent and 58 per cent in the period from 2010 to 2050, according to FAO estimates)[9] and, at the same time, meet the need to reduce greenhouse gas emissions from the livestock sector.

According to the authors of the book *Techno-Fix: Why Technology Won't Save Us or the Environment* (Huesemann and Huesemann 2011), "techno-optimism", the idea that technological progress will solve the environmental crisis, is as widespread as it is unjustified. One of the reasons is that it is impossible to modify natural systems without producing unforeseen and undesirable consequences. This may or may not be true; the case of DDT discussed in Chapter 3, however, seems to offer an important precedent that can prompt reflection on certain geoengineering proposals, for example.

Geoengineering focuses on the development of technologies that can help us to mitigate or adapt to climate change, such as technologies that can be used to remove greenhouse gases from the atmosphere or to alter Earth's climate. Among these are completely reasonable interventions that are already being successfully implemented, such as reforestation. Other proposals are more controversial because, unlike interventions that fairly accurately replicate processes that have been occurring for millions of years (such as the ecological processes at work in forests), they consist of interventions whose effects are difficult to predict and are potentially uncontrollable. Among these is the idea of fertilising the oceans by introducing iron to increase marine productivity and the consequent photosynthetic activity, thereby converting more carbon dioxide into organic matter. However, large-scale ocean fertilisation could have unexpected negative consequences for marine ecosystems and biogeochemical cycles. For example, it could cause oxygen depletion in the ocean depths (consider the "dead zones" discussed in Chapter 3). It is also reasonable to hypothesise that such a significant environmental change could alter the structure of the oceanic microbial community in the long run. For instance, it could hypothetically cause the oceans to become composed of organisms that produce methane and nitrous oxide, greenhouse gases with a greater potential for climate impact than carbon dioxide. The "final" result of the entire operation might be greater damage than the problem it was intended to solve. In general, it is difficult to foresee the full range of the potential effects of ocean fertilisation on the ocean trophic web structure and ocean dynamics (cf. Huesemann and Huesemann 2011, Chapter 4).

While technological progress is viewed by many as our best means of coping with the environmental crisis, others view technology – the main cause of the environmental crisis along with population growth (Park 2001, p. 10) – as powerless in the absence of a drastic change of perspective. This second direction is advocated by a diverse community of authors belonging to different schools of thought, united by the idea that the environmental crisis requires the adoption of a radically different way of thinking from that which the West has adopted up to now.

Let us take as emblematic of this approach the previously mentioned *Staying with the Trouble* by Donna Haraway, the introduction to which clearly illustrates the author's position:

> The book and the idea of "staying with the trouble" are especially impatient with two responses that I hear all too frequently to the horrors of the Anthropocene and the Capitalocene. The first is easy to describe and, I think, dismiss, namely, a comic faith in technofixes, whether secular or religious: technology will somehow come to the rescue of its naughty but very clever children, or what amounts to the same thing, God will come to the rescue of his disobedient but ever hopeful children. . . . The second response, harder to dismiss, is probably even more destructive: namely, a position that the game is over, it's too late, there's no sense trying to make anything any better.

Rejecting these two attitudes, Haraway views the present time as a fruitful opportunity for a comprehensive ontological revision. According to her, the world is not inherently articulated into static dichotomies (organic/inorganic, humans/other species, natural/artificial, and so on). Instead – as she explains in the third chapter, dedicated to Lynn Margulis[10] – it is a disorderly and creatively confused realm that challenges these dichotomies. In response to the Anthropocene, Haraway describes what she calls the *Chthulucene*,[11] a reality of ongoing development and creation, populated by multispecies beings with fluid spatiotemporal boundaries. Consider, for example, holobionts, functional entities comprising a multicellular host (such as a human organism) and its associated microbiome, or the aforementioned bacterial biofilms, or symbiotic associations (from lichens to coral polyps with their zooxanthellae). Haraway's ontology is fundamentally one in which processes (such as association and kinship) are primary, a relational and dynamic ontology that is non-anthropocentric, egalitarian, and anti-exceptionalist. Despite her deliberately imaginative prose, it is a proposal that presupposes – from a biological and ecological perspective – the Extended Synthesis and Eco-Evo-Devo biology that underpin this book (cf. Box 2.1).

As mentioned, Haraway is part of a broader and diverse community of authors. In the introduction to *Staying with the Trouble*, she provides a list of her "allies", as she calls them, who study science, anthropology, and narrative. Among these we find Isabelle Stengers, Bruno Latour, Thom van Dooren, Anna Tsing, Marilyn Strathern, Hannah Arendt, and Ursula Le Guin. This is a somewhat eclectic list, combining living and deceased authors (philosopher Hannah Arendt died in 1975)[12] from various disciplinary backgrounds (Stengers is a chemist and philosopher of science, Latour a sociologist and anthropologist, Tsing and Strathern anthropologists, van Dooren a philosopher, and Le Guin a renowned writer of science fiction and fantasy). Many of them are theoretical touchstones in the *environmental humanities*, sharing key ideas (see Box 5.1).

Despite their clear distance from ecomodernist proposals, the authors on this (non-exhaustive) list do not espouse primitivist views (see Box 4.2), as might be expected. Instead, they encourage us to challenge blind faith in the reparative power of technology, which is often accompanied by climate quietism and techno-optimism. Additionally, they call on us to recognise that the current Western way of conceptualising nature and the environment, and of managing the human environment, is not the only possible one, nor perhaps the best one. Using Haraway's thinking as an example again, what may leave one dissatisfied about the call for ontological revision (typically accompanied by deconstruction and linguistic revision) is the scarcity – if not absence – of indications regarding how this revision should be translated into individual and collective practice and how and why, once translated, it will enable us to address concrete problems related to the environmental crisis.

Box 5.1 The environmental humanities

The environmental humanities are an interdisciplinary and intercultural field of study that emerged in the 2000s. For the environmental humanities, recognising the need for greater collaboration between the natural and the human sciences (which environmental policies increasingly tend to do, as we saw at the end of the previous chapter) is not sufficient to manage the crisis. Science and technology excel in identifying and explaining environmental problems, but there are issues that only the humanities can resolve; for example, designing a perfectly energy-efficient city is scientifically feasible, but persuading people to invest resources in building and living in one is not merely a scientific problem (Emmett and Nye 2017, p. 1). More broadly, and despite significant differences among proponents of the discipline, some key, shared ideas can be identified, as illustrated here (Oppermann and Iovino 2017; Emmett and Nye 2017).

(i) Every entity is defined by its relationships, is part of a network, and only gains meaning in relation to other entities and its surroundings. For instance, one cannot understand a life form by

> isolating it in a laboratory; one must study it within its environment, where its existence is defined by the relationships it maintains with other organisms.
> (ii) Humans are not independent of nature but part of it. The environment and humanity are inseparably connected. Human exceptionalism, like the nature/culture and natural/artificial dichotomies, is outdated.
> (iii) Humans do not have special rights over other species. Animals and plants should not be seen merely as resources for humans but as entities endowed with intrinsic value and an inherent right to exist.
> (iv) Western cultures are not superior to other cultures; a pluralistic and contextual view is therefore necessary. Not all cultures follow the same trajectory, and Western culture does not represent an ideal endpoint for other forms of culture.

5.3 Conserving nature after the end of nature

Like *The Death of Environmentalism*, *The End of Nature* announced in the title of McKibben's aforementioned book reveals a perceived need to rethink a traditional concept that is no longer deemed suitable for the present time. According to McKibben,

> [s]hort of widescale nuclear war, global warming represents the largest imaginable such [i.e. environmental] alteration: by changing the very temperature of the planet, we inexorably affect its flora, its fauna, its rainfall and evaporation, the decomposition of its soils. Every inch of the planet is different; indeed, the physics of climate means the most extreme changes are going on at the north and south poles, furthest from human beings.
>
> (1989/2003, p. xv)

The global dimension of climate change and its anthropic origins have the consequence that *every inch* of the planet is now influenced by human activity; quite simply, nature is *finished*, if "nature" means that which is in no way influenced by humans.

How to deal with the end of nature? According to Steve Vogel, environmentalism should simply divest itself of the concept of nature (and the preservationist model with it) and deal with the human environment, which is the only thing that remains. Regarding the question of how nature can be preserved, which Vogel considers to be the question of traditional environmentalism, he proposes that we replace it with the question "What are the best practices for the realisation and management of the built environment?":

> If the entire environment has become a built environment, would that not then mean that it was time to think about an *environmentalism of the built environment*? ... [I]f most or all of the world that "environs" us is not natural, shouldn't it be the built environment, and not nature, that is the focus of our environmental concern?
>
> (Vogel 2015, p. 4)

From Vogel's perspective (and more generally from the perspective of "post-natural environmentalism"), the distinction between the two aspects of the human environment referenced in the Stockholm Declaration – natural and man-made (artificial, built) – no longer holds. Nature has come to an end; what remains is the built environment, and it is on the best possible management of the latter that we must focus our efforts.

The traditional concept of nature, however, along with the natural/artificial distinction, is not easily eliminated, either from our minds or from policies and practices aimed at environmental management. Although not scientifically well founded, these concepts are firmly rooted in our ordinary interactions with the world, in our perception and language. Furthermore, beyond the theoretical difficulties highlighted in the previous chapter, *naturalness* plays a fundamental role in our policies and practices for managing the human environment. On the one hand, it serves as an *imperative* for conservation: nature must be preserved. Recall, for example, the claim made in the IPCC press release mentioned at the end of Chapter 3: "Safeguarding and strengthening nature is key to securing a liveable future." How can statements of this kind be reformulated without recourse to the concept of nature or the natural environment? On the other hand, naturalness is an *incentive* for conservation: the term "natural" is immediately understandable to the non-expert public and often – although not always – carries a positive value.

An alternative to eliminating the traditional concept of nature from environmental management practices is to reformulate it: recognising its limits and problems, we might revise the concept to make it usable within specific fields. For example, an operational reformulation of the concept of nature will be particularly important in all those applied sciences that have among their objectives the conservation of nature or natural biodiversity, such as ecological restoration and conservation biology. To this end, philosophy – understood as conceptual negotiation, as illustrated in the introduction to this book – can contribute constructively not only by tracing the history of and examining concepts but also by engaging in metaphysical inquiry.

Before proceeding, a clarification is in order. Following a proposal by the logician and metaphysician Achille Varzi (2011), by "metaphysics" I mean the philosophical discipline that deals with answering the question of the ultimate nature of things (or the question "What is x?"). Metaphysics thus distinguishes itself from ontology, which instead deals with answering the question "What entities exist?" When we ask whether the term "nature" refers to something external to our mind (unlike, say, "winged horse"), we are on the ontological level. If we instead ask what nature is, what type of entity it is (and we respond for example, in an Aristotelian manner, that it is a principle of movement), then we are working on the metaphysical level.[13]

Let us proceed with the exposition of a case of "conceptual negotiation in action" (cf. Introduction), which proposes a possible process for revising the traditional concept of nature and, with it, the natural/artificial distinction. The general context in which we intend to operationalise the concept is that of nature conservation. For simplicity, we will break down the revision into three steps.

First step. Initially, it is necessary to show that the assertion that there is no nature left to conserve is unfounded. If this claim were true, the idea of conserving nature or the natural environment would simply be nonsensical. To this end, it is sufficient to adopt the first Aristotelian or the technical Millian meaning of the term "nature", according to which – let us recall – the term refers to all phenomena that are not supernatural or abstract. We can thus affirm that it is not nature that has ended but rather, as McKibben (1989/2003) himself acknowledges, "a certain set of human ideas about the world and our place in it" (p. 7), that is, nature defined in contrast to and in separation from humans, nature as wilderness, "pristine places, places substantially *unaltered* by man" (p. 56). In other words, the claim that nature has ended must be read on an epistemological rather than an ontological level: a certain "set of human ideas", that is, beliefs, no longer correspond to the underlying reality because, given climate change, there are no longer essentially unaltered places. Furthermore, based on the critiques of the wilderness myth discussed in Chapter 4, it could be that these beliefs – at least in some form – have *never* corresponded to the underlying reality. If our ideas and beliefs about nature have become (or have revealed themselves to be) inadequate, then we are in a position to replace them with better beliefs.

Second step. Recognising that the traditional natural/artificial distinction is scientifically unfounded, we can resort to the Millian solution to the impasse proposed in the previous chapter and rely on the common usage of the term. In this regard, an examination of scientific[14] and popular literature shows that the word "*natural* as used in environmental contexts almost always means that which is neither made, changed, nor otherwise affected by humans" (Johnson *et al.* 1997, p. 582). This definition of "natural" will hence be adopted in what follows.

At this point, in a *third step*, we can proceed with the metaphysical inquiry. First, it seems reasonable to claim, for example, that naturalness is normally understood as a property (and not, say, an object or a process). In the case of conservation sciences and their practices, naturalness will be a property of environments, places, ecosystems, habitats, or other conservation targets. What kind of property? We can start by distinguishing between yes/no properties, such as being an Italian citizen (either one is or one is not) and gradable properties (such as being sweet or being expensive) which can be possessed to a lesser or a greater extent (Lalumera 2009, p. 60; Temkin 2011, pp. 166ff.). While naturalness has traditionally been understood as a yes/no property (recall the Aristotelian position: the principle of change is either internal or external to objects), it is perhaps better understood as a gradable property. On closer inspection, it makes perfect sense to claim that, say, a forest is *more natural* than a skyscraper and that a primitive forest is *more natural* than a plantation, just as it seems sensible – and in keeping with conservation practices – to recognise that a zoo is *highly* artificial, a bio-park is *quite* artificial, and a savannah area is *not very* artificial. If naturalness and artificiality are gradable properties, then it will be possible to (i) reformulate the categorical and fixed distinction between natural and artificial entities and processes into a more dynamic one that recognises that absolute naturalness and artificiality do not exist but are ideal extremes of a continuum and (ii) to provide criteria for assessing these two properties (see, for instance, Anderson 1991; Angermeier 2000).

A second relevant distinction is that between intrinsic and relational properties. While the former can be broadly defined as those properties that an object possesses independently of its surroundings (e.g. mass), relational properties are those that an object possesses in virtue of its interaction with other objects (e.g. position).[15] The traditional conception seems to treat naturalness as an intrinsic property (for Aristotle, nature is an *internal* principle of the object). On closer inspection, however, there are two respects in which it could instead be a relational property: an object can be more or less natural in relation to its degree of dependence on human intervention, on the one hand, and in relation to a certain time, on the other. If *naturalness* is conceived of as a relational property, its use in conservation and restoration projects will be more effective. For example, it will allow us to address some of the inconsistencies alluded to in the previous chapter, such as the fact, related to reforestation, that planting new forests would only increase the number of artefacts on the planet. Indeed, from the perspective suggested here, a forest planted by humans will, at the time of its origin, be less natural than a primitive one. If at a later time the human intervention necessary for its maintenance decreases, however (e.g. because the plants no longer need to be watered), then its naturalness will increase.[16]

More generally, if the concept of naturalness is revised along these lines, then environmental conservation and restoration actions will be understood as intended to maintain or improve the naturalness (as opposed to the artificiality) of certain entities, or even to give rise to artificial objects that can then become natural objects. A characterisation of naturalness along the lines just sketched makes it possible to maintain the natural/artificial distinction by making it more dynamic. In this way, it becomes possible, for example, to trace the changes that an entity subject to environmental conservation undergoes over time in its interaction with our species. It should also be noted that the proposed revision does not deny the obvious biological fact that the human species is part of nature. Rather, it considers the fact that, just like any other species, humans modify their environment: from this perspective, conservation actions are an integral part of the ecosystem engineering practised by humans.

Of course, provided such solutions seem convincing, much work remains to be done. Their effectiveness is in fact relative to specific areas and purposes. Could one also speak of a comprehensive revision? And if so, how to proceed? Furthermore, the definition of "natural" adopted in the second passage is clearly peculiar to Western culture. Is it possible (let alone desirable) to integrate the different conceptions of nature held by different human cultures and individuals into a unified account? If so, how? How should we deal with cases where these come into conflict with each other or with the operationalisation proposed within a specific scientific field? If much work remains to be done when it comes to rethinking the concept of nature, even more work remains – as I have tried to illustrate in this chapter – when it comes to overcoming denialism and to arriving at environmental theories, practices, and policies for dealing with the present situation.

Notes

1 Following a discussion lasting about 15 years, on 26 March 2024, a joint statement by the International Union of Geological Sciences and the International Commission on Stratigraphy announced the Subcommission on Quaternary Stratigraphy's rejection of the proposal to recognise the "Anthropocene Epoch" as a formal unit of the geological time scale (setting its beginning in 1952, the year plutonium from hydrogen bomb tests appeared in the sediments of Crawford Lake in Canada). As a result, *geologically* speaking, we are still in the Holocene. The Anthropocene does not meet the formal criteria for being classified as a geological epoch alongside the Holocene and the Pleistocene.
2 A disturbed state is considered irreversible on a given timescale if the recovery time would be significantly longer than the time it took for the system to reach the disturbed state. Among the potentially irreversible phenomena related to climate change, the IPCC lists the collapse of glaciers and the release of carbon from permafrost (ground, typical of the extreme North of the planet, where the soil is perpetually frozen).
3 For illustrative purposes, I shall present Taylor's proposal in a very simplified form, omitting all technical details of his "crisis model". I trust that my presentation faithfully conveys the spirit of the original formulation.
4 The definition reported partly mirrors that proposed by the environmental engineer Stefano Caserini (quoted in Padoa-Schioppa 2021, p. 106), enriched in light of Casetta and Tambolo (2022).
5 See, for example, Dom Phillips's article "Brazil Space Institute Director Sacked in Amazon Deforestation Row", published on the *Guardian*'s website on 2 August 2019.

6 Conservative political leaders who oppose environmental policies have both promoted and benefitted from this attitude. As *The Death of Environmentalism* reports, according to a survey conducted on 1,500 subjects by the market research company Environics, the number of Americans who agree with the statement "To preserve people's jobs in this country, we must accept higher levels of pollution in the future" increased from 17 per cent in 1996 to 26 per cent in 2000. The number of Americans who agree with the statement "Most of the people actively involved in environmental groups are extremists, not reasonable people" rose from 32 per cent in 1996 to 41 per cent in 2000 (Shellenberger and Nordhaus 2004, p. 11).
7 *An Ecomodernist Manifesto* is available on the website of the Breakthrough Institute, the environmental research centre founded in 2007 by Shellenberger and Nordhaus.
8 That technology has the capacity to make humans increasingly independent of ecosystem services is far from certain; see, for example, Costanza *et al.* (1997, p. 255).
9 The data come from the website of the European Environment Agency: https://www.eea.europa.eu/publications/artificial-meat-and-the-environment. Consulted 14 June 2024.
10 We encountered Lynn Margulis in Chapter 2 in our discussion of the Gaia hypothesis. However, her fame is primarily associated with her studies on the role of symbiosis in evolution, particularly in the evolution of eukaryotic cells.
11 The term "Chthulucene", as explained by Haraway in the introduction to her book, derives from the Greek *khtkôn* and *kainos*: "earth" and "now". With *khtkôn*, Haraway refers to chthonic deities, "beings of the Earth [who] romp in multicritter humus". *Kainos*, on the other hand, "means now, a time of beginnings, a time for ongoing, for freshness" (Haraway 2016, pp. 13–14).
12 Haraway includes Hannah Arendt (1906–1975) in her list of "allies" to highlight the importance of an action that is inherently connected with "staying with trouble": *thinking*. It was precisely an absence of thought that constituted the "banality of evil" at the heart of Arendt's analysis (Arendt 1963) of the Nazi criminal Adolf Eichmann. Focused on his bureaucratic task (organising the transports of Jews to extermination camps), Eichmann appeared to Arendt, who attended his trial as a correspondent for the *New Yorker*, not as an extraordinary monster but as a mediocre man, like many others. His actions were monstrous, but what Arendt observed in him was a banal incapacity for thought.
13 Such a characterisation of ontology and metaphysics is neither universally accepted nor without alternatives; for a more complete exposition and defence, see Varzi (2011). For the proposed revision of the concept of nature included in this section, I refer to Casetta (2020).
14 Note that the fact that the natural/artificial distinction is not scientifically well founded does not mean that it is not used – in the sense referred to here – within the scientific literature.
15 Cf. Lewis (1983). For a sceptical position on the existence of intrinsic properties, see Borghini (2010).
16 Note, however, that the issue of the value of the forest (i.e. whether a restored forest is less valuable because it is less natural than a primitive one; cf. Elliot 1982; Katz 1992) remains unsettled.

References

Anderson, J.E. (1991) 'A conceptual framework for evaluating and quantifying naturalness', *Conservation Biology*, 5(3), pp. 347–352.
Angermeier, P.L. (2000) 'The natural imperative for biological conservation', *Conservation Biology*, 14(2), pp. 373–381.

Arendt, H. (1963/2022) *Eichmann in Jerusalem: A Report on the Banality of Evil*. London: Penguin Books.

Borghini, A. (2010) 'Esistono proprietà intrinseche?', *Rivista di estetica*, 43(1), pp. 231–245.

Casetta, E. (2020) 'Making sense of nature conservation after the end of nature', *History and Philosophy of the Life Sciences*, 42(18). https://doi.org/10.1007/s40656-020-00312-3.

Casetta, E. and Tambolo, L. (2022) 'Negazionismo ambientale e crisi dell' expertise', *Paradigmi*, XL(2), pp. 245–264.

Costanza, R. et al. (1997) 'The value of the world's ecosystem services and natural capital', *Nature*, 387, pp. 253–260.

Díaz, S. et al. (eds.) (2019) *Summary for Policymakers of the Global Assessment Report on Biodiversity and Ecosystem Services of the Intergovernmental Science-Policy Platform on Biodiversity and Ecosystem Services*. Bonn: IPBES Secretariat.

Elliot, R. (1982) 'Faking Nature', *Inquiry*, 25, pp. 81–93.

Emmett, S. and Nye, D.E. (2017) *The Environmental Humanities: A Critical Introduction*. Cambridge, MA: MIT Press.

Fekete, H. et al. (2021) 'A review of successful climate change mitigation policies in major emitting economies and the potential of global replication', *Renewable and Sustainable Energy Reviews*, 137, art. n. 110602.

Gluckman, P.D., Hanson, M.A. and Low, F.M. (2019) 'Evolutionary and developmental mismatches are consequences of adaptive developmental plasticity in humans and have implications for later disease risk', *Philosophical Transactions of the Royal Society B: Biological Sciences*, 374, art. n. 20180109.

Haraway, D. (2016) *Staying with the Trouble: Making Kin in the Chthulucene*. Durham, NC: Duke University Press.

Hardin, G. (1968) 'The tragedy of the commons', *Science*, 162, pp. 1243–1248.

Huesemann, M. and Huesemann, J. (2011) *Techno-Fix: Why Technology Won't Save Us or the Environment*. Gabriola Island, BC: New Society.

Jax, K. (2023) *Conservation Concepts: Rethinking Human–Nature Relationships*. London: Routledge.

Johnson, D.L. et al. (1997) 'Meaning of environmental terms', *Journal of Environmental Quality*, 26, pp. 581–589.

Katz, E. (1992) 'The big lie: Human restoration of nature', *Research in Philosophy and Technology*, 12, pp. 231–241.

Lalumera, E. (2009) *Cosa sono i concetti*. Roma-Bari: Laterza.

Latour, B. (2017) *Facing Gaia: Eight Lectures on the New Climatic Regime*. Translated by C. Porter. Cambridge, UK and Malden, MA: Polity.

Le Quéré, C. et al. (2020) 'Temporary reduction in daily global CO_2 emissions during the COVID-19 forced confinement', *Nature Climate Change*, 10, pp. 647–653.

Lees, A.C. et al. (2020) 'Biodiversity scientists must fight the creeping rise of extinction denial', *Nature Ecology & Evolution*, 4, pp. 1440–1443. https://doi.org/10.1038/s41559-020-01285-z.

Lewis, D. (1983) 'Extrinsic properties', *Philosophical Studies*, 44, pp. 197–200.

Mann, M.E. (2021) *The New Climate War: The Fight to Take Back Our Planet*. Melbourne and London: Scribe.

McKibben, B. (1989/2003) *The End of Nature*. London: Bloomsbury.

Meneganzin, A., Pievani, T. and Caserini, S. (2020) 'Anthropogenic climate change as a monumental niche construction process: Background and philosophical aspects', *Biology & Philosophy*, 35, art. n. 38.

Morton, T. (2013) *Philosophy and Ecology after the End of the World*. Minneapolis, MN: University of Minnesota Press.

Nature Editorial (2023) 'COP28: The science is clear – fossil fuels must go', *Nature*. Dec; 624(7991), p. 225. https://doi.org/10.1038/d41586-023-03955-x.

Nichols, T. (2017) *The Death of Expertise: The Campaign against Established Knowledge and Why It Matters*. New York: Oxford University Press.

Olson, R.L. and Rejeski, D. (2018) 'Slow threats and environmental policy', *Environmental Law Reporter*, 48(2), art. n. 10116.

Oppermann, S. and Iovino, S. (eds.) (2017) *Environmental Humanities: Voices from the Anthropocene*. London and New York: Rowman & Littlefield.

Oreskes, N. and Conway, E.M. (2010) *Merchants of Doubt: How a Handful of Scientists Obscured the Truth on Issues from Tobacco Smoke to Global Warming*. London: Bloomsbury.

Ostrom, E. (1990) *Governing the Commons: The Evolution of Institutions for Collective Action*. Cambridge: Cambridge University Press.

Padoa-Schioppa, E. (2021) *Antropocene. Una nuova epoca per la Terra, una sfida per l'umanità*. Bologna: il Mulino.

Park, C. (2001) *The Environment: Principles and Applications*, 2nd edition. London and New York: Routledge.

Pörtner, H.-O. et al. (eds.) (2022) 'Summary for policymakers', in Pörtner, H.-O. et al. (eds.) *Climate Change 2022: Impacts, Adaptation and Vulnerability. Contribution of Working Group II to the Sixth Assessment Report of the Intergovernmental Panel on Climate Change*. Cambridge, UK and New York, NY: Cambridge University Press, pp. 3–33. https://doi.org/10.1017/9781009325844.001.

Russill, C. (2015) 'Climate change tipping points: Origins, precursors, and debates', *WIREs Climate Change*, 6, pp. 472–434.

Schlaepfer, M.A., Runge, M.C. and Sherman, P.W. (2002) 'Ecological and evolutionary traps', *Trends in Ecology and Evolution*, 17, pp. 474–480.

Shellenberger, M. and Nordhaus, T. (2004) *The Death of Environmentalism*. Available at: https://s3.us-east-2.amazonaws.com/uploads.thebreakthrough.org/legacy/images/Death_of_Environmentalism.pdf (Accessed 14 June 2024).

Taylor, M.S. (2009) 'Innis lecture: Environmental crises: Past, present, and future', *The Canadian Journal of Economics/Revue canadienne d'Economique*, 42(4), pp. 1240–1275.

Temkin, L.S. (2011) *Rethinking the Good: Moral Ideals and the Nature of Practical Reasoning*. Oxford: Oxford University Press.

Tollefson, J. (2020) 'How Trump damaged science', *Nature*, 586, pp. 190–194.

UN Environment (2019) *Global Environment Outlook – GEO-6: Summary for Policymakers*. Nairobi. https://doi.org/10.1017/9781108639217.

Varzi, A.C. (2011) 'On doing ontology without metaphysics', *Philosophical Perspectives*, 25, pp. 407–423.

Vogel, S. (2015) *Thinking Like a Mall: Environmental Philosophy after the End of Nature*. Cambridge, MA: MIT Press.

Wurgaft, B.A. (2020) *Meat Planet: Artificial Flesh and the Future of Food*. Berkeley, CA: University of California Press.

Conclusion

In the introduction to this volume, I highlighted how, just over 50 years ago, interest in environmental issues was the preserve of a few, who were mostly ridiculed or, at any rate, not taken seriously. The sciences of conservation and environmental management did not exist as independent fields, or played only a marginal role. The systemic approach to studying the planet was viewed with some suspicion (consider the criticisms that greeted the Gaia hypothesis), and little was known about the functioning of the biosphere.

In general, we now know much more about environmental issues than we did back then. With the emergence of sciences specifically dedicated to the conservation of the natural environment (from restoration ecology to conservation biology) and to understanding the functioning of the planet (the Earth System Science), along with significant global investments, our knowledge of the impact of human activities has advanced at an unprecedented rate. In just over 50 years, public awareness has also greatly increased, at least concerning climate change. We are undoubtedly behind schedule (and this delay has been, and continues to be, exacerbated by environmental denialism). Compared to 50 years ago, however, we are now engaged with the problem, and I agree with Haraway (2016, p. 1) when she writes that

> Staying with the trouble does not require such a relationship to times called the future. In fact, staying with the trouble requires learning to be truly present, not as a vanishing pivot between awful or edenic pasts and apocalyptic or salvific futures, but as mortal critters entwined in myriad unfinished configurations of places, times, matters, meanings.

Being truly present as interconnected creatures means, from the perspective I have adopted, recognising that the human environment is part of the environment of all living beings. Staying with the trouble requires resisting simplifications, whether the myth of the noble savage and the golden age, the Hobbesian state of nature, or what Sahotra Sarkar (2005, p. 32) calls "an inexorable faith in human ingenuity", the blind belief that technology will save us from catastrophe, a belief that is counterbalanced, of course, by the conviction that *there will* be a catastrophe. The catastrophist attitude risks having the same paralysing outcomes as primitivism based on the myth of the golden age or blind faith in technological solutions. If the only way to manage the environmental crisis is to return to an ideal Arcadian state of harmony between humans and nature, then little can be done beyond invoking the providential advent of such a state. If, on the other hand, one thinks that technology will save us, then it will suffice to wait for the development of adequate technologies. If, finally, undetermined catastrophes continue to threaten, then a "crying wolf" effect will be generated. In all cases, as Emilio Padoa-Schioppa (2021, p. 104) observes, there is a risk of obscuring the necessity of rethinking the current economic paradigm and the consumption of natural resources.

With this volume, I have sought to make a contribution – a drop in the ocean – to meeting the evolutionary challenge that the environmental crisis poses to our species. In particular, from the perspective of philosophy as conceptual negotiation, I have pursued a specific goal: that of highlighting the causal relationships between life – both human and non-human – and the environment. If these relationships are now a bit clearer, environmentalism – understood as a set of policies, ethics, and practices aimed at the conservation and management of the environment of living beings – should no longer be viewed as the sole preserve of hippie tree-huggers or intellectuals who don't need to worry about earning a living. In fact, health, development, and the evolution of all organisms, including humans, depend on the environment. With that in mind, shouldn't we all define ourselves as environmentalists?

References

Haraway, D. (2016) *Staying with the Trouble: Making Kin in the Chthulucene*. Durham, NC: Duke University Press.
Padoa-Schioppa, E. (2021) *Antropocene. Una nuova epoca per la Terra, una sfida per l'umanità*. Bologna: il Mulino.
Sarkar, S. (2005) *Biodiversity and Environmental Philosophy. An Introduction*. Cambridge: Cambridge University Press.

Index

2°C 1, 39, 95, 101n10, 148; *see also* threshold

abiogenesis hypothesis 68
adaptation 9–12, 21, 39, 42, 45–51, 57, 58, 74, 84, 88, 98, 145
Adaptedness 45, 48
affordance 26, 34n11
agriculture 80, 83, 87, 96, 99, 101n6, 126–129, 138
Alberti di Villanova, Francesco 10
Alembert, J-Baptiste Le Rond d' 125
Amazon: rainforest 2, 131, 150 tribes 39, 40, 72, 83–84, 131
Amrita Devi 7
Andina, Tiziana 94
anthropocene 85, 95–97, 102n11, 144, 153–156, 162n1
Arendt, Hannah 157, 163n12
Aristotle 26, 101n4, 106–109, 112, 114, 139n3, 161
artificial meat 155
Ashoka (Indian emperor) 126
atmosphere 17, 41–42, 61–63, 66, 68n4–5, 95–96, 99, 117, 118, 155

bacteria 42, 60–61, 77, 79, 84, 95–96, 112, 119, 120, 156; *see also* microorganisms
balance of nature 23, 28–32, 34n13
Beaver dam 2, 55–56, 60, 82, 111–115; *see also* niche construction theory
Bees 51, 81, 101n8
behavioural flexibility 27, 74, 98, 100n2, 151
Bentham, Jeremy 140n17
Bernard, Claude 19–20, 61–63
Bichat, Xavier 18, 34n6

biodiversity 1, 3, 9, 40, 42, 47, 85, 93, 94, 97, 133, 140n14, 146, 149, 159; crisis 40, 47; *see also* Convention on Biological Diversity; extinction
biogeochemical cycles 62, 63, 118, 155; *see also* biosphere
biosemiotics 25, 39
biosphere 2, 8, 41–42, 66, 67, 68n4, 85, 97, 99, 118, 120, 166; theory 39, 56, 61–64, 94
Boggs, Carol 97
Bolsonaro, Jair 84, 150, 151
Bonpland, Aimé 16, 17, 34n4
Borghini, Andrea 119
Botkin, Daniel 30
Brandon, Robert N. 45–46, 50, 68n6
Brundtland Report 93; *see also* human future generations; sustainability
Buffon, G.-Louis Leclerc de 26

Callicott, J. Baird 113, 115, 130, 136, 140n13
Canguilhem, George 3, 7n2, 9, 10
cap-and-trade 153, 154
Capitalocene 83–86
carbon dioxide 17, 42, 61, 95, 96, 99, 118, 152, 155; *see also* greenhouse gas
carbon sinks 118, 121
Carlyle, Thomas 20
Carson, Rachel 8, 89–93, 99
Casati, Roberto 5
Caserini, Stefano 100, 162n4
catastrophe view *see* climate catastrophe view
causation and causal relations 6, 11, 12, 13, 15, 18, 22, 38, 41, 44, 46, 50–56, 58, 64, 73, 75–76, 78, 79, 90, 107, 133, 140n12, 146, 167

Index

CBD (Convention on Biological Diversity) 1, 47, 68n8
cells: cancer or tumour 61, 78; differentiation 50; environment 76, 77; eukaryotic 163n10; human 9; immune 79
charismatic megafauna 88, 101n8
chemosynthesis 42
Chthulucene 156, 163n11; *see also* Anthropocene
circumstances or conditions 6, 10, 11–22, 28, 41, 42, 48, 49, 59–61, 74–76, 78, 82, 86, 87, 97, 114, 120, 151–152
Clements, Frederic 31, 32
climate catastrophe view 95
climate change 3, 8, 17, 25, 39, 40, 47, 48, 54, 73, 93, 94, 97–99, 105, 113, 120, 121, 124, 133, 144–155, 158, 160, 162n2, 166; *see also* denialism; IPCC
climate change convention 1, 93, 101n10
climate crisis 5; *see also* climate change
climate modelling 64
Club of Rome 2
cognitive biases 152–153
Cold War 67
Coleridge, Samuel Taylor 122
colonialism 34n7, 88, 126–128, 130; *see also* environmentalism: birth of
Comte, Auguste 9, 18–21, 26, 34n6, 88
conservation biology 159, 166
conservation sciences 39, 166; *see also* conservation biology
conservation vii, 1, 2, 4, 30, 32, 47, 48, 72, 88, 100, 101n8, 105, 124, 126–139, 140n14, 159, 160–162, 167; *see also* biodiversity; conservation biology; cultural heritage; cultural landscapes; ecological livelihood; environmental stewardship; forests; restoration ecology; resourcism; preservationism
coral bleaching 120
coronavirus 9, 80; *see also* viruses
correspondence 15, 19–21, 26, 38, 42–43, 49, 57, 59, 61, 63–66, 73, 84; *see also* organism-environment dyad or pair
Crutzen, Paul 96
cultural heritage 92, 132
cultural landscapes 134, 140n15

cultural niche construction 80–83, 90; *see also* human niche construction
cultural primitivism 123–125, 127, 129, 167; *see also* transcendentalism
cybernetic system 64, 66
cybernetics 39, 56

Daisyworld model 64, 65–66, 149
Darwin, Charles 21–23, 26, 27–29, 43, 45, 56, 57, 82, 87
Darwin, Erasmus 12
Dawkins, Richard 41, 66–67
DDT 89–92, 155
dead zones 99, 155
deep ecology 101n5
deforestation 6n1, 8, 17, 39, 40, 83–84, 89, 96, 127–128, 138, 140n12, 146, 150; *see also* Amazon; forests
denialism 144, 149–153, 162, 166
Descartes, René 112
developmental biology 4, 43, 44, 76, 77
Diderot, Denis 125
DNA 41–42, 45, 50, 77, 92; DNA methylation 76; *see also* gene expression
Dobzhansky, Theodosius 43
domestication and domesticated organisms 80, 87, 113, 119, 126, 129, 131

earth system 61–67, 95, 96, 138; science 67, 68n10, 166; *see also* biosphere
Eco-Devo (Ecological Developmental Biology) 44, 50, 51, 79
Eco-Evo-Devo (Ecological Evolutionary Developmental Biology) 44, 156
ecofeminism 110n5
ecological engineering 32
ecological footprint 136
ecological livelihood 129, 136
ecology 4, 9, 14, 15, 23, 34n12, 39, 43, 44, 55, 62, 63, 102n12, 136; definition of 27–28; origin of 26–32, 46
ecomodernism 157, 163n7
economy of nature 28–32
ecosystem 16, 25, 30, 31, 46, 47, 62–63, 66, 68n8, 85, 90, 92, 94–98, 118, 120, 121, 133–138, 139n7, 139n10, 140n16, 145, 146, 155, 161; design 32; engineering 53, 55–56, 58, 59, 73, 79, 86–89, 118, 162; restoration

32; services 32–33, 90, 123, 137, 154, 163n8; stress 139n8
Elliot, Robert 134
Elton, Charles 31
embryogenesis 11–12
Emerson, Ralph Waldo 121–123
emissions: containment and reduction 1, 117, 145, 148, 150, 152; market (*see* cap-and-trade)
empiricism 122
energy 41, 45, 57, 61, 67, 75, 82, 86, 88, 99, 118, 121, 152, 157; flow 62, 118; regime 8, 96; solar 41–42, 62, 63; transition 150, 154
Engelke, Peter 84, 98
environment: as an anthropocentric concept 5, 119, 137; artificial 2, 6, 72, 82, 105, 106, 108, 111–117, 128, 129, 159, 161; built 159 (*see also* artificial); concept of 3, 4, 6, 8–21, 28, 38–41, 73, 126, 144; cultural (*see* cultural landscapes; cultural niche construction); developmental 50–52, 75–79, 92; ecological 42–52, 73–75, 79, 82, 83, 92; edible 119; external 19, 20, 46, 48, 60, 64, 77; and genes 43, 59, 77, 79 (*see also* gene expression and genes-environment); global 2, 39, 40, 67, 95, 154; human 2, 5, 6, 38, 49, 72–104, 117–120, 128, 138, 157–159, 166; internal 19, 28; natural 2, 4, 32, 39, 40, 72, 105, 106, 109, 113–138, 145, 159, 160, 166 (*see also* conservation; nature; natural/artificial distinction); and organism (*see* organism-environment dyad or pair); and organism health 2, 9, 11, 30, 73, 89, 99, 117, 121, 127, 147, 167; selective 48–49, 68n6, 75, 82 (*see also* selective pressures); subjective 23–26, 57
environmental crisis 3, 5, 6, 15, 86, 114, 119, 144, 145–150, 153–157, 167; *see also* biodiversity: crisis; climate crisis
environmental ethics 4, 83, 136
environmental humanities 157
environmentalism 4, 6, 15–16, 138, 144, 167; birth of 30, 127–130, 140n12; definition of 126; history of 89, 93; manifesto of 1; death of 153–157; post-natural 158–159

environmental philosophy 2, 3, 40, 68n8
environmental policies vii, 2, 32, 84, 94, 105, 115, 116, 126, 137, 138, 140n12, 148, 154, 157, 159, 162, 163n6, 167
environmental protection 7n1, 93, 105, 106, 116, 126–138, 140n12; *see also* conservation
environmental restoration 113, 133–134, 161; *see also* ecosystem: restoration
environmental sciences 68n9, 106
environmental sex determination 51–53, 97
environmental signals 51, 76–79, 151; *see also* phenology
environmental stewardship 129, 136–137
environmental studies 40, 67n3
epigenetic processes or mechanisms 76, 78
epigenetics 44
ethology 25, 39
European Biodiversity Strategy for 2030 105, 113, 118, 120
Evo-Devo (Evolutionary Developmental Biology) 44
evolution: cultural 42, 80–83; as development 11; of eukaryotic cells 163n10; human (*see* human evolution); Lamarckian 12, 14; of life (*see* life: evolution of); by natural selection 34n12, 42, 43, 44, 53, 56, 58, 59, 66–67, 89, 97, 98, 115, 120, 146, 167
evolutionary biology 4, 6, 9, 43, 44, 56, 84, 100n2, 112, 113
evolutionary psychology 152
evolutionary theory: by natural selection 21–23, 27–28, 43, 46–47, 57, 81, 112; extended (*see* Extended Evolutionary Synthesis); Lamarckian 9, 10, 12–15, 81
evolutionary traps 98, 151–153
explorations 8, 16
extended evolutionary synthesis 43–44, 84, 156
external conditions 6, 11, 15, 20, 28, 61; *see also* circumstances
extinction 39, 40, 46, 47, 52, 74, 87–89, 96, 98, 116, 120, 136, 149; *see also* mass extinctions

Index

feedback 19, 23, 52, 56, 58, 61, 65, 67, 78, 84, 97, 138, 148; *see also* cyclic causation
Feldman, Marcus 58
Ferraris, Maurizio 81, 111, 115
fitness 22, 33n2, 45, 46, 58, 60, 66, 74, 80, 89, 90, 98, 99, 151, 152
Fixism 12
fluid 10, 12–14, 18, 77, 78; *see also* medium
food 11, 27, 32, 40, 51, 55, 74, 77, 78, 81, 87, 90, 99, 119, 137, 151, 152
Foote, Eunice 17
forests 2, 15, 17, 23, 45, 83–84, 85, 90, 105, 106, 115, 117–119, 121, 124, 126–129, 131, 133–136, 138, 139n11, 140n12, 146, 155, 161, 163n16; *see also* deforestation
fossil fuels 8, 15, 96, 99, 118, 148; *see also* emissions
functional cycles 24
future human generations 82, 92–94, 129

Gaia hypothesis 39, 56, 63–67, 94, 163n10, 166
garbage patches 115, 117, 139n4
gene expression 53, 75–76, 92; *see also* genes-environment; genotype
genes-environment 43
genome 45, 76, 77; *see also* genotype
genotype 45–46, 48, 49, 50, 54, 75, 110; *see also* DNA; gene expression; genes-environment
GEO (Global Environment Outlook) 1, 2, 145
geoengineering 97, 155
Gibson, James J. 25–26, 34n11
global warming 1, 3, 40, 48, 88, 145–146, 149, 152; *see also* climate change
globalisation 49, 79
Godfrey-Smith, Peter 112
goods 32–33, 121, 123, 136, 137; *see also* tragedy of the commons
great acceleration 98
great oxidation 61, 95
greenhouse gas 1, 95, 99, 117, 148, 155; *see also* emissions
growth: economic 1–2, 93–94, 152; of organisms 11, 12, 65, 78, 99; of population 15, 27, 46–48, 60, 88, 98, 121, 147, 156

habitat 14, 29, 55, 74, 85–88, 98, 101n3, 134, 136–138, 161
Haeckel, Ernst 27–28
Haldane, John B.S. 68n5
Haraway, Donna 144, 156–157, 163n11, 166
Hardin, Garrett 147
harmony 18–19, 26, 125, 127, 167
Hippocrates 11
Hobbes, Thomas 124–125
homeostasis 19–20, 63–64, 66–67
human evolution 72–75, 80–83, 151, 152
human exceptionalism 111–117, 154, 156, 158
human nature 124
human niche construction 82–100
Humboldt, Alexander von 9, 14–18, 20, 21, 23, 26, 27, 30, 34n4, 62, 63, 67, 124, 127, 128
Hume, David 54, 110
Hume's law 110
Huneman, Philippe 32
Hutchinson, George Evelyn 62

ice melting 149
indigenous people 4, 83–84, 125, 131, 139n6
information 24, 45–46, 50, 51, 75, 77–78, 80–82, 112
inheritance: of acquired traits 13, 43; behavioural 44; cultural 44, 82; ecological 44, 59, 82, 129; epigenetic 44, 76, 92; genetic 43, 44, 59, 76; symbolic 44
intergenerational equity, principle of 93–94
IPBES (Intergovernmental Science-Policy Platform on Biodiversity and Ecosystem Services) 47, 145, 146, 149
IPCC (Intergovernmental Panel on Climate Change) 1, 62, 88, 100, 145, 149, 159, 162n2

Jablonka, Eva 44, 45, 76, 81
Jonas, Hans 93

Kant, Immanuel 23–24, 34n7, 122
Katz, Eric 133–134
Khejarli massacre 6n1
Kyoto Protocol 1, 148

Laland, Kevin N. 58
Lamarck, J.-Baptiste de 9, 10, 12–15, 18, 20, 22, 23, 26, 33n1, 34n3, 45, 77, 78
Lamb, Marion 44, 45, 76, 81
Latour, Bruno 150–151, 156, 157
Le Guin, Ursula 157
Leopold, Aldo 135–136, 138
Lévêque, Christian 131
Lewontin, Richard C. 50, 57–58
life: conditions of 11, 63 (*see also* circumstances); evolution of 13, 61; origin of 41, 42, 61, 63, 68n5, 95–96; quality of 83–84, 94; right to 2, 101n5; theories of 18, 20, 34n6; *see also* biosphere; correspondence; Gaia hypothesis
Linnaeus 26, 28–30
Locke, John 122
Lovelock, James 63–66
Lyell, Charles 18

Mace, Georgina 137, 138
maladaptive behaviour or choice 151–152; *see also* adaptation
malaria 90, 92, 99, 101n9
Malthus, Thomas Robert 27
Margulis, Lynn 63, 66, 156, 163n10
Marsh, George Perkins 128–129
mass extinctions 95, 96, 100
McKibben, Bill 117, 158, 160
McNeil, John 84, 96, 98
medium 6, 10, 13, 19, 42, 54, 60, 65, 77
Mendel, Gregor 43
Meneganzin, Andra 100
metabolism 9, 33n2, 55, 61, 74
metaphysic 160, 163n13; *see also* ontology
microenvironment 77–78, 92
microorganisms 42, 62, 86, 119; *see also* bacteria
microplastics 116, 139n4, 139n7
Milieu or *Milieux* 7n2, 10–13, 18, 21, 34n3, 78; *see also* medium
Mill, John Stuart 110, 114–116, 140n17
Millennium Ecosystem Assessment 122, 139n10
modern synthesis 34n12, 43–44, 57, 76; *see also* evolutionary theory: by natural selection
Moore, Jason 84–86
Morton, Timothy 152–153

Muir, John 129–130, 136
mutations 33n2, 88, 92, 112
myths: Edenic 131; of the golden age 125–126, 167; of the noble savage 125–126, 166; of the wilderness 160; *see also* wilderness

Naess, Arne 101n5
natural capital 32–33, 83
natural or environmental resources 2, 3, 10, 16–17, 27, 30, 33, 46–47, 55, 56, 59, 74–75, 78, 79, 83–88, 93, 99, 105, 106, 117–121, 127–129, 134–137, 146–148, 155, 158, 167; *see also* tragedy of the commons
natural reserve 130, 132–135, 136, 138, 140n12
natural sciences 20, 21, 108–110, 138
natural selection 21–23, 29, 34n7, 50–52, 57, 59, 67, 73, 88, 97, 112; *see also* evolution: by natural selection
natural/artificial distinction 2, 6, 105, 106, 113–117, 119, 128, 134, 139n11, 144, 156, 158–162, 163n14
naturalness 110, 111, 113–117, 159–162
nature: Aristotle's view of 106–109, 114, 133, 160, 161; and art 18, 107–109, 115, 134–135 (*see also* cultural heritage); and culture 122, 124–125, 130, 132, 138, 158; concept of 5, 6, 8, 9, 144, 153, 158–160, 162, 163n13; conservation of (*see* conservation); end of 117, 144, 158–159; exploitation of 3, 16, 17, 33, 34n7, 47, 79, 84–86, 127, 135, 146 (*see also* natural or environmental resources; sustainability; value); force of 13–14; holistic or systemic view of 17–18, 30, 63, 90; Humboldt's view of 17, 18, 30, 62, 63, 124; integrity of 93; Mill's view of 115–117; monetization of 33 (*see also* ecosystem services); humans and 9, 33, 105, 127, 132, 136–138, 167 (*see also* natural/artificial distinction); pristine 40, 117–118, 121, 129, 131, 133, 137 (*see also* wilderness; wildness); teleological view 33; *see also* balance of nature; economy of nature;

environment: natural; natural/
artificial distinction; natural or
environmental resources; value:
instrumental
network or web: of causes 50, 152;
biospheric 101n5; of genes 53, 75;
of relations 6, 8, 18, 22, 27, 28, 30,
157; trophic 155
niche construction theory 23, 39, 44,
53, 56–61, 80, 82
Niger Delta 85–86
Nordhaus, William 95

Odling-Smee, John 58
oil 85–86, 96, 118–120
ontology and ontological 66, 94, 113,
132, 156, 157, 160, 163n13; see also
metaphysics
Oparin, Alexander 68n5
organism: development of 11–12, 14,
25, 39, 43–46, 50–53, 58, 59, 68n6,
73, 75–79, 89, 102n12, 106, 107,
109–110, 146, 156, 167 (see also
embryogenesis; gene expression;
phenotypic plasticity); and
environment (see environment: and
organism); functioning 19, 29; model
50; physiology 11, 21, 28, 56–57, 59,
80, 114, 152
organism-environment dyad or pair 6,
8, 9, 11, 18–21, 61
Ostrom, Elinor 147

Padoa-Schioppa, Emilio 150, 167
Paris agreement 1, 101n10, 148
Peccei, Aurelio 2
perturbations 29, 32, 64, 148
pesticides 88, 89, 99; see also DDT
phenology and phenological 98,
102n12, 124, 146
phenotype 44, 45, 50–52, 59, 68n6, 75,
78–79, 109–110; see also genotype;
phenotypic plasticity
phenotypic plasticity 44, 51–52, 59,
68n7, 73, 78–80, 88, 98, 110,
151, 153
photosynthesis 62, 118; see also great
oxidation
Pievani, Telmo 98, 100
Pinchot, Gifford 135, 136
plastic 59, 113, 116, 117, 139n7,
146; see also garbage patches;
microplastics

Pleistocene 74, 79, 80, 82, 88, 96,
100n1, 152, 162n1
Plumwood, Val 101n5, 111
pollination 90, 98, 112; see also
ecosystem services
pollution 1, 3, 47, 49, 54, 82, 86, 89,
93, 101n5, 116, 128, 146, 153,
163n6; see also Niger Delta; plastic
Pope Francis 67n1
POPs (Persistent Organic Pollutants) 90,
92, 99; see also DDT
population boom 99
positivism 18
preadaptation 77, 78, 87, 101n3
prebiotic soup 41–42
Preiffer, Ida Laura 21
preservationism 129–132, 135–137,
158
progress 23, 96, 155–156

reductionism 50, 135
reforestation 117, 129, 133, 155, 161
resilience 32, 34n13, 68n10
resourcism 129, 132, 135, 136, 137
responsibility 85, 88, 145; ethics
of 93; intergenerational 93–94;
imperative of 93
restoration ecology 166; see also
environmental restoration
revolution: agricultural 87; Copernican
5; Darwinian 5; industrial 8, 14, 16,
30, 48, 54, 96; scientific 8
Rio Conference (United Nations
Conference on Environment and
Development) 1; see also Rio
Declaration
Rio Declaration 105
Romanticism 121, 122, 131
Roosevelt, Franklin Delano 135
Rousseau, J.-Jacques 125–126
Russell, Bertrand 52

Sarkar, Sahotra 68n8, 166
scientific community 8, 20, 31, 40, 47,
64, 65, 127, 131, 140n12, 145, 146,
148, 149
selective pressures 56, 58, 59, 60, 82,
84, 90, 97, 98; see also natural
selection
self-regulation 20, 31, 62, 63, 65, 66,
148; see also homeostasis
Singer, Peter 101n5
Sober, Elliott 110, 111, 113, 134

species: diversity of 83 (*see also* biodiversity); endangered or threatened 39, 54, 134 (*see also* extinction); exotic 48, 146; evolution of 12, 73, 75, 89 (*see also* evolution); human 24, 27, 82, 85, 89, 95, 111, 151, 162; invasive 47–49, 96, 136, 139n8; native 48, 139n11; thermophile 98; transformation of (*see* evolution: Lamarckian); wild 87 (*see also* wildlife)
speciesism 101n5
Spencer, Herbert 9, 18, 20–21, 34n7
Standing Bear, Luther 131
Steffen, Will 96
Stengers, Isabelle 156
Stockholm Conference (United Nations Conference on the Human Environment) 1, 2, 5, 72, 128; *see also* Stockholm Declaration
Stockholm Declaration 6, 72, 105, 117, 159
Stoermer, Eugene 96
Strathern, Marilyn 157
struggle for existence 23, 27–29, 42, 46, 47
sublime 122
superorganism 64–67
sustainable development 93, 136, 137
sustainable use 1, 120
symbiosis and symbiotic 79, 120, 156, 163n10

Tansley, Arthur 66n8
Taylor, Michael Scott 147–148, 150
techniques 87, 129, 135, 150; *see also* progress; technology
technology 80, 93, 97, 112–115, 139n3, 154–157, 166, 167, 173n8; *see also* geoengineering
techno-optimism 155, 157; *see also* ecomodernism
Theophrastus 26
Thoreau, David Henry 121, 123–124
threshold 67, 95, 100, 120, 137, 148, 151
tragedy of the commons 147; *see also* natural or environmental resources
transcendental construction 21, 24–25, 57, 86; *see also* subjective environment
transcendental idealism 122
transcendentalism 121–123, 129–132
transformism *see* evolutionary theory: Lamarckian
Treviranus 33n1
Trump, Donald 150
Tsing, Anna 157

Umwelt theory 23–26, 34n6, 34n10, 43, 57
UNEP (United Nations Environment Programme) 1, 145, 149
United Nations Millennium Declaration 137, 140n18
urbanisation 88, 96, 128; *see also* environment: built; urban
utilitarianism 140n17

value 159, 163n16, 101n5, 116, 121, 132, 134; aesthetic 136; anthropocentric 33; economic 32–33; intrinsic 33, 158; moral 140n17; normative 109–110; scientific 134, 136; spiritual 122; instrumental 33; *see also* ecosystem services
Van Doreen, Thom 156–157
variations 21, 22, 42, 43, 45, 59, 82, 98
Vernadsky, Vladimir Ivanovich 61–63
viruses 33n2, 61, 67n2, 77, 79, 84, 96, 119
Vogel, Steven 131, 158–159
Von Uexküll, Jacob 9, 21, 23–26, 34, 34n10, 57, 86

Waddington, Conrad Hal 44
Wallace, Alfred Russel 21, 22, 26, 27, 43, 45
Weismann, August 43
West-Eberhard, Mary Jane 51
Western culture 4, 8, 158, 162
Whitehead, Alfred North 44
wilderness 106, 121–124, 129–135, 137, 140n14, 160; *see also* nature: pristine
Wilderness Act 132–133
wildlife 105, 124, 126, 137
wildness 133, 137
Wordsworth, William 122
Worster, David 30
Wulf, Andrea 16, 124, 128

Yellowstone Park 121
Yosemite Park 130

Printed in the United States
by Baker & Taylor Publisher Services